GLOBAL
SURFARi
THE SURFER'S TRAVEL ATLAS

GLOBAL
SURFARi
THE SURFER'S TRAVEL ATLAS

Managing director	Chryl Campbell
Publishing manager	Sarah Anderson
Art director	Kylie Mulquin
Project manager	Scott Forbes
Consultants	Matt Butel, Chris Tola (Surfrider Foundation Australia)
Contributors	Andrew C. Abel, Alan Atkins, Chris Binns, Sam Bleakley, Paul Botha, John Seaton Callahan, Mike Cianciulli, Paul Evans, Dave Foster, Paul Kennedy, Zoe Lally, Andrew Lewis, Miles Masterson, Ben Matson, Jim Michell, Brenda Miley, Adrian Nelson, John Philip, Ross Phillips, Keith Redman, Jeff Schorr, Paul Scott, Alex Smalley, Alvaro Solari, Andrew Wafer, Byron W. Yagual de la Rosa, Alex Zadnik
Editors	Scott Forbes, John Mapps, Bronwyn Sweeney
Map editor	Anne Matthews
Map checker	Alan Edwards
Cover design	Kylie Mulquin
Designer	Cathy Campbell
Design concept	Jacqueline Richards
Map illustrator	Lionel Portier
Map technician	Paula Kelly
Picture research	Tracey Gibson
Index	Jon Jermey
Proofreader	Kevin Diletti
Production	Ian Coles
Contracts	Alan Edwards
Foreign rights	Kate Hill
Publishing assistants	Katie Holmes, Christine Leonards

First published in the United Kingdom 2008 by
Aurum Press Ltd
7 Greenland Street
London NW1 0ND
www.aurumpress.co.uk

This publication and arrangement
© Global Book Publishing Pty Ltd 2007
Text © Global Book Publishing Pty Ltd 2007
Maps © Global Book Publishing Pty Ltd 2007
Photographs are credited on page 256

A catalogue record for this book is available from the
British Library.

ISBN-10   1 84513 298 X
ISBN-13   978 1 84513 298 9

The moral rights of all contributors have been asserted.

Printed in China by SNP Leefung Printers Limited
Colour separation Pica Digital Pte Ltd, Singapore

Photographers Global Book Publishing would be
pleased to hear from photographers interested in
supplying photographs.

Cover photo Tasmanian surfer Michael Hoult rides
a wave at Bingin on Bali's Bukit Peninsula, Indonesia,
by Paul Kennedy/pkphotos.com.

Contents

Consultants

SURFRIDER FOUNDATION The Surfrider Foundation is a not-for-profit organization dedicated to the protection and enjoyment of our oceans, waves, and beaches. All over the world, it campaigns for the sustainable management and use of the coastal environment and has helped shape and improve government management and conservation programs. For more information, see www.surfrider.org.

MATT BUTEL Matt is a director of Surfrider Foundation Australia. Father of two and a chiropractor with his own practice on Australia's Gold Coast, he lives and works by the beach. He has been involved in surfing events around the globe for over a decade, as a therapist for the Australian team and the ASP World Championship Tour. Matt is a keen surfer and member of his local Kirra Surfriders Club.

CHRIS TOLA Chris is currently chair of Surfrider Foundation Australia, and has been a director and branch representative for many years. He works as Business Development Manager at Coastalwatch (www.coastalwatch.com) and has previously worked with Coastcare and Keep Australia Beautiful. Chris has traveled and surfed around the planet; he lives in Australia with his wife and children.

Contributors

ANDREW C. ABEL In 1998, when he was just 19 years old, Andrew set up the Surfing Association of Papua New Guinea (SAPNG) to raise the profile of PNG as a surfing destination and to channel revenue from surf tourism into local communities. He remains president of the association and is also on the PNG Tourism Board and the National Museum Board.

ALAN ATKINS Alan began surfing at the age of ten, at Lorne, Victoria, Australia. He has been a state and national surfing team member, has held several national shortboard and longboard titles, and still competes in senior divisions. A pioneer of surf coaching, he oversaw the development of Surf Victoria and Surfing Australia, and currently holds a vice president's position in the International Surfing Association. He is now based at Byron Bay, New South Wales.

CHRIS BINNS Raised in Western Australia, Chris has surfed in every ocean and worked as a ski instructor in Canada, a barman in London, a water-ski instructor in the USA, a deckhand in the Indian Ocean, and an organizer at Club Med. He is now Assistant Editor at Australia's *Surfing Life* magazine, where he delights in coming to work barefoot and surfing at lunchtime.

SAM BLEAKLEY A professional surfer and writer from Sennen Cove in Cornwall, England, Sam is also a graduate of Cambridge University, with a BA and MA in Geography. He has twice been European Longboard Champion and several times British Longboard Champion. He currently specializes in surf exploration to far-flung coastlines with photographer and surf writer John Seaton Callahan.

PAUL BOTHA After learning to surf on a hollow wooden surfboard in Cape Town in the late 1950s, Paul Botha helped pioneer many of South Africa's now-popular surf spots. He has since surfed in more than 30 countries and become a full-time surfing promoter. In preparing his contributions to this book, Paul was ably assisted by Rhodes University journalism student Craig Ritchie.

JOHN SEATON CALLAHAN Constantly traveling the world, John photographs with passion and specializes in tropical places and top surf spots. He operates his own photographic agency, Tropicalpix (www.tropicalpix.com), and his work is published all over the world. Originally from Hawaii, USA, he now lives in Singapore.

MIKE CIANCIULLI Mike is an ardent surfer, traveler, and writer. His passion for writing developed while he drafted journal and online entries documenting his search for waves across five continents. His work has since appeared in various American surfing publications, both print and online versions. A native of Florida, he now resides in Southern California.

PAUL EVANS Originally from England, Paul now lives and works in Hossegor, southwest France, where he is the editor-in-chief of *Surf Europe* magazine. When he's not traveling or in the office, he likes reading John Fante, eating Mexican food, drinking coffee, and watching soccer.

DAVE FOSTER From Cornwall, England, Dave has been surfing for 20 years and is a former British Surfing Team member. He is currently employed by the British Surfing Association at Fistral Beach, Newquay, UK, and regularly surfs many of the local spots.

PAUL KENNEDY Based in New Zealand, Paul is a roving freelance surf and travel photojournalist. He makes regular visits to South America and Indonesia seeking out photo, story, and surfing opportunities.

ZOE LALLY Zoe is the Development Officer for the Irish Surfing Association (ISA; www.isasurf.ie), the governing body of surfing in Ireland. Zoe's contributions to this guide were gathered with the assistance of members of the ISA.

ANDREW LEWIS Andrew has represented Barbados at international contests since 1988 as a judge and was also manager of the Barbados team at the World Junior Surfing Games in Brazil in 2006. He is currently the president of the Barbados Surfing Association.

MILES MASTERSON Miles Masterson is a writer and photographer based in Cape Town, South Africa. He began his career in 1992 at *Wavelength* surfing magazine in the UK, then became a co-founder of *blunt*, an award-winning boardriding, music, and lifestyle magazine. Miles recently resigned from *blunt* to resume traveling, writing, and photography at surf spots around the world.

BEN MATSON Ben is the founder of and Chief Swell Forecaster for Swellnet, Australia's leading source of real-time surfing information. He learned to surf in the cold and sharky waters of South Australia, but now lives on Sydney's Northern Beaches. Ben provides the official forecasts for many events on the ASP World Championship Tour.

JIM MICHELL A freelance journalist and photographer based in north Cornwall, UK, and formerly editor of *Wavelength* (Britain's longest-running surfing magazine), Jim contributes to a wide range of surfing magazines and national newspapers, and runs Barefoot Media, a public relations consultancy specializing in action sports.

BRENDA MILEY Brenda is a former women's surfing champion who operates two of Australia's leading surf schools at Sydney's Bondi and Maroubra beaches. Brenda has introduced tens of thousands of people to surfing, founded the Bondi Girls Surfriders club, and is National Women's Director of Surfing Australia.

ADRIAN NELSON Adrian is a surfer and environmentalist based in British Columbia. He spends most of his time scouring the West Coast of Canada filming surfing and snowboarding.

JOHN PHILIP A founding member of the Fiji Surfing Association and its current president, John has been surfing in Fiji since 1980. He also enjoys wave sailing some of the known surfing breaks in Fiji.

ROSS PHILLIPS Having searched dozens of countries for that perfect wave, Ross founded Tropicsurf (www.tropicsurf.net), a company that specializes in vacations for surfers looking to escape the crowds, stay in comfort, and improve their surfing. Tropicsurf operates primarily from a boat in the Maldives, but also at Noosa Heads in Australia, Nihiwatu in Indonesia, the Marshall Islands, and the Mentawai Islands.

KEITH REDMAN A keen surfer and weather-watcher, Keith launched New Zealand's first online surf report service, www.surf.co.nz. Managing the service allows him the luxury of being able to surf almost daily.

JEFF SCHORR Jeff was born and bred on Australia's Gold Coast, and now resides in Japan, where he runs the number-one English-language Japanese surf website, JapanSurf.com. Jeff can be heard each week on Osaka's airwaves presenting radio programs in both Japanese and English.

PAUL SCOTT A lecturer in the Communication program at the University of Newcastle, New South Wales, Australia, Paul also writes for a range of Australian publications, and is media manager for the annual World Qualifying Series surfing events at Newcastle and the Central Coast. In 2004, he produced *Swell Dreaming*, an award-winning radio series on surfing, for the Australian Broadcasting Corporation.

ALEX SMALLEY Alex graduated with First Class Honours in Environmental Sciences from the University of East Anglia, England. He has a strong interest in creating new methods to communicate scientific research, and in 2006 he received the Alan Preston Prize for outstanding work in oceanography.

ALVARO SOLARI A pioneer of surfing and other adventure sports in Chile, Alvaro co-founded Chilean boardriding magazine *Surfeando*. He has been a Chilean representative at various international surf associations, including the ISA, ASP, and PASA (Pan-American Surfing Association), and was the director of the only Chilean stop on the ASP Tour, the Mormaii Cristal World Tour, at Iquique in 1993.

ANDREW WAFER A surfer and physiotherapist, Andrew can usually be found chasing waves south of Newcastle in Australia. In over 15 years of surfing, he has traveled and surfed throughout Australia, Indonesia, Peru, Costa Rica, Mexico, Spain, and France.

BYRON W. YAGUAL DE LA ROSA A marine biologist and journalist as well as a surfer, Byron has been head judge and president of the Ecuadorian Judging Association, and ISA development program for Ecuador.

ALEX ZADNIK After graduating from the University of Melbourne, Australia, Alex undertook further studies in atmosphere–ocean interaction at the University of New South Wales. Now based in Victoria, he works as a meteorologist for the Australian surf forecasting company Swellnet, and regularly surfs off the beaches of the Mornington Peninsula.

Foreword

In recent years, surfing has become one of the most popular sports on the planet, appealing to all age groups and both genders. At the same time, the availability of cheap travel and the ubiquity of glamorous images of exotic surfing locations have created huge interest in the concept of the surfari — a journey made to experience the sport in other locations, often in the context of other cultures, and usually in pursuit of the perfect wave.

Whether you prefer to join an organized tour or travel independently, a vast spectrum of travel options is now available. But for all of us, and especially those whose trips are constrained by budget and by work and family obligations, it is vital that we research our surf trip thoroughly to ensure that we make the most of our time and resources. Will the conditions suit our ability, what is the best time of year to travel, what equipment do we need to bring? To find answers to these and other questions, you could ask your mates at your local beach, trawl the Internet, or wade through back-issues of surfing magazines. Far quicker and more reliable, however, to consult a comprehensive, up-to-date, thoroughly researched guide like this one.

Compiled by experienced surfers with sound local knowledge, the information in these pages spans the globe, covering more surf spots in more detail than any other comparable guide. All of it is presented in a format that makes it quick and easy to consult. For every surf spot, there is a brief description, followed by helpful listings, including the average wave height, swell direction, best tide, and optimum time of year, as well as an indication of the skill level required.

As surfers, we tend to be more aware of the environment, and our impact on it, than the average citizen. When we travel, it is important to try to limit our impact on the places we visit, and their communities and beaches. That can be done through small gestures, such as not throwing your wax wrapper on the beach, but it should also extend to displaying consideration for those we encounter, in and out of the water. Local surfers can be territorial, but a little respect and understanding go a long way. Your attitude will make a big difference to how enjoyable your trip will be.

With this in mind, it is great to have this book endorsed by the Surfrider Foundation, which is a global organization committed to preserving the oceans and coastline. Give them your support, so that more of the places in this guide will be preserved for future generations.

Even if you are not about to set off on a surf trip, this book will help you daydream and start planning that "one day" adventure. Whenever you head off, enjoy it, and have a great trip. I hope you get the waves of a lifetime, and have a barrel for me.

Mark

Born and raised in Newcastle, Australia, Mark Richards had a remarkable career as a professional surfer, winning, among many other titles, four world championships, in 1979, 1980, 1981, and 1982 — only Kelly Slater holds more men's world titles. At the same time, Mark established himself as a pioneer of surfboard shaping, paving the way toward acceptance of the twin-fin surfboard design. Mark still lives, works, and surfs in Newcastle, where he runs a board-shaping business and surf shop. He is also a patron of Surfrider Foundation Australia, and was recently awarded an honorary doctorate by the University of Newcastle.

How to Use This Book

This comprehensive guide contains all the information you need to plan a trip to any of the world's top surf spots. An introductory section, Oceanography, explains the topography of the oceans, the timing of tides, how surf forms, and how we can all help protect our oceans and coastlines. The remainder of the book is divided into nine regions. Within these regions, we've identified the major surf areas, and within these areas we've selected the top surf spots. Each surf spot is covered by a detailed entry, including a concise description, more detailed information on when to go, what to avoid, and how to get there, and the icons shown below.

The introduction to each region includes a map showing the locations of the surf areas covered in that section. In addition, each surf area feature includes a detailed map pinpointing the surf spots and the major towns, roads, and other geographical features in the area. A key to the icons and symbols that appear on the maps is shown here.

Map icons and symbols

AUSTRALIA	Country
CALIFORNIA	State, region, district, province
Cape Verde	Territory
	National border
	State/territory border (Canada, USA, Australia)
◎ Washington DC	National/territory capital
◉ Richmond	State capital
● Ocean City	City, town
INDIAN OCEAN	Ocean
Bali Sea	Sea
Lombok Strait	Bay, gulf, channel, strait, reef, cape, point
HINAKO ISLANDS	Island group/Major island
Long Island	Island
Short River	River
York Peninsula	Peninsula
Central Range	Mountain range
Mount Wilhelm	Mountain peak
Mauna Loa	Volcano
Fiordland National Park	National park or other major reserve
BUSSELL HWY	Major road
Caves Road	Minor road
9	Surf spot
🛆	Lighthouse
✈	Airport

Surf Spot icons

 BEGINNER

 INTERMEDIATE

 ADVANCED

 ALL LEVELS

 ATTRACTS BIG WAVES
Indicates that the surf spot regularly has waves of 10 ft (3.1 m) or more

 MOST CONSISTENT WAVE
Indicates that the surf spot is the most consistent in its surf area

 WORLD FAMOUS
Indicates that the surf spot is known around the world

CHAPTER 1

Oceanography

The Oceans

A brief look at any global map quickly reveals the startling magnitude of our oceans. From the great basins of the Pacific and Atlantic oceans, to the warm waters of the Indian Ocean, and the cold depths of the Arctic and Southern oceans, these deep blue expanses govern our planet and its atmosphere.

The Pacific is the largest of our oceans, followed by the Atlantic. Both of these huge bodies of water stretch from high latitudes in the Northern Hemisphere down to Antarctica's great encircling Southern Ocean. Each of their basins possesses strongly varying temperature characteristics that help drive the vigorous atmospheric circulation responsible for our weather. The third-largest ocean, the Indian Ocean, has a tropical climate and supports some of the rarest and most beautiful life-forms on earth, from tiny, highly endangered reef species to great whales. In the far north, the Arctic Ocean is our smallest and perhaps most important ocean, for in these remote waters extremely cold and deep currents are formed that help to ventilate the unfathomable depths of the world's oceans and maintain an ocean circulation that supports the global climate.

Mountains and Valleys

Far below the surface waters, the seafloor terrain is as varied and treacherous as the topography of the world's great mountain ranges. The relatively shallow continental shelf of coastal margins can give way to enormous drops in depth. At actively subducting plate boundaries, where giant slabs of Earth's crust are forced beneath each other, deep trenches have formed. The Mariana Trench in the western Pacific has a record depth of over 36,000 ft (11,000 m), while the Indian Ocean's Java Trench descends more than 23,000 ft (7,000 m). Volcanoes often form along the edge of these subducting plates, as is the case in Indonesia and the Philippines.

Mirroring the trenches, seamounts rise from the vast monotony of the seafloor's abyssal plains, in places reaching 2½ miles (4 km) in height and often breaching the sea surface. The Hawaii–Emperor Island chain provides the classic example. A great hotspot of hot and viscous mantle material has been

The map shows the world's oceans and principal seas, as well as the major features of the seafloor, including mid-ocean ridges, trenches, and seamounts.

The shape of the seafloor on coastal margins has a strong bearing on wave size and form.

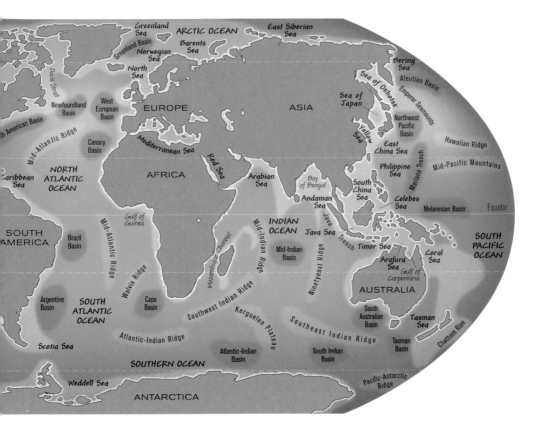

effusing from the seafloor here for tens of millions of years, gradually forming the Hawaiian Island chain and, incidentally, one of the best surfing coastlines in the world.

Seamounts also form along the tectonic plate boundaries, such as along the Mid-Atlantic Ridge between the continents of Africa and South America. These seamounts are often regions of seafloor spreading, where new crust is formed. Amid a baptism of fire and seismic tremors, rising magma forces the adjacent oceanic plates in opposite directions, in turn pushing the oceans' bounding continents apart at up to 2½ inches (64 mm) per year.

Shallow Margins

The world's oceans have a typical depth of about 2–2½ miles (3–4 km). In contrast, the world's marginal and continental-shelf seas are much shallower, occasionally confined to depths of just 150 ft (45 m). These locally important seas include the North Sea (western Europe), the Bering Sea (southern Alaska) and the Gulf of Carpentaria (northern Australia).

Such areas can be extremely biologically productive, and often sustain local fishing industries and economies.

The oceans are characterized by highly complex wind and current systems. Ocean currents at times bear a strong resemblance to air currents in the atmosphere. Confined and rotating eddies traverse the ocean, carrying water of different temperatures and salinities to new locations. Regions of coastal upwelling provide nutrients that sustain great blooms of biological activity, whereas the interiors of the Pacific and Atlantic oceans are, by comparison, oceanic deserts that are largely devoid of life.

The oceans have remained a mystery throughout most of history, and only in the last century has science made the theoretical and technical breakthroughs necessary to allow us to begin to unravel the myriad of secrets locked in their depths. Yet, while glass jars and thermometers have been replaced with highly sophisticated remote sensing satellites and deep-diving submersibles, many of our questions remain unanswered.

Currents and Wind

The oceans and atmosphere comprise an inextricably coupled system. The global imbalance in oceanic surface temperatures drives vigorous winds and an atmospheric circulation that delivers our familiar weather patterns. In turn, these surface winds help to mix the upper portions of the sea — to a depth of 3,300 ft (1,000 m) — and power the great currents that traverse the ocean basins.

The large-scale movement of fluids across Earth's surface is far from simple. We live on a planet that is not only spherical, but also rotating. This creates an apparent force that deflects motion away from a straight line. The Coriolis effect, as this is known, causes the motion of winds and currents to bend to the right in the Northern Hemisphere and to the left in the Southern Hemisphere. The effect diminishes in lower latitudes, reaching zero at the equator, allowing the narrow equatorial currents to traverse in almost straight lines.

Atmospheric Circulation

The equator receives the largest amount of energy from the sun, raising temperatures and evaporation to provide the fuel for a vast uprising of air. As this air rises, it cools, dries, and spreads poleward. The cooling air then sinks at around latitudes 30° north and south to form broad areas of subtropical high pressure and the clear, sunny skies of Mediterranean climates. At the surface a return flow of air heads back toward the equator and, deflected by the Coriolis effect, forms the easterly trade winds. Other air currents flow around subtropical high-pressure systems (clockwise in the Northern Hemisphere and counterclockwise in the Southern Hemisphere), forming anticyclones. These rotating weather systems act upon the ocean surface to drive the great ocean gyres. The gyres exist in each large basin, and are characterized by a broad weak flow of surface waters that mirrors the atmospheric winds.

Energy from the sun drives Earth's wind systems and, in turn, its ocean currents.

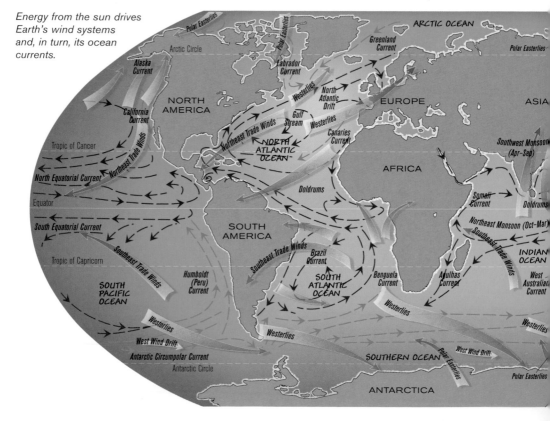

A combination of prevailing winds and strong ocean currents can create intensely powerful wave action.

MAP KEY

— — >— — Warm ocean current
— >— — — Cool ocean current
———————> Westerly winds
<————————— Easterly winds

Oyashio
(Kamchatka)
Current

North Pacific
Current

Kuroshio
(Japan)
Current

NORTH
PACIFIC
OCEAN

Northeast Trade Winds

Equatorial Counter Current

AUSTRALIA

East
Australian
Current

Antarctic Circumpolar
Current

Luckily for oceanographers, our picture of ocean currents extends well beyond the immediate simplicity of a surface-wind-driven circulation. We know, for example, that the western boundaries of the Atlantic, Pacific, and Indian oceans are dominated by the strong, warm, poleward flows of the Gulf Stream, Kuroshio, and Agulhas currents, respectively, and that these currents play a crucial role in the global distribution of heat. Western Europe, for example, has a winter climate some 9°F (5°C) warmer than comparative latitudes on the west coast of the Atlantic Ocean, mostly attributable to the atmospheric transfer of heat from the ocean.

The influence of the Coriolis effect provides explanation for one of the great banes of surfing. Several stretches of coastline around the world witness persistently cool water temperatures, despite high land temperatures and favorable climates. It is not uncommon for example, for San Diego in southern California to see winter ocean temperatures of 57°F (14°C), while the nearby Mexican coast is bathed by waters some 9°F (5°C) warmer. The reason for this is that along the Californian coast the winds come predominantly from the north. These winds push coastal surface waters to the right, or west, due to the effect of the Coriolis force and a resulting physical process known as the Ekman Transport. As each layer of water pulls along the layer beneath, a spiral westward flow forms, with the main flow eventually directed perpendicular to the wind — offshore, in other words. Cold, deep water rises to replace the warmer surface water, bringing with it nutrients that fuel and maintain high levels of biological productivity, and, in turn, also keeping surfers rather chilly.

How Surf Forms

Waves are generated by winds that blow across the surface of the ocean. However, the high-quality swells sought by surfers require a particular set of weather events to occur over a certain period of time.

When strong winds blow across a large expanse of ocean for an extended duration, energy is imparted into the sea surface. This energy creates small wavelets that build in size and strength as winds persist. The longer and stronger that winds blow, the larger the waves become.

Of equal importance to wave size is the distance or area that the winds blow over, which is known as the fetch. If the length of a given fetch is limited by a landmass or by an enclosed bay, the potential wave height from this source will be capped. Therefore, the largest waves tend to occur in large expanses of open oceans, such as the Atlantic, Pacific, and Indian oceans. For example, powerful and slow-moving low-pressure systems over the North Pacific Ocean are responsible for large swells that regularly bombard the Hawaiian Islands each winter.

A surfer attempts to outride a monster wave in Hawaii. Such waves are often generated by swells that have traveled all the way from the Indian Ocean.

Swell and Wave Height

As waves build in size, they also increase in strength. The strength of a swell is indicated by its wavelength, or period. Measured in seconds, the swell period is the time it takes for two successive wave crests to pass a particular point. Large swell periods are associated with powerful waves, due to the close relationship between the swell period and its forward speed. For example, swells with 20-second periods travel at approximately 34 miles per hour (55 kph) through deep water, while swells exhibiting 10-second periods travel at only 17 miles per hour (28 kph).

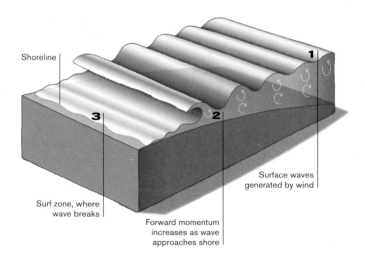

Shoreline

3

2

1

Surface waves generated by wind

Surf zone, where wave breaks

Forward momentum increases as wave approaches shore

1 Waves are generated by winds blowing over the surface of the sea. The strength and duration of the winds, combined with the area that they blow over (the fetch), determine the size and strength of the swell.
2 Water molecules have very little forward momentum in deep water, and generally move in circular orbits as waves pass. As they enter shallower ocean, however, they start to move in a more elliptical orbit, with greater forward motion.
3 Waves break in the surf zone when the depth of the water becomes roughly two-thirds that of the wave height.

Long-period swells, also known as ground-swells, can travel huge distances, often reaching coastlines many thousands of miles away. In contrast, short-period swells lose their size and strength quite quickly upon leaving their source, especially if they encounter opposing winds or currents. Waves with a period of under six seconds are known as chop or windswell, and are usually weak and poor for surfing.

When long-period swells approach the coastline, they tend to slow and "stand up" as they encounter shallower waters. As frictional effects increase, water molecules within the wave start to gain a greater forward momentum. This momentum causes waves to break when the depth of the ocean is approximately two-thirds of the wave height, but local winds and opposing rips are also important factors.

The depth to which swell energy penetrates the ocean is proportional to the swell period; that is, the longer the period, the deeper the swell will penetrate. As a result, long-period swells begin to "feel" and react to the shape of the seafloor much sooner than short-period swells do. This allows them to bend around points and islands much more efficiently. Such bending is known as refraction, and is an important factor in the creation of quality waves at point breaks and beaches that are sheltered from the swell direction.

The measurement of waves by surfers is highly subjective and open to interpretation. Most surfers refer to wave heights in feet, even where the metric system is standard, and the measurement normally refers to the height of the face of the wave. Many government agencies maintain offshore wave buoys that continuously record wave data, the output of which is usually represented by two wave height readings. The first is "significant wave height" (Hsig), which refers to the average of the highest third of all recorded waves in a set time period, and the second is "maximum wave height" (Hmax), which is the single largest wave recorded in the set time period. The latter is a less reliable guide to surf size, as the maximum wave height is often the result of a number of wave crests passing the buoy at the same time.

Real-time buoy readings are available on the Internet, but it is difficult to gauge the exact size and quality of surf from these alone. You can, however, get an idea of whether winds are light in the vicinity of the buoy. Strong winds can exaggerate wave heights at the buoy by generating additional short-period windswell that is of little value for surfing.

An understanding of tides will greatly enhance your chances of a successful outing and help ensure safety.

Tides

The daily, rhythmic motion of the oceans' tides has a profound influence upon the world we live in; for example, tides are responsible for an enormous amount of energy dissipation that ultimately influences both the climate of the ocean and the atmosphere. Tides are, of course, also a major determiner of surf conditions, so, for the surfer, good tidal knowledge is as important as remembering to bring your wax.

Tidal movements result from the interaction of the gravitational forces of the moon, sun, and Earth. These forces are hugely important astronomical phenomena, responsible for the deformation of entire planetary bodies, not just surface fluids such as our oceans. The gravitational pull of the moon varies across our planet and is at its highest, not surprisingly, on the side nearest the moon. There, it creates a bulge in the ocean, raising its open ocean surface by over 3 ft (0.9 m). On the opposite side of Earth, a similar bulge forms as the

Moon pulls our planet away from the water. Thus as Earth rotates about its axis, a single coastal point will experience two tidal bulges, creating two high tides in just over 24 hours.

The sun exerts a similar effect upon the world's oceans, but since it is much farther away its influence is diminished to roughly half that of the moon. However, when the sun and moon line up with Earth (that is, the moon is directly between the sun and Earth), their influences combine to create especially high tides known as spring tides. When the sun and moon pull at right angles to each other, the lowest tides — neap tides — occur.

Predicting Tides

Unfortunately, tides do not propagate around the world in a single, easily predictable motion. Furthermore, approximately 400 orbital characteristics influence their variation — a headache for any would-be tidal forecaster! Fortunately, coastal tides can be largely determined from historical tide-gauge data, making prediction in populated areas relatively straightforward.

However, tidal range can be influenced by a number of other, temporary factors. Intense low-pressure systems, often the creators of classic swells, can act to raise the surface of the ocean by 2½ inches (1 cm) for every millibar of extra pressure at their center. The vigorous winds associated with these systems also pile water up against the coastline, both in the direction of the wind and perpendicular to it. Furthermore, the large breaking waves often associated with such systems raise water levels in the surf zone. All of these influences can occur simultaneously, at times producing a low tide similar in level to a normal high tide, and an exaggerated high tide with the potential for devastating effects. This is often referred to as a storm surge, and is usually the most destructive component of a hurricane.

The shape of the seafloor along the coastline can significantly enhance the effects of tides. At long, flat, shallow beaches, the watermark may recede over half a mile (1 km) into the distance at low tide. Narrow, shallow estuaries can focus tidal energy into a single propagating wave or tidal bore; in such cases (the Severn Estuary in England is a good example), tidal bores can be ridden for up to an hour, covering distances of tens of miles.

An understanding of the actions of tides can help you avoid dangers and get more out of your surfing. For example, low tides may expose dangerous rock shelves or make an outer sandbank just shallow enough to start firing.

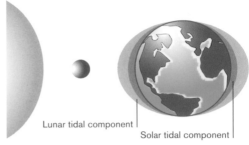

Lunar tidal component | Solar tidal component |

Very high tides, called spring tides, occur when the sun and moon pull in the same direction.

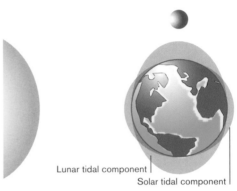

Lunar tidal component | Solar tidal component |

Low tides known as neap tides occur when the sun and moon pull at right angles to each other.

Importantly, areas with a large tidal range often see increased wave heights in the hours preceding high tide, as the tide literally helps push the incoming swell. Furthermore, tidal currents are responsible for redistributions of sand and sediment that can completely obscure or reveal reef structures, and obliterate or construct a perfect sandbank.

Waves crashing onto rocks at Neals Harbour, Nova Scotia, Canada. Changing tides can expose or hide potential dangers.

Preserving the Oceans

As surfers, we are in a unique position to observe firsthand the state of our oceans and coastlines. This should inspire us to act to help maintain and protect these environments.

Pollution of our oceans and beaches isn't just a visual blight; in some circumstances it can affect your health. One of the main contributors to pollution along our beaches is stormwater runoff from city streets after heavy rain. Any litter that is thrown onto the street or sidewalk quickly washes through the stormwater system and eventually ends up in the ocean. Plastic bags and bottles not only look ugly on our beaches, but also can choke marine animals such as whales and dolphins. We can all do our bit to minimize such waste and dispose of it carefully. It's also important to clean up after our pets, as animal droppings in stormwater may carry diseases that are potentially a source of ill health for surfers.

In some parts of the world, partially treated human waste is pumped directly into the ocean. This can cause ear, nose, and throat infections in surfers who frequent neighboring waters and boost nutrient levels in the ocean to such a level that toxic algal blooms result. It is up to local communities, including surfers, to band together and lobby local politicians to stop such practices. If sewage is treated properly, it can become a valuable source of fresh water for industrial, agricultural, and residential use.

If you notice pollution entering the ocean from nearby industry, you should alert your local environmental protection agency or an environmental organization such as the Surfrider Foundation (see box, right). Oil slicks along the coast should also be reported to appropriate authorities so that poorly maintained ships can be tracked down.

Surfrider Foundation

Numerous groups around the world work hard to improve conditions in coastal areas. One of the most prominent is the Surfrider Foundation. Founded in 1984, this non-profit grassroots association of surfers, kayakers, and other enthusiasts now has offices in the United States, Australia, Brazil, Japan, and Europe, and more than 40,000 members in total.

The Surfrider Foundation aims to heighten awareness of the ways in which indiv-iduals, businesses, and governments impact on oceans and coastlines, and encourage a more environ-mentally responsible use of these resources through conservation, activism, research, and education. Around the world, Surfrider has helped reduce pollution, improve coastal manage-ment, and enhance enjoyment of our oceans. For further information, see www.surfrider.org.

Campaigners from Surfers Against Sewage protesting in London against coastal pollution

Without controls, the ocean becomes a dumping ground. Garbage and sewage pollute beaches worldwide.

An Everchanging Scene

Land clearing and development along the coastal fringe can alter the movement of sand along the beach and add heavy sediment loads to the ocean. This sediment can block out light and affect the health of marine ecosystems. If large amounts of sand are stripped from the beach, there can be a negative impact on the quality of surf breaks in the area. Large dune systems often help replenish offshore sand repositories, so the construction of parking lots and buildings along the coastal fringe will often deprive surfing breaks of the sand needed to create good surfing waves. On rare occasions, such changes have a positive impact on surf breaks. On Australia's Gold Coast, for example, the Tweed River Entrance Sand Bypassing Project, a sand dredging and pumping operation, created a very long and hollow sand-bottom point break, now known as The Superbank; however, this came at significant cost, with the world-famous waves of nearby Kirra now but a distant memory.

A major threat to the world's oceans and coastlines is climate change. An increase in average global temperatures is expected to raise sea levels over coming decades, leading to greater coastal erosion in many areas. The rise in sea level, in combination with rising temperatures, may also affect the health of tropical coral reefs. We can play a small role in helping to minimize the impact of climate change by reducing our greenhouse gas emissions; this can be done by, for example, using less energy, switching to renewable energy sources, and leaving the car at home whenever possible.

Introduction

The West Coast of the United States was the site of modern surfing's birth and adolescence. Americans first saw surfing on the mainland in 1885, when a trio of Hawaiian princes rode planks carved from redwood at the mouth of the San Lorenzo River in Santa Cruz. But it wasn't popularized until the appearance of Hawaiian-born duo George Freeth, who surfed Southern California's Venice Beach in 1907, and Duke Kahanamoku, who surfed a number of Southern California beaches in 1915.

Surf Culture Spreads

But this popularity was nothing compared to the craze that swept the country in 1959 after *Gidget* — the Hollywood movie adaptation of a novel chronicling the adventures of a Southern Californian teenager at Malibu. More surf films followed, along with surf music, surf photography, and surf magazines. California's Rincon, Steamer Lane, and Malibu were soon etched into the global surfing imagination.

California can be divided into three geographical areas. "NorCal" begins at the Oregon border and ends at San Francisco. From there to Point Conception is Central California, while "SoCal" runs from Point Conception to the Mexican border.

September through November is the best time to surf Central California and SoCal. September can bring cleaner and warmer water conditions than the summer months of June to

Surf locales in North America range from Canada's beaches to the tropics of Mexico.

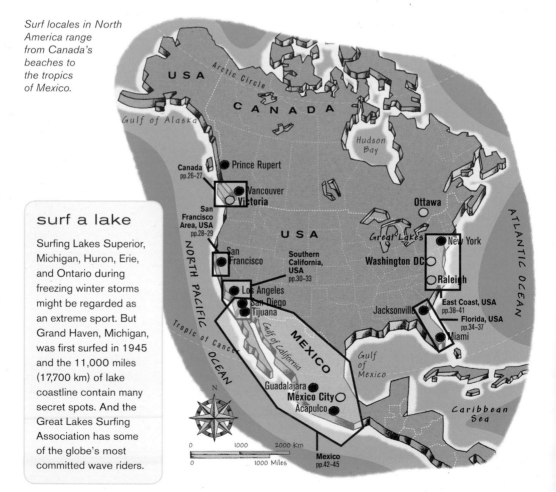

surf a lake

Surfing Lakes Superior, Michigan, Huron, Erie, and Ontario during freezing winter storms might be regarded as an extreme sport. But Grand Haven, Michigan, was first surfed in 1945 and the 11,000 miles (17,700 km) of lake coastline contain many secret spots. And the Great Lakes Surfing Association has some of the globe's most committed wave riders.

USA
Arctic Circle
CANADA
Gulf of Alaska
Hudson Bay

Canada pp.26–27 · Prince Rupert
Vancouver
Victoria
San Francisco Area, USA pp.28–29

Ottawa

NORTH PACIFIC OCEAN

San Francisco
USA
Southern California, USA pp.30–33
Great Lakes
New York
Washington DC
Raleigh
ATLANTIC OCEAN

Los Angeles
San Diego
Tijuana
Tropic of Cancer
Gulf of California
MEXICO
Jacksonville
East Coast, USA pp.38–41
Florida, USA pp.34–37
Miami

Gulf of Mexico

N

Guadalajara
Mexico City
Acapulco

Caribbean Sea

0   1000   2000 Km
0   1000 Miles

Mexico pp.42–45

August. SoCal can receive swell in summer from hurricanes off the coast of Mexico. A northwest swell in late fall and winter (October to February) comes from the same North Pacific Aleutian storms that see some of the planet's biggest waves hit Hawaii. This swell can slam the entire West Coast, with areas north of Point Conception receiving bigger swell than SoCal. Wind direction can be a problem, though. But when complex lows are fanned by hot, dry 25–50-knot gusts of the Santa Ana winds, you can experience ideal conditions.

Farther north, along the wet and wild west coast of Canada, surfing is growing in popularity. There are more surfers here than you might expect, and waves have been ridden regularly since the early 1960s at least. Vancouver Island offers some of the best breaks, especially between August and December.

On the Atlantic Ocean side of the continent, the 2,100-mile (3,380-km) US coast can be divided into three geographical areas. From the Canadian border to New York State's Long Island, it's mostly rocky coastline. The mid-Atlantic has sandy barrier islands. Then there's the long white-sand strips of Florida.

Surfing the left break in the shadow of the Golden Gate Bridge in San Francisco

The entire East Coast can be affected by Atlantic Ocean hurricanes and their big swells from June to November. The most intense hurricane period is August and September, but the best surf really gets underway in September and October. You can also find surf on the East Coast in winter and spring too, but come summer, there can be weeks at a time when barely a ripple stirs the coast all the way from New England to Florida.

Down Mexico way, you'll find three distinct surfing areas: Baja California, the Gulf Coast, and mainland Mexico. Baja offers world-class surf spots within a few hours' drive of the US border. The limited surf on the Gulf Coast comes from boosts in wind-swell due to the same winter cold fronts and summer hurricanes that hit the US East Coast. Mainland Mexico has many excellent breaks and waves year-round along its Pacific coast, thanks to swell from both the North and South Pacific Ocean.

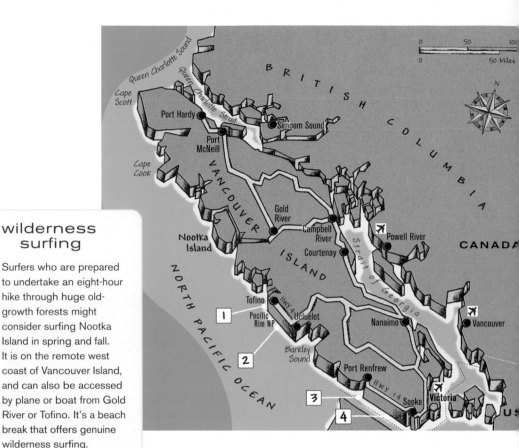

wilderness surfing

Surfers who are prepared to undertake an eight-hour hike through huge old-growth forests might consider surfing Nootka Island in spring and fall. It is on the remote west coast of Vancouver Island, and can also be accessed by plane or boat from Gold River or Tofino. It's a beach break that offers genuine wilderness surfing.

Canada

With its seemingly endless rain falling from seemingly endless gray skies, the west coast of Canada is not usually thought of as a surfer's paradise. But British Columbia, from the US border north to Prince Rupert, an area that also includes Vancouver Island, is a region of secret surf spots.

Secret spots are just that. Even less-secret spots can often only be reached by bumping down gouged logging roads in a four-wheel-drive. From a dead-end in a forest, you might need to hike through land inhabited by bears, cougars, and wolves to get to the waves.

Vancouver Island, off the west coast of Canada, is open to the regular swell from the immense Pacific Ocean. The waves that break here year-round are surprisingly good, although August through to December is the best time

to surf because the weather isn't really cold yet but the swell-generating storms in the North Pacific are becoming more frequent.

Tofino is Vancouver Island's surf capital, and Long Beach is its most accessible surf location, offering miles (kilometers) of surfable beach breaks, with a few points. Water temperatures in summer generally sit around 50°F (10°C). In winter, both air and water are around 39°–45°F (4°–7°C). Parks Canada strongly suggests a full-body wetsuit and booties year-round — most of its ocean rescues are of people not wearing wetsuits. And when the snow starts, you'll need a balaclava, gloves, and a titanium rash vest, too.

If you find yourself surfing a part of this coast where there are no hard-surfaced roads, and the only thing you have to dodge for waves is the kelp, you won't have any regrets.

1 Cox Bay

This little bay just south of Tofino provides great summer action and can be a little more consistent than Long Beach to the south. Although it will handle a larger swell than Long Beach, it can't handle the crowds, so you may want to avoid it on the busy weekends.

WAVE TYPE Left and right

WAVE HEIGHT 3–15 ft (0.9–4.6 m)

BREAK TYPE Beach

BEST SWELL W–NW

BEST WIND E–SE

BEST TIDE All

BEST TIME June–September

HAZARDS Rips, logs, weekend crowds

DIRECTIONS Drive south from Tofino on Hwy 4 and turn right at the Pacific Rim Beach Resort. Drive to the end of the road and park in the gravel lot. Follow the path to the beach.

2 Long Beach

Probably the best-known spot in British Columbia, Long Beach is a 6-mile (9.7-km) stretch of sandbars and shore break. It's a great spot for beginners or for enjoying the small summer waves with friends. It can be a little busy, but there are always plenty of peaks to choose from.

WAVE TYPE Left and right

WAVE HEIGHT 3–10 ft (0.9–3.1 m)

BREAK TYPE Beach

BEST SWELL W–NW

BEST WIND E–SE

BEST TIDE Mid–high

BEST TIME June–September

HAZARDS Rips, logs, weekend crowds

DIRECTIONS Drive south from Tofino on Hwy 4 to Pacific Rim National Park. Turn off into the Long Beach day parking lots.

3 Sombrio

Located on the southern end of Vancouver Island, Sombrio consists of three main breaks: Firsts, Seconds, and Chickens. Firsts and Seconds are more ledge–reef setups, while Chickens is more a beach break. The locals can get a little heavy at Firsts, and rightly so, as there are a couple of exposed rocks in the takeoff zone.

WAVE TYPE Left and right

WAVE HEIGHT 6–20 ft (1.8–6.1 m)

BREAK TYPE Reef and beach

BEST SWELL NW

BEST WIND E–SE

BEST TIDE All

BEST TIME October–April

HAZARDS Rips, logs, rocks, weekend crowds

DIRECTIONS Drive 5 miles (8 km) south of Port Renfrew on Hwy 14. Turn right at the Sombrio Beach Trailhead marker. Park in the lot at the end of the road and follow the trail to the beach.

4 Jordan River

Jordan River consists of two breaks: The Point and Sewers. When this wave starts to fire, it can serve up nice, long, clean rides all the way from The Point through to Sewers. It has a history of localism, and is one of the more heavily guarded breaks in British Columbia.

WAVE TYPE Left and right

WAVE HEIGHT 3–15 ft (0.9–4.6 m)

BREAK TYPE Point

BEST SWELL NW

BEST WIND E–SE

BEST TIDE Mid–high

BEST TIME October–April

HAZARDS Rips, logs, weekend crowds, territorial locals

DIRECTIONS Drive north on Hwy 14 from Sooke. The highway passes right through the small town of Jordan River and you can see the break on the left.

San Francisco Area, USA

North of the Santa Barbara Channel in California lies some rocky coastline, some pretty cold water, some fairly strong winds, and some mighty big waves. In fact, this region attracts the biggest waves in California.

This stretch of coast has three main surf regions: San Francisco, Santa Cruz, and the Monterey Peninsula. Around San Francisco, you'll find some of the most consistent and challenging surf in all of California. About 25 miles (40 km) south of the city, Pillar Point forms one of the few harbors on the Californian coast. A few miles north of Half Moon Bay and 400 yards (400 m) out to sea, Maverick's (named after a surfer's dog) is a place where men ride mountains. The surf season here peaks in December and January.

South of Half Moon Bay, 50 miles (80 km) of open coastline stretch along central California until you reach Santa Cruz. This cold-water playground, where Jack O'Neill finessed the wetsuit after settling here in 1959, has surf all year round. But fall and winter (September to February) are the most reliable seasons for delivering bigger and more consistent swell to the approximately 70 breaks along Santa Cruz's 45-mile (72-km) S-shaped coastline. You'll find isolated spots along this stretch, where the city's crowds are a memory. Farther south, much of the rocky coastline is inaccessible — search out the breaks of the Monterey Peninsula between Lover's Point and Carmel Beach.

The water rarely exceeds 60°F (15.5°C), so you'll need a minimum of a steamer all year.

1 Ocean Beach

Where the city meets the sea: San Francisco's Ocean Beach is a moody, 4-mile (6.4-km) stretch of beach-break peaks that vary with the tide, sandbars, and swells. They are best during large winter swells and offshore winds. Ocean Beach has been compared to Mexico's Puerto Escondido because when it's on, the barrels are enormous.

WAVE TYPE Left and right

WAVE HEIGHT 3–20 ft (0.9–6.1 m)

BREAK TYPE Beach

BEST SWELL SW–NW

BEST WIND E

BEST TIDE Varies depending on sandbars

BEST TIME September–March

HAZARDS Currents, sharks, cleanup sets, crowds, cold

DIRECTIONS From downtown San Francisco, head west until you reach the Great Hwy, which runs along the coast. There are 4 miles (6.4 km) of beach breaks between Kelly's Cove and Sloat Street. Parking is easy.

2 Maverick's

This is NorCal's premiere big-wave venue. Mav's is as deadly as it looks, having claimed the life of legendary big-wave surfer Mark Foo. Massive swells come out of deep water, creating inverted drop-ins over a jagged rock shelf and scattered boulders. For experts only.

WAVE TYPE Left and right

WAVE HEIGHT 12–40 ft (3.7–12.2 m)

BREAK TYPE Rock shelf

BEST SWELL NW

BEST WIND E

BEST TIDE Low–mid

BEST TIME September–March

HAZARDS Hold-downs, rocks, sharks, cold, broken boards

DIRECTIONS Head south from San Francisco on Hwy 1. Turn right on Capistrano Rd, right on Harvard Ave, right on West Point Ave, and park at the foot of the Navy Radar Towers. Take the path west to the beach. And look out to sea. Or go to Princeton Harbor and try to charter a boat.

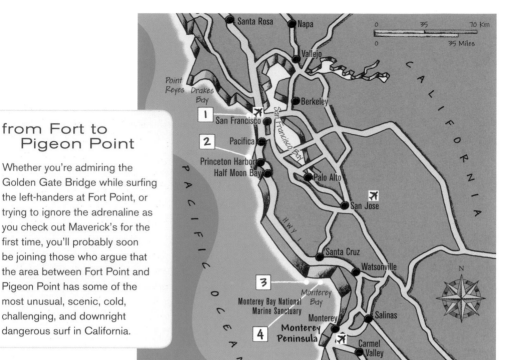

from Fort to Pigeon Point

Whether you're admiring the Golden Gate Bridge while surfing the left-handers at Fort Point, or trying to ignore the adrenaline as you check out Maverick's for the first time, you'll probably soon be joining those who argue that the area between Fort Point and Pigeon Point has some of the most unusual, scenic, cold, challenging, and downright dangerous surf in California.

3 Steamer Lane

Steamer Lane is Santa Cruz's West Side wonder, with four varied spots. The Point offers hollow rights on a south swell. The Slot allows you to take off next to the cliff for a shorter, punchier right-hander. Middle Peak (with First, Second, and Third Reefs) pops up during a nice northwest swell, while most of the crowd congregates at Indicators farther along the cove. This truly top-notch wave has a crowd that reflects its quality.

WAVE TYPE Left and right

WAVE HEIGHT 2–20 ft (0.6–6.1 m)

BREAK TYPE Reef, point

BEST SWELL S–NW

BEST WIND E, NW

BEST TIDE Mid

BEST TIME Year-round

HAZARDS Crowds, kelp, seals, rocks, cliff

DIRECTIONS Head along West Cliff Dve on Santa Cruz West Side to Lighthouse Point. There's parking along the point and at the Mark Abbott Memorial Lighthouse.

4 Pleasure Point

A very enjoyable wave, as the name implies, Pleasure Point can provide multiple sections over a stretch of four peaks. Beginning with Sewer Peak farthest outside, there's a dumpy, hollow right on a north swell and a fun left on a south. First Peak is a long right with a short left that fields a lot of longboarders, while Second Peak is less crowded but also a softer ride. Insides is a friendly wave over a reef peak that gives beginners and longboarders something to play with. Crowds are abundant.

WAVE TYPE Right and occasional left

WAVE HEIGHT 2–12 ft (0.6–3.7 m)

BREAK TYPE Rock, sand

BEST SWELL SW–NW

BEST WIND E, NW–N

BEST TIDE Low–mid

BEST TIME Year-round

HAZARDS Kelp, crowds, groms

DIRECTIONS Head along Opal Cliffs Dve on Santa Cruz East Side. There's parking at the top of the point.

Southern California, USA

There's *California Dreaming. California Girls. Hotel California. Californication. California Here I Come.* Is there any place on Earth that has inspired more song titles? While Hawaii is the ancient and spiritual home of surfing, SoCal has been its cultural capital and commodity incubator since the 1940s, inspiring music, film, and fashion.

Mention California and surfing, and Malibu, in Los Angeles County, soon pops into the conversation. Once described as the "exact spot on Earth where ancient surfing became modern surfing," Malibu's rise to fame also saw it become the first place to suffer really badly from crowds. Today, with an estimated population of about 750,000 surfers in California and nearly 10 million residents in Los Angeles County alone, both the crowd levels and water quality in Santa Monica Bay can get toxic.

Santa Barbara, Ventura, Orange, and San Diego Counties also offer quality breaks and their own surf scenes. Rincon, bordering Santa Barbara and Ventura, is America's best right point break, and rides up to 500 yards (500 m) long are rare but possible when conditions align.

The cool Pacific Ocean demands a wetsuit for most of the year. A 3/2 full wetsuit and booties will see you through winter. Even in summer, you'll want a springsuit.

SoCal has 200 miles (320 km) of surfing possibilities and a great climate. It's big, bold, and its beaches can provide a barrel bonanza.

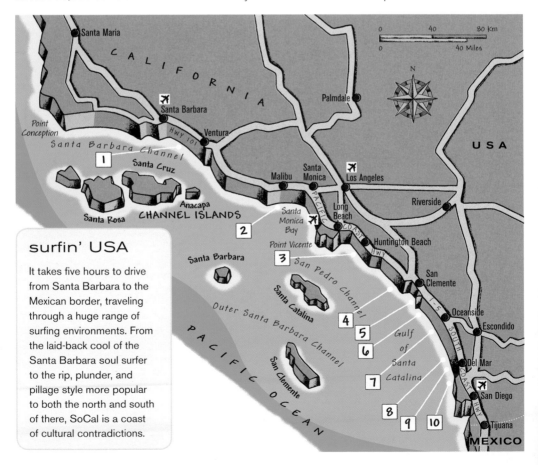

surfin' USA

It takes five hours to drive from Santa Barbara to the Mexican border, traveling through a huge range of surfing environments. From the laid-back cool of the Santa Barbara soul surfer to the rip, plunder, and pillage style more popular to both the north and south of there, SoCal is a coast of cultural contradictions.

1 Rincon

The textbook Californian point break, Rincon is truly world class when it's doing its thing. Known as the "Queen of the Coast," this long, reeling right-hander offers multiple barrel sections from the river mouth at the top of the point all the way to the beach. It's always crowded, but well worth it.

WAVE TYPE Right

WAVE HEIGHT 2–12 ft (0.6–3.7 m)

BREAK TYPE Point

BEST SWELL SW–NW

BEST WIND NE

BEST TIDE Low

BEST TIME September–March

HAZARDS Crowds, thieves

DIRECTIONS Head south on Hwy 101 from Santa Barbara. Take the Bates Rd exit. There's some free parking.

2 Malibu

Another classic Californian point break, Malibu almost always has a dense crowd. With movie stars' homes on the hill overlooking the point, it's a trendy SoCal surf spot but also a top-shelf wave. It has three distinct mini-points (Third, Second, and First), and during a southwest swell, Malibu can be one of the longest waves in the area.

WAVE TYPE Right

WAVE HEIGHT 1–12 ft (0.3–3.7 m)

BREAK TYPE Point

BEST SWELL S–WSW

BEST WIND NE

BEST TIDE Mid

BEST TIME April–October

HAZARDS Crowds, pollution

DIRECTIONS Head north along the Pacific Coast Hwy from Santa Monica. There is pay parking at the beach or free parking along the highway.

3 Huntington Beach

Surf City USA! Huntington has been the arena for many large-scale surfing contests over the years. Consistent beach-break peaks are scattered along the city's beaches, with the most energy (and competition) focused on The Pier. There are ridable waves all year, but during fall when the Santa Ana winds mix with combo swells, that's when HB really fires.

WAVE TYPE Left and right

WAVE HEIGHT 1–10 ft (0.3–3.1 m)

BREAK TYPE Beach

BEST SWELL S–NW

BEST WIND E

BEST TIDE Mid

BEST TIME Year-round

HAZARDS Localism, crowds, pier pilings, pollution

DIRECTIONS From I-405 in Huntington Beach, take the Beach Blvd exit and drive west. Pay parking is plentiful.

4 Salt Creek

This popular beach has something for everyone. To the north, a hollow, shallow sandbar known as Gravels dishes up grinding barrels. Middles sees hoards of bodyboarders and surfers mixing in the scattered beach-break-style peaks. To the south is The Point, which offers an exceptional left or right, depending on the swell direction. Great light makes Salt Creek a stage for countless pros and photographers trying to nail their next cover shot.

WAVE TYPE Left and right

WAVE HEIGHT 1–12 ft (0.3–3.7 m)

BREAK TYPE Beach with rock point

BEST SWELL S–NW

BEST WIND E–S

BEST TIDE Mid–high

BEST TIME September–April

HAZARDS Localism, crowds, shallow sandbars

DIRECTIONS Travel just north of Dana Point on the Pacific Coast Hwy. There's lots of pay parking at Salt Creek Beach Park.

5 Trestles

The most high-performance SoCal wave, Trestles is fed by a cobblestone river mouth and is separated into two main points: Uppers and Lowers. Lowers is a perfect A-frame wave that offers a long, rippable right and a shorter, more bowly left. Best on an overhead south swell, it's usually very crowded. Upper Trestles is a right point, unless the river is flowing, when it offers a short left into the mouth.

WAVE TYPE Left and right

WAVE HEIGHT 1–12 ft (0.3–3.7 m)

BREAK TYPE Point

BEST SWELL S–W

BEST WIND NE–E

BEST TIDE Mid

BEST TIME Year-round

HAZARDS Crowds, thieves, pollution, long hike

DIRECTIONS On I-5, just south of San Clemente, turn right at the Christianitos Rd exit. Turn left onto El Camino Real. Park at the free lot near Carl's Jr. Take the trail under the train trestle.

6 San Onofre

An extremely popular wave with longboarders, San Onofre is more about the surfing lifestyle than your wave-riding ability. Bring your beach chair, volleyball, barbecue, and longboard for a day at the beach. Three main breaks – Point, Old Man's, and Dogpatch – provide fun, rolling breakers that are considered the mainland equivalent of Waikiki.

WAVE TYPE Left and right

WAVE HEIGHT 1–8 ft (0.3–2.4 m)

BREAK TYPE Soft reef

BEST SWELL SW

BEST WIND E

BEST TIDE Mid

BEST TIME May–August

HAZARDS Crowds, loose longboards, nearby San Onofre Nuclear Power Plant, sharks

DIRECTIONS On I-5, just south of San Clemente, take the Basilone Rd exit. Turn right on the Old Pacific Hwy and follow the signs to San Onofre State Beach. There's pay parking.

7 Oceanside

Oceanside is a reliable stretch of coast that picks up most swells. It has several scattered peaks but two main surfing areas: Oceanside Pier and Harbor. At Harbor there are two jetties with consistent, punchy waves to be had. The Pier is often slightly smaller and mushes out on the higher tide.

WAVE TYPE Left and right

WAVE HEIGHT 1–8 ft (0.3–2.4 m)

BREAK TYPE Beach, pier, jetty

BEST SWELL SW–NW

BEST WIND E

BEST TIDE Mid

BEST TIME Year-round

HAZARDS Pollution from nearby harbor

DIRECTIONS On I-5 at the north end of San Diego County, take the Harbor Dr exit for Oceanside. Take Harbor Dr to the left until you reach North Pacific St. South Jetty is right in front of you. Turn right on North Pacific for North Jetty and left for The Pier. There's day parking at both.

8 Cardiff

Cardiff, a small series of flat reefs in front of a lagoon, can be a window of perfection during winter swells. South Peak offers a longer right, which ends in the channel. Cardiff's serious wave is Suckouts, a ledgy, right-hand barrel with a tight takeoff over a shallow reef. To the north is Tippers, which provides a faster left and a short right. The lineup is visible from the road.

WAVE TYPE Left and right

WAVE HEIGHT 2–10 ft (0.6–3.1 m)

BREAK TYPE Reef

BEST SWELL W–NW

BEST WIND E

BEST TIDE Low–mid

BEST TIME December–February

HAZARDS Crowds, reef at low tide

DIRECTIONS Drive just north of Cardiff-by-the-Sea along the South Coast Hwy 101. Look out for Sea Cliff County Park on the left. There's a pay parking lot in front of the break or free street parking farther north.

Bruce Irons takes to the air at The Pier at Huntington Beach in the 2003 Philips Fusion US Open of Surfing.

9 Blacks

Blacks is one of the best beach breaks in California. A deep-water canyon just offshore allows winter swells to jack up when they reach the beach's sandbars, so large swells hold form when it really starts pumping. There are three distinct peaks hucking out barreling lefts and rights when the wind is offshore. Blacks is almost always worth the hike in and the crowd.

WAVE TYPE Left and right

WAVE HEIGHT 1–15 ft (0.3–4.6 m)

BREAK TYPE Beach

BEST SWELL SW–NW

BEST WIND E–SE

BEST TIDE Low–mid

BEST TIME December–February

HAZARDS Falling cliffs, long hike, cleanup sets, currents, naked old men

DIRECTIONS Head south from Del Mar on Camino Del Mar. Turn right onto North Torrey Pines Rd, then right on La Jolla Farms Rd to Blackgold Rd. Hike down a steep path to the beach.

10 La Jolla

A long stretch of quirky reefs can dish up some serious perfection when the elements combine. San Clemente Island blocks west swells, but waves like The Cove, Windansea, Horseshoe, and Big Rock give plenty of options. The Cove is a thick, epic left that breaks when everywhere else is closed out. Windansea is one of the most popular breaks in San Diego County. Get out of your car every ½ mile (0.8 km) or so to evaluate which reef is the best that day.

WAVE TYPE Left and right

WAVE HEIGHT 2–25 ft (0.6–7.6 m)

BREAK TYPE Reef

BEST SWELL SSW–NW

BEST WIND E

BEST TIDE Varies depending on the reef

BEST TIME Year-round

HAZARDS Crowds, aggressive locals, reefs, caves

DIRECTIONS Search along the coast from La Jolla Cove south to PB Point and you're bound to find a reef that's working. There's street parking.

Florida, USA

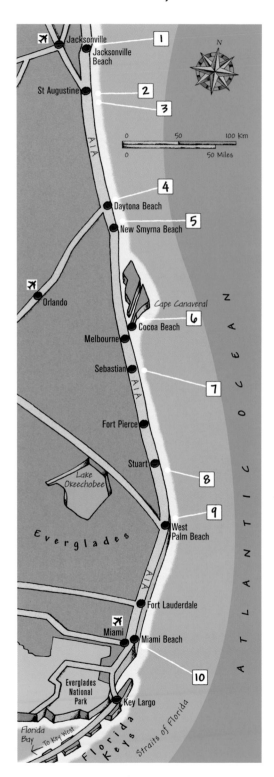

Florida's entire coast is bordered by a wide continental shelf and barrier islands such as The Bahamas, which stop much of the incoming swell dead. The fall hurricane season, from September to November, is the best time to surf, because of the strong groundswells that make it all the way to Florida's 580-mile (930-km) eastern coastline. Winter and spring provide fairly consistent windswells, and the occasional groundswell can have considerable grunt. Forget summer – it's all tourists, gridlock, stifling humidity, and flat surf.

The northern east coast of Florida, from Jacksonville to New Smyrna Beach, has many long, flat, hard-packed beaches that you can drive along. But it's the central coast, from rocket-launching Cape Canaveral south to Sebastian Inlet, that holds the area's most famous surf breaks, including Cocoa Beach. It's here that Kelly Slater first learned to launch himself from the water. Most spots south from Fort Pierce Inlet only get occasional ground-swells from sources north and northeast of the Bahama Bank. And the Florida Keys, a 150-mile (240-km) string of islands southwest of Florida, is not known for quality breaks.

Florida has subtropical weather, and even in winter the ocean rarely gets colder than 60°F (15.5°C). It's the ideal place for surfing – if you exclude June to August, with its humidity, heavy rain, and pancake-flat ocean.

shark attack capital

There's no escaping it. Florida is the shark attack capital of the world. Most aren't fatal. George Burgess, director of the International Shark Attack File at the University of Florida, estimates there were 62 recorded shark attacks worldwide in 2006. Florida had 23 of them. Burgess says Volusia County and particularly New Smyrna Beach are shark magnets – on a square mile basis, this area has more attacks than anywhere else in the world.

1 Mayport Poles

This long jetty at the southern end of St. Johns River is the best bet when a big nor'easter is pushing through. Although there are peaks along the beach at Hannah Park, the jetty keeps things relatively clean compared to elsewhere in the region. It provides a long, powerful ride.

WAVE TYPE Left and right

WAVE HEIGHT 1–12 ft (0.3–3.7 m)

BREAK TYPE Beach

BEST SWELL N–S

BEST WIND W

BEST TIDE All

BEST TIME October–March

HAZARDS Currents, sharks, pollution

DIRECTIONS From Jacksonville Beach, head north on A1A/3rd St, which turns left into Atlantic Ave. Make a right on Mayport Rd and head toward the Mayport US Naval Station. Enter through Hannah Park (there's a fee), park in lots 1–6, and walk north toward the jetty.

2 Blowhole

Once the best wave around thanks to an open inlet, Blowhole still serves up decent, punchy peaks even though the sand has filled in and the inlet is non-existent. It likes a lower tide and a southeast swell, but can hold at a higher tide with a bigger northeast swell. Other quality peaks exist within Anastasia State Recreation Area. Driving on the beach is now prohibited.

WAVE TYPE Left and right

WAVE HEIGHT 2–12 ft (0.6–3.7 m)

BREAK TYPE Beach

BEST SWELL E–SE

BEST WIND W

BEST TIDE Low–mid

BEST TIME Year-round

HAZARDS Crowds, floating debris

DIRECTIONS Head south from St. Augustine on A1A. Turn left on Anastasia Park Rd, enter the Anastasia State Recreation Area, and park at the end of the road. Walk ½ mile (0.8 km) north along the beach.

3 Matanzas Inlet

With no rock jetties securing the inlet, Matanzas sees many moods. Constantly shifting sands allow it to turn on or shut off for weeks at a time. Long lefts often peel into the inlet from the north, while multiple peaks that rely on optimal swell direction grace the south beach. It's very sharky.

WAVE TYPE Left and right

WAVE HEIGHT 2–10 ft (0.6–3.1 m)

BREAK TYPE Inlet

BEST SWELL NE–SE

BEST WIND W

BEST TIDE All

BEST TIME February–May

HAZARDS Sharks, currents, driving in soft sand

DIRECTIONS Head south from St. Augustine along A1A. Matanzas is the next inlet. Beach driving is allowed (a four-wheel-drive is best) via an on-ramp on the north side of the inlet, just before the bridge. There's free lot parking on the north side and free street parking on the south side.

4 Main Street Pier

Once ground zero for Daytona Beach's surf scene and for college students' springtime revelries, Main Street Pier these days isn't the hotspot it was back in the 1980s. However, good sandbars still build up along The Pier's pilings, offering fun rights and lefts. The heavy localism isn't as prevalent as it once was and you can usually rely on The Pier's consistency.

WAVE TYPE Left and right

WAVE HEIGHT 2–12 ft (0.6–3.7 m)

BREAK TYPE Beach

BEST SWELL NE–SE

BEST WIND W

BEST TIDE All

BEST TIME September–March

HAZARDS Crowds, tourists, jellyfish, drunk spring breakers

DIRECTIONS Drive east from downtown Daytona Beach on Main St. Take the Main Street Bridge straight to A1A and Main Street Pier is right in front of you. Pay parking is abundant.

5 Ponce Inlet and New Smyrna Beach

At this top-quality Florida inlet, the Ponce (north) side is best during a bigger south swell, which sends long, often barreling rights reeling down the beach. The New Smyrna (south) side is one of the most consistent breaks in Florida and the crowds reflect that. It has a tight local crew.

WAVE TYPE Left and right

WAVE HEIGHT 1–12 ft (0.3–3.7 m)

BREAK TYPE Inlet with jetty, beach

BEST SWELL E–SE

BEST WIND W

BEST TIDE All

BEST TIME September–May

HAZARDS Sharks, crowds, beach drivers, grumpy locals, jellyfish, jet skis

DIRECTIONS For Ponce Inlet, take South Atlantic Ave south from Daytona Beach to the end. Turn left onto the beach. For New Smyrna Beach, exit I-95 on Route 44. Head east until North Peninsula Ave and turn left. Turn right at Beach Way on-ramp and drive north on the beach.

6 Cocoa Beach

Home of eight-time ASP World Champion Kelly Slater, Cocoa Beach is the hub of the Central Florida surf scene. It offers fun waves on all swells, which are accentuated by the Cocoa Beach Pier. There is something for everyone here, whether you're an expert or a wannabe. However, when a good south swell is pulsing, you'll find better waves a quick drive south at Sebastian Inlet.

WAVE TYPE Left and right

WAVE HEIGHT 2–8 ft (0.6–2.4 m)

BREAK TYPE Beach

BEST SWELL NE–S

BEST WIND W

BEST TIDE High

BEST TIME September–March

HAZARDS Crowds, anglers

DIRECTIONS Take the A1A south from Cape Canaveral and you'll soon find yourself at the East Coast's version of Huntington Beach.

7 Sebastian Inlet

Sebastian Inlet is Florida's most high-profile wave. Of its three peaks, the most notorious is the side-wedging right at First Peak, often a high-quality barrel. A south swell and offshore winds send the wave and the crowds through the roof, but you'll find a mellower lineup at the northern end of the beach. On the inlet's south side is Monster Hole – an elusive deepwater sandbar that is sharky, and a marathon paddle, but holds long lefts on a north swell.

WAVE TYPE Left and right

WAVE HEIGHT 2–12 ft (0.6–3.7 m)

BREAK TYPE Inlet with jetty

BEST SWELL NE–SE

BEST WIND W

BEST TIDE Mid

BEST TIME September–March

HAZARDS Anglers, sharks, jellyfish, crowds

DIRECTIONS From Melbourne Beach, head south on A1A to Sebastian Inlet State Recreation Area. There's a small entry fee, and parking.

8 Stuart Rocks

This is a quality series of reefs that work best on a north swell, when Stuart Rocks can get just about perfect. The spread of peaks helps disperse the overabundance of surfers, although the local vibe can get heavy. There's a serious pecking order in this lineup, but if you wait your turn and are polite, you can be rewarded with some of the area's best waves.

WAVE TYPE Left and right

WAVE HEIGHT 2–12 ft (0.6–3.7 m)

BREAK TYPE Reef

BEST SWELL N–NE

BEST WIND W

BEST TIDE Low–mid

BEST TIME September–March

HAZARDS Crowds, territorial locals, reef

DIRECTIONS From Fort Pierce, take the South Causeway to A1A. Turn right and head south along the coast for about 2 miles (3.2 km). There's street and lot parking.

9 Reef Road

Florida's fabled big-wave spot is not for everybody. This large left-hander peaks up on an outside coquina reef near the southern side of Palm Beach Inlet and re-forms onto a sandy inside bank. Big nor'easters or hurricane swells fuel Reef Road's power. If the wind isn't off-shore, things can get a bit disorganized and ugly. You'll need high skill levels for this wave.

WAVE TYPE Left

WAVE HEIGHT 6–20 ft (1.8–6.1 m)

BREAK TYPE Reef

BEST SWELL N–NE

BEST WIND W

BEST TIDE Low–mid

BEST TIME September–March

HAZARDS Cleanup sets, currents, territorial locals

DIRECTIONS Head north from West Palm Beach along North Ocean Blvd. There's no parking within a mile (1.6 km) of the spot, which means a hike in. Walk along North Ocean Blvd to the beach at Dolphin Rd.

10 South Beach

This trendy (and fickle) place is quintessential Miami Beach. It can offer some of the best waves in the area when swells enter its window. The Bahamas block a lot of action, but when a solid pulse leaks through, hollow peaks are the norm and an epic right will occasionally reel off the north side of a jetty.

WAVE TYPE Left and right

WAVE HEIGHT 2–12 ft (0.6–3.7 m)

BREAK TYPE Beach

BEST SWELL NE–SE

BEST WIND W

BEST TIDE All

BEST TIME September–March

HAZARDS Crowds, pollution

DIRECTIONS From downtown Miami, take I-195 east to A1A. Head south to the end of A1A. South Beach is the southernmost beach before the start of the Florida Keys.

Summer crowds create gridlock on the hard-packed sand of Daytona Beach, near Main Street Pier.

1 Montauk Point

A lighthouse on the tip of New York's Long Island indicates you've reached the end of the road. It is also the home of some of New York's best point surf. Two distinct spots, North Bar and Turtle Cove, offer fast, down-the-line right-handers on southeast swells. Turtle Cove can handle some size and throw out the occasional barrel, while North Bar gets good when a large east or southeast swell wraps around the point. Watch the strong currents.

WAVE TYPE Right

WAVE HEIGHT 2–12 ft (0.6–3.7 m)

BREAK TYPE Point

BEST SWELL E–S

BEST WIND SW–W

BEST TIDE Mid

BEST TIME September–March

HAZARDS Crowds, sharks, jellyfish, currents

DIRECTIONS Take I-495 east from New York City to Long Island. Exit right on Sagtikos Parkway and continue on to Hwy 27. Turn left and head east as far as you can go.

2 Rockaway Beach

Rockaway is the closest surfing beach to New York City, so it sees all sorts. The lineups can be as crowded as Times Square even though these beach-break peaks rarely get epic. In fact, it takes a pretty powerful swell just to push sizable surf in here. Don't expect Rockaway to be a friendly, clean, or safe place to surf.

WAVE TYPE Left and right

WAVE HEIGHT 2–8 ft (0.6–2.4 m)

BREAK TYPE Beach

BEST SWELL E–S

BEST WIND NW

BEST TIDE All

BEST TIME September–March

HAZARDS Pollution, crowds, thieves

DIRECTIONS From Brooklyn, take the Marine Parkway Bridge to Rockaway. Parking is a few blocks from the beach.

East Coast, USA

The Outer Banks of North Carolina are a 130-mile (210-km) string of sandy barrier islands, or banks, that stretch into the Atlantic Ocean and cup the shoreline. Shipping crews know them as "The Graveyard of the Atlantic." But a graveyard to sailors can be a birth suite for surfers, and the Outer Banks deserves its reputation for consistency and quality.

A wide continental shelf squashes incoming swells along much of the East Coast. But the Outer Banks' narrow shelf means waves reach the beach unhindered. Its exposed locale attracts the full whack of all low-pressure systems, as well as nor'easters and other tropical and non-tropical events. The most popular area is around Cape Hatteras; the most popular time, the Atlantic Ocean's hurricane season from June to November. The hurricanes are what East Coast surfers live for, boosting North Carolina's resident surf population of about 10,000 as visitors arrive from all over.

To the north, surfing in Virginia occurs mostly around Virginia Beach at First Street Jetty. The State is notorious as the only place in the United States where surfers are required by law to wear leashes. Delaware has a small surfing scene, while New Jersey has 130 miles (210 km) of coast, mainly consisting of beach breaks that work best when near jetties. New York's most consistent and sizable offerings along its 127-mile (204-km) Long Island coast are the point breaks around Montauk.

Winter on the East Coast from Montauk Point to the Outer Banks is for the hardcore only. Water temperatures drop as low as 30°F (1°C), making booties, gloves, a hood, and a sealed 4/3 wetsuit a must. In spring and fall, you'll at least need a steamer and booties.

3 Belmar

A fun stretch of jetties put in place to reduce erosion around nearby coastal homes, Belmar, south to Sea Girt, can get all-time when the right elements are in place. Constantly moving sand will typically make one peak much better than the next, depending on the tide. While it can't hold as big a swell as Manasquan, Belmar really shines when offshore winds mix with overhead surf.

WAVE TYPE Left and right

WAVE HEIGHT 2–10 ft (0.6–3.1 m)

BREAK TYPE Beach

BEST SWELL NE–S

BEST WIND W

BEST TIDE Low–mid

BEST TIME September–March

HAZARDS Crowds, submerged stormwater drains

DIRECTIONS From the New Jersey Turnpike, take I-195 east, which becomes Route 138. Continue straight until you reach Belmar. Go north on Route 71, then turn right on 5th St. There's pay parking.

4 Manasquan Inlet

Manasquan Inlet is possibly the best wave in New Jersey when it's cranking. It goes off thanks to deep water outside the inlet, a long jetty, and optimal sandbars. Amazing barrels develop with a south to southeast swell and offshore winds. The Inlet can hold some serious size and the crowds tend to thin out as the wave heights climb. Good waves can also be found at a series of smaller jetties up the beach.

WAVE TYPE Left and right

WAVE HEIGHT 2–15 ft (0.6–4.6 m)

BREAK TYPE Beach

BEST SWELL SE–S

BEST WIND W

BEST TIDE Low–mid

BEST TIME September–March

HAZARDS Crowds, localism, currents, thick lips

DIRECTIONS From the New Jersey Turnpike, take I-195 east to Route 34. Turn right and drive on to Manasquan. Turn left before the bridge and take Green Ave. At Brielle Rd, turn right, then take 3rd Ave to the beach. There's pay parking.

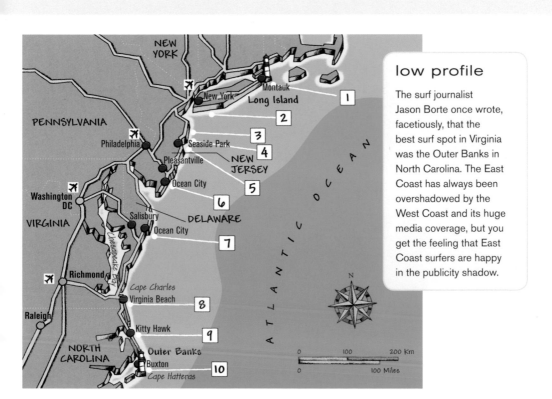

low profile

The surf journalist Jason Borte once wrote, facetiously, that the best surf spot in Virginia was the Outer Banks in North Carolina. The East Coast has always been overshadowed by the West Coast and its huge media coverage, but you get the feeling that East Coast surfers are happy in the publicity shadow.

5 Seaside Heights

A classic New Jersey pier setup, replete with amusement rides and a boardwalk, Seaside Heights can also be tube city for surfers. Peaks either side of the pier's roller-coaster ride can produce pristine tubes in the right conditions. South of the pier a few hundred yards (meters) is Seaside Park, where plenty of quality rogue peaks can pop up. Parking is a nightmare during tourist season (from June to August).

WAVE TYPE Left and right

WAVE HEIGHT 2–12 ft (0.6–3.7 m)

BREAK TYPE Beach

BEST SWELL NE–SE

BEST WIND W

BEST TIDE All

BEST TIME September–March

HAZARDS Crowds, lack of parking, distracting amusement rides

DIRECTIONS From the Garden State Parkway, take Route 37 east until you hit the beach. There is pay parking.

6 Ocean City, New Jersey

Constantly moving sands create ideal setups along a series of jetties and rocks at Ocean City, giving surfers plenty of options. The rights are good on a south swell and the lefts are best on a north. The area's accessibility, consistency, and larger sets mean that it draws the crowds. It gets so packed, surfing is restricted to before 9:30 AM and after 5 PM from Memorial Day to Labor Day (late May to early September).

WAVE TYPE Left and right

WAVE HEIGHT 2–18 ft (0.6–5.5 m)

BREAK TYPE Beach

BEST SWELL NE–SE

BEST WIND W–NW

BEST TIDE All

BEST TIME September–March

HAZARDS Surfing restrictions, storm pipes, crowds

DIRECTIONS From Pleasantville, take Route 9 over the bridge to Ocean City. Turn left on Wesley Ave, then right on 3rd, 5th, or 12th Streets, and continue on to the beach. There's pay parking.

At Virginia Beach, a surfer takes advantage of the swell, courtesy of a hurricane heading toward the coast.

7 Ocean City, Maryland

Ocean City may be a popular mid-Atlantic tourist destination, but it also gets great surf. The two best bets here are The Pier and The Inlet. While there's nearly always something to ride at The Inlet, the nice stretch of peaks between the north jetty and The Pier is somewhere else to consider when it gets ultracrowded.

WAVE TYPE Left and right

WAVE HEIGHT 2–12 ft (0.6–3.7 m)

BREAK TYPE Beach

BEST SWELL NE–S

BEST WIND W

BEST TIDE Mid–high

BEST TIME September–March

HAZARDS Currents, crowds

DIRECTIONS From Ocean City, take Ocean Gateway (Route 50) and turn right on South Philadelphia Ave, then left on South 1st St for The Inlet. Take another left on South Boardwalk for The Pier. There's lots of parking.

8 Virginia Beach

While far from perfect, Virginia Beach has a cruisy, typically mid-Atlantic atmosphere for surfers and tourists alike, plus surf. The Pier is always reliable, but there are better waves to the south toward Croatan Beach. Hoards of visitors mean surfing is restricted to before 10 AM and after 4 PM from Memorial Day to Labor Day (late May to early September).

WAVE TYPE Left and right

WAVE HEIGHT 2–10 ft (0.6–3.1 m)

BREAK TYPE Beach

BEST SWELL NE–SE

BEST WIND W

BEST TIDE All

BEST TIME September–March

HAZARDS Seasonal surfing restrictions, crowds, anglers, parking

DIRECTIONS From downtown Virginia Beach, drive east on Hwy 58. Turn right on Pacific Ave, then take 14th St. The Pier is at Atlantic Ave and 14th. There's metered parking.

9 Nags Head

Nags Head is a stellar Outer Banks wave, although its quality comes and goes with the everchanging sand bottom. The Nags Head Pier was an extremely popular spot in the 1960s and can still get pretty epic when the sand is in the right spot, offering hollow barrels off either side of the pier's pilings.

WAVE TYPE Left and right

WAVE HEIGHT 2–15 ft (0.6–4.6 m)

BREAK TYPE Beach

BEST SWELL NE–SE

BEST WIND W

BEST TIDE All

BEST TIME June–November (hurricane season)

HAZARDS Crowds, anglers

DIRECTIONS From Kitty Hawk, drive south on State Hwy 12 to Jockey Ridge State Park in Nags Head. Park at the nearby pier.

10 Cape Hatteras Lighthouse

Exposed to virtually all swells, the three groins at the Cape Hatteras Lighthouse provide some of the best and most consistent waves in the region. Since it's hanging virtually all alone in the mid-Atlantic, Cape Hatteras is constantly overrun by hurricanes. But if the storms stay far enough off the coast, the miles of shifting sandbanks around the Lighthouse can throw out some of the East Coast's biggest tubes.

WAVE TYPE Left and right

WAVE HEIGHT 2–12 ft (0.6–3.7 m)

BREAK TYPE Beach

BEST SWELL NE–SE

BEST WIND W

BEST TIDE Low–mid

BEST TIME June–November (hurricane season)

HAZARDS Crowds, rocks, floating debris

DIRECTIONS Drive south on State Hwy 12 to Buxton. Turn left on Cape Hatteras Lighthouse Rd. There are parking lots.

the Gulf Coast

The Mexican stretch of coast along the Gulf of Mexico is probably best described as reliably unreliable. What surf it does get comes from boosts in windswell from cold fronts in winter and hurricanes in summer. But like nearly all the unreliable places in the world, the right time and right place can bring some good scores. Most surfing here happens in the resort areas of Cancun and Cozumel.

Mexico

With more than 6,000 miles (9,660 km) of coastline, Mexico offers a vast range of surfing possibilities. There can be waves year-round along the 775-mile (1,250-km) peninsula of Baja California. May is the most consistent month for south swell, while in fall (September to October) you'll get remnants of this swell along with the season's more common north swell. Winter (December to March) can see Killers, off the island of Todos Santos, deliver massive waves.

The 2,500-mile (4,020-km) Pacific coast of mainland Mexico gets waves year-round, too. June to October consistently provides waves of 3–6 ft (0.9–1.8 m). The southern half of Mexico tends to fire up more around this time, while the northern stretch attracts more waves in winter. South-facing beaches get the best swell from May to October, mainly from storms tracking east from below New Zealand. Arctic storms bring swell to the west-facing beaches in winter.

There are international airports in major cities throughout the country, and buses and local minibuses will get you to most places. The climate and the air temperatures vary from desert to tropical. Cold-water upwelling in Baja makes a steamer necessary at all times. On the Pacific coast north of Puerto Vallarta, you might need a springsuit at times. To the south, boardshorts and a rashguard will get you through the year in the 80°F (27°C) water.

Sharks, pollution, and theft can be problems. Violent crime occurs in tourist areas, while some spots off the beaten track offer the joy and danger of surfing in splendid isolation. Get the necessary inoculations and antimalarial medicines before you leave, and pack an insect repellent that contains DEET.

1 Todos Santos

Todos Santos is a thumping, big-wave spot that is 12 miles (19 km) off the coast of North Baja California. A very heavy right catches all available swell. The aptly named Killers is the main break and it catches the most swell. This means that you can at least double whatever swell is hitting Baja's coast.

WAVE TYPE Right

WAVE HEIGHT 5–20 ft (1.5–6.1 m)

BREAK TYPE Reef

BEST SWELL NW

BEST WIND NE–E

BEST TIDE Rising

BEST TIME April–October

HAZARDS Rips, hold-downs, cold

DIRECTIONS Take a boat from Ensenada Harbor to the island of Todos Santos.

2 Patoles

Patoles is an epic, barreling left, renowned for its consistency, that rivals the barrels of Indonesia, without the crowds. Not only that, there are lots of other point breaks right nearby that are just as good.

WAVE TYPE Left

WAVE HEIGHT 5–8 ft (1.5–2.4 m)

BREAK TYPE Point

BEST SWELL S–SW

BEST WIND NE

BEST TIDE Mid

BEST TIME March–June

HAZARDS Rocks, rips, access road

DIRECTIONS It's a two-hour drive from Mazatlán, and a four-wheel-drive is recommended — although in the rainy season (May–September), access is near impossible. Heading north on the toll road from Mazatlán, take the Km 69 exit. Drive for 3 miles (4.8 km), then turn left at the bottom of the hill. Turn right under the second railroad underpass. Continue to the beach.

3 Stoners

This right-hand point break can be fun when there's enough swell. It's not the most consistent wave in the area, but when it's on, it can really fire. This is a semisecret spot, so respect the locals and you'll be respected in return.

WAVE TYPE Right

WAVE HEIGHT 5–12 ft (1.5–3.7 m)

BREAK TYPE Point

BEST SWELL S–SW

BEST WIND NE

BEST TIDE Low–mid

BEST TIME April–October

HAZARDS Rocks, rips, crocodiles and sharks near river mouth

DIRECTIONS In San Blas, head to the town's main beach, Playa Borrega. Walk south to the river mouth. Paddle across the river (keeping an eye out for crocs and sharks), then follow the path through the jungle. This will bring you to Stoners Point.

4 Pascuales

A seriously heavy wave, Pascuales stands toe to toe with Puerto Escondido for the title of Mexico's premier beach break. It catches plenty of swell, particularly from the south. A fast, pitching wave, it has plenty of rewards for experienced tube riders. That said, there are serious consequences for the unprepared.

WAVE TYPE Left and right

WAVE HEIGHT 3–12 ft (0.9–3.7 m)

BREAK TYPE Beach

BEST SWELL SE–S

BEST WIND NE

BEST TIDE All

BEST TIME April–October

HAZARDS Rocks, rips

DIRECTIONS From downtown Tecomán, follow the signs to Boca de Pascuales. It's about 7 miles (12 km) south of Tecomán.

5 La Ticla

This very consistent point break has waves all year round. It has lots of variety, and serves up nice barrels and very workable faces. It can get pretty crowded when the swell is on.

WAVE TYPE Left and right

WAVE HEIGHT 3–12 ft (0.9–3.7 m)

BREAK TYPE Point

BEST SWELL SW–W

BEST WIND NE–SE

BEST TIDE All

BEST TIME April–October

HAZARDS Rocks, rips, crowds

DIRECTIONS Head south from Tecomán on Hwy 200 for about 50 miles (80 km). Turn off on the road marked with the La Ticla sign. It's about 2½–3 miles (4–4.8 km) to the beach.

6 Río Nexpa

This beautiful, long, tubing left can run up to 300 yards (300 m) on the right swell. The biggest of these happen during the rainy season (June to September), but Río Nexpa is surfable year-round. There's not much to do here apart from surf perfect waves.

WAVE TYPE Left

WAVE HEIGHT 6–16 ft (1.8–4.9 m)

BREAK TYPE River mouth

BEST SWELL S–SW

BEST WIND N–NE

BEST TIDE All

BEST TIME April–October

HAZARDS Rocks, rips, sharks, crocodiles

DIRECTIONS Take a bus or fly to Zihuatanejo. From there, take a taxi directly to Río Nexpa or, more economically, take the bus from Zihuatanejo to Lázaro Cárdenas and then on to Caleta de Campos. Then hire a taxi to drive you the last 6 miles (10 km) to Río Nexpa.

7 El Rancho

El Rancho is a fast reef break that catches all available swell. It isn't a particularly tuby wave but it has fun, long walls nonetheless. The A-frame setup keeps feuding goofyfoots and natural footers happy.

WAVE TYPE Left and right

WAVE HEIGHT 3–8 ft (0.9–2.4 m)

BREAK TYPE Reef

BEST SWELL S–SW

BEST WIND NE

BEST TIDE Low–mid

BEST TIME April–October

HAZARDS Rocks, rips, deep water, remote location

DIRECTIONS Head north from Zihuatanejo on Hwy 200 and turn off to one of the small fishing villages along the coast. Take a ride with one of the more sturdy fishing boats — the fishermen will know where you want to go. Alternatively, drive north from Zihuatanejo on Hwy 200 for about one hour until the left turnoff for El Rancho. Follow the dirt road.

8 Chacahua

Ever wanted to feel like the only surfer on the planet? This is the place. A tiny fishing village nestled among a national park of lagoons, with a fantastic right point break. It feels as though it goes on forever, and there's no one out! You can negotiate with the locals for a room.

WAVE TYPE Right

WAVE HEIGHT 3–8 ft (0.9–2.4 m)

BREAK TYPE Point

BEST SWELL S

BEST WIND N–NE

BEST TIDE Low–mid

BEST TIME April–October

HAZARDS Rocks, rips, lots of biting insects (bring a repellent with DEET)

DIRECTIONS Head north from Rio Grande on Hwy 200. To go in by boat, take the Zapotalillo turnoff and ask local fishermen for a ride to Lagunas de Chacahua. In a four-wheel-drive, take Hwy 200 to San José del Progreso. Turn left and go to El Azufre. Take a long sand track to the beach.

9 Puerto Escondido

Puerto Escondido has the world-famous, sand-bottom "Mexican Pipeline," so named because it breaks with similar ferocity to its famous Hawaiian namesake. Bring a longer board with heavy glass. If you're willing to commit, you will get some insanely hollow barrels or a beating you'll never forget. Most waves are found on the stretch of beach called Zicatela. The World Masters Championship is held here in August.

WAVE TYPE Left and right

WAVE HEIGHT 3–16 ft (0.9–4.9 m)

BREAK TYPE Beach

BEST SWELL S–SW

BEST WIND NE

BEST TIDE Low–mid

BEST TIME April–October

HAZARDS Rocks, rips

DIRECTIONS From downtown Puerto Escondido, head south on Oaxaca Ave. Turn left on Hwy 200, then right on Calle del Morro, which runs along Playa Zicatela.

10 La Punta

La Punta is the left point break at the southern tip of Puerto Escondido's main beach. A little easier to negotiate than the beach breaks of Puerto, this wave can be a quite challenging, but fun, alternative.

WAVE TYPE Left

WAVE HEIGHT 3–16 ft (0.9–4.9 m)

BREAK TYPE Point

BEST SWELL S–SW

BEST WIND NE

BEST TIDE Mid–high

BEST TIME April–October

HAZARDS Rocks, rips, sea snakes

DIRECTIONS From downtown Puerto Escondido, go south on Oaxaca Ave. Turn left on Hwy 200 then right on Calle del Morro. Head for the southern end of the beach and the bay.

Tony Ray heads down Killers at Todos Santos. No matter what size it breaks at, this wave is a challenge.

Introduction

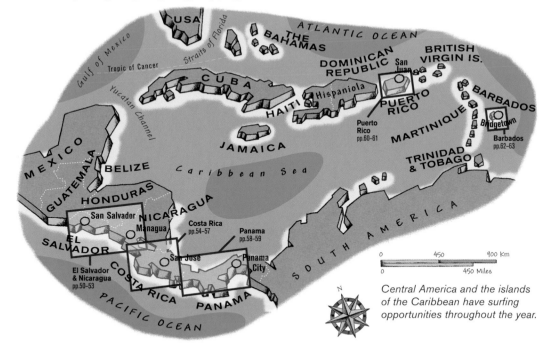

Central America and the islands of the Caribbean have surfing opportunities throughout the year.

Central America and the Caribbean islands may be a very small area, but it's one with lots of quality waves. The islands extend from Puerto Rico and Hispaniola in an arc southward to Trinidad and Tobago. Central America has a Caribbean and a Pacific coastline. With long, cobblestone point breaks on the Pacific coast and shallow coral reef breaks on the Caribbean side, long-term groundswell and short-term windswell, as well as powerful hurricane surf, this area has something for every surfer.

Surf the Four Seasons

During the winter months (November to February), the Atlantic sides of the Caribbean islands enjoy their best season, with strong north swells from winter storms off the US East Coast. Breaks on the deep-water coral reefs of Puerto Rico can get up to 15 ft (4.6 m), with 30-ft (9.1-m) wave faces. Breaks on islands such as Hispaniola (Haiti and the Dominican Republic), Tortola (in the British Virgin Islands), Martinique, and Barbados are smaller.

The winter swells in the Caribbean drop off in March. Then the springtime action shifts to the Pacific coast of Central America. El Salvador, Nicaragua, and Costa Rica have some of the widest swell windows of anywhere on the planet, being open to groundswell from nearly 180 degrees. Dry-season offshore winds still blow through April, while strong southwest swells travel thousands of miles (kilometers) across the Pacific from the Southern Hemisphere. So at this time of year, this coast is one of the most consistent surfing areas anywhere.

Bathsheba, on Barbados's east coast, has quality breaks such as Soup Bowl, Parlors, and High Rock nearby.

Summer sees the swell energy continue on the Pacific coast, with nonstop southwest swells from June to August. The rainy season (May to October) brings afternoon thunderstorms and onshore winds from Panama all the way to southern Mexico. It's best to get out in the morning, before the waves blow out. The Caribbean islands lack solid groundswell, but those islands exposed to the northeast trade winds, such as Jamaica, the Dominican Republic, and Barbados, get consistent windswell from high-pressure systems in the Atlantic.

In mid-August, the swell energy shifts again. The islands of the western Caribbean get windswells, while on the Atlantic side of the islands from Barbados to Puerto Rico, hurricane-generated groundswells from storms in the Atlantic Ocean roll in. Sustained high-pressure areas in the Gulf of Mexico can produce solid windswell along the Caribbean coasts of Nicaragua, Costa Rica, and Panama, too. The result: powerful waves up to 10 ft (3.1 m) hit the many reef and beach breaks in this area.

The water is warm to downright hot, particularly on the Pacific coast. You'll only want a wetsuit for tempering windchill from strong offshore winds. A long-sleeved rashguard is a good idea though, given the intense tropical sun.

Occasional political instability can occur in this region, and countries such as Jamaica, Costa Rica, and Panama have high levels of street crime. Mosquitoes are everywhere, and nearly everyone gets a gastrointestinal bug at some stage. Dengue fever is common in Central America. Check government travel advisories and get inoculations and medicines before you leave. Then prepare for the quality waves that can be found here at any time of the year.

Atlantic hurricanes

Hurricanes mostly form well out in the Atlantic Ocean between longitude 5 and 15 degrees north of the equator, off West Africa. Once a storm system begins to spin counterclockwise and head west, it gathers strength and wind speed, generating powerful groundswell in many directions. Hurricanes are unpredictable. High winds and flooding bring destruction and terrible loss of life when storm systems make landfall. But they also bring epic surf conditions to the Caribbean and Central America.

El Salvador and Nicaragua

El Salvador and Nicaragua are becoming more and more popular with visiting surfers. Many are Americans, heading south in the classic quest for quality, uncrowded waves — and this is one place that won't disappoint.

The waves have always been there, but the destruction and political upheaval of civil wars, plus zero or rudimentary facilities for visitors, have kept all but the most determined surf travelers away until recently. Now all that has changed. Growing political stability has attracted investment, and deluxe surf lodges have sprung up along the Pacific coast. Several places, most notably around San Juan del Sur in Nicaragua, are veritable surfing boomtowns, with day-boat charters, accommodation, restaurants, and real estate agencies sprouting overnight to cater for the gringo *surfistas* and their US dollars.

The rugged coastline facing the Pacific Ocean, from the long-established surfing area of La Libertad in El Salvador to the new boomtown of San Juan del Sur in southern Nicaragua, is one of the most consistent surf zones on the planet. It gets regular groundswell from distant storms in both the Northern and Southern Hemispheres. Consistent offshore winds predominate during the dry season (November to April). In the rainy season (June to October), morning offshore winds are the rule — get out then, before the afternoon deluge sets in and the waves blow out.

Point breaks abound, thanks to the frequent rains washing rocks and sand into the ocean. These form long sandbars, which are ideal for receiving clean groundswell and shaping it into long and perfect surfing waves.

1 Km 61, El Salvador

This right-hand point is slightly mellower than its next-door neighbor, Km 59. Because it's a fair distance from La Libertad, it is often less crowded than other waves in the region, and it produces long, workable walls that break over a rock bottom. It can be tricky to get out, though — if it's too difficult off the beach, paddle out from Km 59.

WAVE TYPE Right

WAVE HEIGHT 3–6 ft (0.9–1.8 m)

BREAK TYPE Reef

BEST SWELL S–SW

BEST WIND N–NE

BEST TIDE All

BEST TIME May–September

HAZARDS Rocks

DIRECTIONS Take the Carretera del Litoral (Central America 2) west along the coast from La Libertad. The beach is at the Km 61 mark.

2 Km 59, El Salvador

Km 59 is in a gated community and it's hard to access unless you're staying in one of the surf camps on the point. However, with a bit of effort, you can get in on foot from the main road. It's a fast, barreling right, and a good proposition if you can get to it because of its consistency and the lack of crowds.

WAVE TYPE Right

WAVE HEIGHT 4–8 ft (1.2–2.4 m)

BREAK TYPE Reef

BEST SWELL S–SW

BEST WIND N–NE

BEST TIDE All

BEST TIME May–September

HAZARDS Rocks

DIRECTIONS Take the Carretera del Litoral (Central America 2) west along the coast from La Libertad. The beach is at the Km 59 mark. Park and then clamber through the forest to the beach.

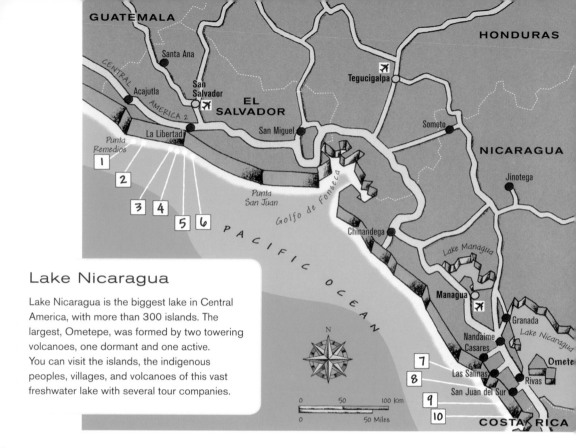

Lake Nicaragua

Lake Nicaragua is the biggest lake in Central America, with more than 300 islands. The largest, Ometepe, was formed by two towering volcanoes, one dormant and one active. You can visit the islands, the indigenous peoples, villages, and volcanoes of this vast freshwater lake with several tour companies.

3 Sunzal, El Salvador

Arguably the longest break in El Salvador, Sunzal produces waves on even the smallest swells. There are a number of hotels right in front of the break, and it is very popular with surf tourists, so watch out for an inexperienced crowd throwing their boards when set waves roll through. The local surfers are good and don't like to give up their waves easily. It is very deep out the back but can produce a nice bowl section through the inside on a lower tide.

WAVE TYPE Right

WAVE HEIGHT 4–8 ft (1.2–2.4 m)

BREAK TYPE Reef

BEST SWELL S–SW

BEST WIND N–NE

BEST TIDE Lower

BEST TIME May–September

HAZARDS Inexperienced crowds, territorial locals

DIRECTIONS Take the Carretera del Litoral (Central America 2) 5 miles (8 km) west of La Libertad.

4 La Bocana, El Salvador

One of the few lefts in El Salvador, La Bocana is a very fun, rippable wave when everywhere else is small. The localism can be very heavy, although it's mainly on the weekends, when the "locals" drive down from San Salvador. They love to tell foreigners to get out – forcibly. Watch your ankles when you walk out across the boulders, as they roll around on the bottom.

WAVE TYPE Left

WAVE HEIGHT 3–6 ft (0.9–1.8 m)

BREAK TYPE Reef

BEST SWELL S–SW

BEST WIND N–NE

BEST TIDE Medium–high

BEST TIME May–September

HAZARDS Rocks, territorial locals

DIRECTIONS Take the Carretera del Litoral (Central America 2) 4¼ miles (7 km) west of La Libertad.

5 Punta Roca, El Salvador

The Punta is the most famous wave in El Salvador, a long, racing right point break capable of barreling for hundreds of yards (meters) and throwing up long, whackable sections. It breaks out the back and then peels through the cove in front of the cemetery in the town of La Libertad. You need to be very careful in La Libertad though – it's a dangerous and unwelcoming place.

WAVE TYPE Right

WAVE HEIGHT 4–12 ft (1.2–3.7 m)

BREAK TYPE Reef

BEST SWELL S–SW

BEST WIND N–NE

BEST TIDE Medium–high

BEST TIME May–September

HAZARDS Rocky bottom, crowds, pollution, dangerous town

DIRECTIONS Walk to the point at the western end of the beach, Playa La Paz, which is right in front of La Libertad.

6 La Paz, El Salvador

Inside Punta Roca is a tamer section of beach known as La Paz. This can get really crowded with longboarders and beginners, but it's a gentle, easy wave where learners and kids can hone their skills. It can occasionally get good. But if La Paz is good, Punta Roca will be firing!

WAVE TYPE Left and right

WAVE HEIGHT 2–4 ft (0.6–1.2 m)

BREAK TYPE Sand, rock

BEST SWELL S–SW

BEST WIND N–NE

BEST TIDE All

BEST TIME May–September

HAZARDS Crowds, pollution, dangerous town

DIRECTIONS Go to the beach right in front of La Libertad. Look for the break between Punta Roca and the pier.

Jimmy Rotherham in the air at Punta Roca. This point break has some of the best waves in Central America.

7 Popoyo (Papollo), Nicaragua

Popoyo, or Papollo, is one of the busiest surf locales in Nicaragua. Before the creek, there's a long stretch of highly variable beach breaks. Inside Reef is across the creek, a left and right that breaks on a flat rock shelf. Boat access is the only way to get to the fabled Outer Reef. This huge, powerful, barreling left breaks over a shallow reef – for experts only.

WAVE TYPE Left and right

WAVE HEIGHT 2–6 ft (0.6–1.8 m)

BREAK TYPE Beach, rock shelf, reef

BEST SWELL SW

BEST WIND NE

BEST TIDE All

BEST TIME May–September

HAZARDS Crowds

DIRECTIONS Take the road southwest out of Nandaime. There's a maze of unsigned dirt roads to the coast road, so a guide is a good idea. Once on the coast road, head south until the road ends at a creek south of Las Salinas.

8 Manzanillo, Nicaragua

Manzanillo is a long, long left point with many barrel sections and workable walls. It's in an inaccessible part of Rivas Province, and chartering a boat from San Juan del Sur is the only option for surfing this fickle, yet legendary, wave. Do NOT risk crossing private land to get to the point.

WAVE TYPE Left

WAVE HEIGHT 4–12 ft (1.2–3.7 m)

BREAK TYPE Reef

BEST SWELL SW

BEST WIND NE

BEST TIDE Mid

BEST TIME May–September

HAZARDS Heavy wave

DIRECTIONS Charter a boat from San Juan del Sur.

9 Madera, Nicaragua

Set amidst picturesque scenery in the middle of nowhere, Madera boasts a number of beach break peaks along its bay. It's often crowded with backpacker learners and hard-core locals, but if you exercise courtesy in the water, you should have a lot of fun. The best break is directly in front of the *cabina* on the beach.

WAVE TYPE Left and right

WAVE HEIGHT 2–6 ft (0.6–1.8 m)

BREAK TYPE Beach

BEST SWELL SW

BEST WIND NE

BEST TIDE All

BEST TIME May–August

HAZARDS Crowds

DIRECTIONS Take the dirt road north from San Juan del Sur along the coast. After five to ten minutes, turn left at a little restaurant and follow the road for five to ten minutes. At a chicken farm, take the left fork, go over a big hill (use a four-wheel-drive after rain), and you're there.

10 Playa El Yanqui, Nicaragua

Playa El Yanqui is a fun wave that can get quite hollow at times. It has well-defined left and right breaks about 200 yards (200 m) apart. It attracts more swell than surrounding areas, so it's a great option on a smaller swell when other places are flat.

WAVE TYPE Left and right

WAVE HEIGHT 2–6 ft (0.6–1.8 m)

BREAK TYPE Beach

BEST SWELL SW

BEST WIND NE

BEST TIDE All

BEST TIME May–September

HAZARDS None

DIRECTIONS Take the road south out of San Juan del Sur for 6 miles (10 km).

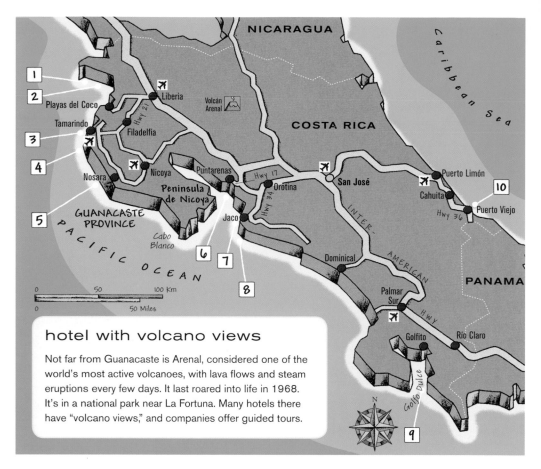

hotel with volcano views

Not far from Guanacaste is Arenal, considered one of the world's most active volcanoes, with lava flows and steam eruptions every few days. It last roared into life in 1968. It's in a national park near La Fortuna. Many hotels there have "volcano views," and companies offer guided tours.

Costa Rica

Costa Rica has been called a "Surfer's Paradise," and if the thousands of surfers who travel there every year — many of them repeat visitors — are any indication, then it must be true. With waves on two coasts, a peaceful and civilized society by Central American standards, and a government and tourism industry that caters to the needs of surfers, Costa Rica must be one of the most surfer-friendly countries in the world.

The long Pacific coast, from dry and arid Guanacaste Province in the north to the wet and humid far south, has literally hundreds of breaks, several of them world-class.

The Guanacaste area is extremely popular. The surfer town of Tamarindo has plenty of hotels, and several top breaks nearby, including Playa Grande and Playa Negra. In central Costa Rica, Boca Barranca and Caldera Jetty are outstanding. At the reef and beach breaks at Mal País, on the tip of the Nicoya Peninsula, you'll find droves of Europeans learning to surf or just enjoying the relaxed atmosphere from a hammock strung between two coconut trees. The south has popular beach breaks in the Dominical area. Even farther south, near the border with Panama, Matapalo and Pavones draw surfers from around the world during the summer south-swell season.

The Caribbean coast has some of the biggest and most powerful waves in the country. Salsa Brava is in the funky Afro-Caribbean banana town of Puerto Viejo, and it can deliver solid 10-ft (3.1-m) barrels over coral reef. The nearby beach breaks at Punta Cocoles and Playa Uva can be just as good on smaller days.

1 Ollie's Point (Portrero Grande)

Ollie's Point, or Portrero Grande, is a right point in front of a river mouth that offers long, quality rides, which longboarders and shortboarders will enjoy. It needs decent-sized swell though, as the window is small. There are no hotels or public roads here and the break is extremely isolated. Keep an eye out for crocodiles, too.

WAVE TYPE Right

WAVE HEIGHT 3–12 ft (0.9–3.7 m)

BREAK TYPE Point

BEST SWELL SW

BEST WIND N–NE

BEST TIDE Low

BEST TIME December–April

HAZARDS Crocodiles, isolation

DIRECTIONS You'll need to take a boat out of Playas del Coco or Tamarindo. Book a day trip for a dawn departure to beat the wind. To get to Playas del Coco, take Hwy 21 from Liberia toward Filadelfia. Turn right after Comunidad. It's 9 miles (15 km) to Playas del Coco.

2 Witch's Rock

Playa Naranjo was made famous in the movie *Endless Summer 2*. It's a 2–3-mile (3–5-km) stretch of sand-bottom beach breaks. The best banks are closest to the huge Witch's Rock (Roca Bruja), which makes a terrific backdrop. These beach breaks can get hollow and perfect, although they need a decent swell to fire up.

WAVE TYPE Left and right

WAVE HEIGHT 3–15 ft (0.9–4.6 m)

BREAK TYPE Beach

BEST SWELL SW

BEST WIND NE–E

BEST TIDE All

BEST TIME December–April

HAZARDS Crocodiles, isolation

DIRECTIONS It's most practical to take a boat — normally out of Playas del Coco, but also out of Tamarindo. Book a day trip the day before for a dawn departure to beat the wind.

3 Tamarindo

Tamarindo is Costa Rica's best-known surf town. You'll find punchy beach breaks just north at Playa Grande, and great rights and lefts at the mouth of Río Tamarindo. For beginner waves, try the Playa Tamarindo break. And anything from mushy burgers to tubing rights occur at Pico Pequeño, in the heart of town.

WAVE TYPE Left and right

WAVE HEIGHT 1–10 ft (0.3–3.1 m)

BREAK TYPE Beach, river mouth, rock shelf

BEST SWELL NW

BEST WIND NE–SE

BEST TIDE All

BEST TIME December–April

HAZARDS Thieves — don't leave valuables unattended at any time

DIRECTIONS From Liberia, take Hwy 21 toward Filadelfia. Just after Belén, turn right and follow this road 15 miles (24 km) to Huacas. Turn left and go to Villarreal. Then it's 2½ miles (4 km) to Tamarindo. Or fly in from San José.

4 Playa Negra

This is one of the best waves in Costa Rica. A fast ride with high-performance opportunities and some barrels as well, it's quite consistent and always popular. Ideally, you'll surf it on a morning high tide, especially in the rainy season (May–October), before the waves blow out.

WAVE TYPE Right

WAVE HEIGHT 3–12 ft (0.9–3.7 m)

BREAK TYPE Reef

BEST SWELL SW

BEST WIND NE–SE

BEST TIDE Mid–high

BEST TIME April–October

HAZARDS Shallow reef on low tide, thieves, crocodiles

DIRECTIONS Head out of Tamarindo to Villarreal. Turn right onto the coast road and go about 7½ miles (12 km) south to Paraíso. Turn right at the soccer field and follow the signs to Hotel Playa Negra. The trip is easier in the dry season (November–March), with a four-wheel-drive.

5 Nosara

Nosara is a quiet, spread-out little town with a stretch of soft and easy beach breaks. There are a number of surf schools here because the waves suit the learner or the longboarder looking for a pleasant, rolling beach break with long rides. It's fairly reliable as well.

WAVE TYPE Left and right

WAVE HEIGHT 2–12 ft (0.6–3.7 m)

BREAK TYPE Beach

BEST SWELL SW, NW

BEST WIND NE–SE

BEST TIDE Low

BEST TIME Year-round

HAZARDS Thieves

DIRECTIONS Head out of Tamarindo to Villarreal. Turn right and take the coast road south to Nosara. Only try it in the dry season, when you probably won't need a four-wheel-drive. To stay on all-season roads, head south from Nicoya to Samara, then take the coast road north via Garza to Nosara. Or fly in from San José.

6 Boca Barranca

One of the longest waves you'll ever see, this wave peels seemingly endlessly and can actually get hollow. It's perfect for longboarders looking for the ultimate nose ride. In fact, a number of nose-riding contests and even World Titles for longboarders have been held here. It gets crowded.

WAVE TYPE Left

WAVE HEIGHT 2–12 ft (0.6–3.7 m)

BREAK TYPE River mouth

BEST SWELL Large SW

BEST WIND E–SE

BEST TIDE Low

BEST TIME June–September

HAZARDS Polluted water, thieves, strong currents during rainy season (May–October)

DIRECTIONS Travel south from Puntarenas on Hwy 17 for about 3 miles (5 km). Turn right before the bridge that crosses the main river, the Barranca. It's best to pay for secure parking.

7 Playa Jaco

Jaco (pronounced with an H) is a touristy town with easy, average beach breaks and lots of places to stay and eat. It's two hours from the capital, San José, so there are plenty of people. It's not a bad starting point for your first Costa Rican experience. It's also good for accessing better waves, such as Playa Escondida (an excellent, hollow, A-frame peak) and Roca Loca (a challenging right reef on bigger swells).

WAVE TYPE Left and right

WAVE HEIGHT 2–15 ft (0.6–4.6 m)

BREAK TYPE Beach

BEST SWELL SW

BEST WIND NE–SE

BEST TIDE All

BEST TIME April–October

HAZARDS Thieves

DIRECTIONS Take Hwy 1 west out of San José. Take the turnoff left to Atenas, San Mateo, and Orotina. Hwy 34 eventually runs close to the coast, and the Jaco turnoff signs are huge.

8 Playa Hermosa

Playa Hermosa is one of Costa Rica's most consistent surf spots. It's a black-sand stretch of beach tucked in front of mountains and rain forest. The waves are powerful by local standards – tubes and hold-downs are frequent once the swell gets bigger. Simply walk south along the 7 miles (11 km) of beach toward Tulín for some less crowded waves.

WAVE TYPE Left and right

WAVE HEIGHT 2–15 ft (0.6–4.6 m)

BREAK TYPE Beach

BEST SWELL SW

BEST WIND NE–SE

BEST TIDE High

BEST TIME April–October

HAZARDS Thieves, rips

DIRECTIONS Take Hwy 34 south from Jaco for about 5 miles (8 km). You can see the start of the Playa Hermosa beach strip from near the road.

Witch's Rock, at the river mouth on Playa Naranjo, serves up fast, hollow waves in a remote corner of paradise.

9 Pavones

One of the world's longest waves, with rides of more than a mile (1.6 km), Pavones suits all boards. It is a classic setup, but it needs a very big swell to break properly. These days, due to internet swell forecasting, it gets very crowded when the swells are good. Still, it's a fast, epic ride that's worth the effort.

WAVE TYPE Long left

WAVE HEIGHT 3–12 ft (0.9–3.7 m)

BREAK TYPE Point

BEST SWELL Big S–SW

BEST WIND E–SE

BEST TIDE Low

BEST TIME April–August

HAZARDS Thieves, road during rainy season

DIRECTIONS Head south on the Inter-American Hwy. Outside Río Claro, take the right turn to the Río Coto Colorado crossing. Catch the ferry to Pueblo Nuevo. It's another 9 miles (15 km) to Conte, the last town before Pavones. Or catch a bus to Golfito and take a taxi from there.

10 Salsa Brava

At Puerto Viejo on the Caribbean coast, you'll find Costa Rica's best and heaviest wave. Salsa Brava means "angry sauce" in Spanish, and this wave is the real deal. It's shallow, heavy, and dangerous. Booties, helmets, and thicker boards are recommended. The locals can be territorial, and it's crowded too, but for the patient, advanced surfer who shows respect, epic barrels await.

WAVE TYPE Left and right (right is best)

WAVE HEIGHT 5–18 ft (1.5–5.5 m)

BREAK TYPE Reef with two peaks

BEST SWELL NE–E

BEST WIND S–SW

BEST TIDE Mid–high

BEST TIME December–March

HAZARDS Thieves, sharp coral reef, locals

DIRECTIONS Travel south from Puerto Limón on Hwy 36 past Cahuita. Take the Puerto Viejo turnoff left. It's about 3–4 miles (5–6 km) to the town and the break.

1 P Land

Off Silva Island near Morro Negrito, this world-class spot can get big, hollow, and powerful. The wave requires a committed takeoff before it bowls up into a heaving barrel section and rifles off down the line. Beware of the end section on lower tides – rocks loom close in the clear water. Not for the fainthearted!

WAVE TYPE Left

WAVE HEIGHT 3–18 ft (0.9–5.5 m)

BREAK TYPE Reef

BEST SWELL SW

BEST WIND E

BEST TIDE Mid–high

BEST TIME March–October

HAZARDS Rocks, especially on lower tides

DIRECTIONS Head west from Santiago on the Inter-American Hwy. After about 50 miles (80 km), take the Morro Negrito turnoff. To surf Silva Island, you must either stay at Morro Negrito Surf Camp or have your own boat. All the island's waves are accessed by motorboat.

2 Sand Bar

Also off Silva Island, this fun, consistent wave is easy to surf even when it's big. Lefts and rights provide long walls, sometimes with barrel opportunities. But big sections where you can go through your full repertoire of maneuvers are more common. Sand Bar is the ideal wave to surf daily and get paddle-fit, charging waves that have minimal consequences.

WAVE TYPE Left and right

WAVE HEIGHT 3–15 ft (0.9–4.6 m)

BREAK TYPE River-mouth sandbar

BEST SWELL SW

BEST WIND NNE

BEST TIDE Low–mid

BEST TIME March–October

HAZARDS Rips

DIRECTIONS As with P Land, the only way to surf the breaks of Silva Island is to stay at Morro Negrito Surf Camp or to have a boat of your own. All the island's waves, including Sand Bar, are accessed by motorboat.

Panama

Panama has been called the younger, rougher surfing cousin of Costa Rica. There's the same two-coast scenario producing high-quality waves, but with a lot fewer surfers around to enjoy them. Surfing started in Panama around the same time as in Costa Rica, in the early 1970s, when locals and US residents from the former Panama Canal Zone took to the waves of the Pacific coast with enthusiasm.

Panama's Pacific coast receives solid groundswell from the Southern Hemisphere, and has all-day offshore winds in the dry season (December to April). Along with the perfect right reef break at Santa Catalina – the most famous wave in Panama – many of the best waves on this coast are in isolated parts of the Azuero Peninsula, a rugged area of few and bad roads that has limited facilities for visitors. If you make it this far, there are few if any surfers to share the waves with.

Bastimentos Island

Take a boat from the town of Bocas del Toro, on Colón, to Bastimentos Island. There are no roads or cars here, but the forest has sloths and monkeys, and the national marine park offers fine snorkeling and scuba diving among coral gardens and underwater caves. Ask the locals in Old Bank for directions to Wizard Beach, where clean, uncrowded peaks over a sand bottom are the reward for an hour's hike.

The Caribbean side of Panama has much to offer surfers, especially in the province of Bocas del Toro. When the sun comes out and it stops raining for a few minutes, this former banana-growing area reveals many beautiful islands. The main one is Colón. Quality coral reef breaks, plus the Bluff Beach beach break, are accessed by one particularly bad road. Equal to any world-class sand-bottom barrel for sheer power, it's famous for breaking boards and the occasional surfer's neck, so choose your waves carefully.

3 Santa Catalina

Santa Catalina is Panama's most popular wave, with good reason. The right is the main course, but the left is also good. This spot is very consistent and can be ridden anywhere from 3–20 ft (0.9–6.1 m). Big drops, deep barrels, long open faces to carve, and no shortage of power – this wave has it all, despite a relatively small takeoff area.

WAVE TYPE Left and right

WAVE HEIGHT 3–20 ft (0.9–6.1 m)

BREAK TYPE Reef

BEST SWELL S–SW

BEST WIND N

BEST TIDE Mid–high; low possible in big swell

BEST TIME March–November

HAZARDS Urchins, rocks on lower tides, crowds

DIRECTIONS Head southwest from Santiago for about 30 miles (48 km) on the road to Soná. Just before Soná, turn left at the Santa Catalina turnoff. After another 30 miles (48 km), turn left at El Tigre Amarillo and travel to Santa Catalina.

4 Punta Brava

A ledgy wave that is both hollow and powerful, Punta Brava is a swell magnet. It's usually much bigger than nearby Santa Catalina or anywhere else, so it's the go for big-wave chargers, or when other waves are too small to surf. Take a spare leash as paddle-outs and duck-diving are testing when it's sizable.

WAVE TYPE Left

WAVE HEIGHT 4–18 ft (1.2–5.5 m)

BREAK TYPE Reef

BEST SWELL S–SW

BEST WIND N

BEST TIDE Low

BEST TIME March–October

HAZARDS Rocks, no channel

DIRECTIONS From the beach in Santa Catalina, walk east for about 45 minutes along the coast to Punta Brava.

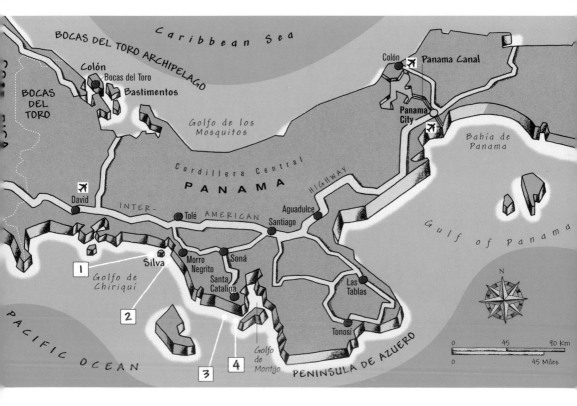

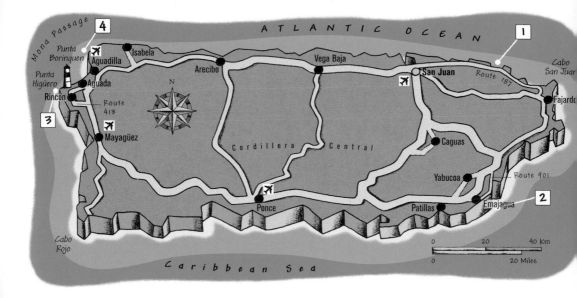

Puerto Rico

Puerto Rico deserves its reputation as the Hawaii of the Caribbean. It has consistent waves for much of the winter season (October to April), and the occasional triple-overhead swell that sends locals and visitors scrambling for their biggest boards. Ever since it hosted the World Championships in 1968 in Aguadilla, Puerto Rico has been on surfers' radar for quality reef breaks.

The many high-quality reef breaks along the north coast from Arecibo to the capital and international gateway, San Juan, catch swell from a wide window into the North Atlantic. The best time is in the morning, before the prevailing northeast trade winds blow onshore and make the waves unridable. Many breaks are hidden and hard to access — befriend knowledgeable locals to find and ride good surf around here.

The south coast has the best offshore wind conditions, but in a cruel twist of fate, receives the least swell. Several days of strong northeast trade winds or a hurricane passing to the south will send swell to the Patillas area and Ponce. The reefs are sharp and shallow, with fire coral everywhere. You won't be surfing alone, but crowds are less intense here than around Puerto Rico's surfing heartland.

Gas Chambers

The best local surfers live for Gas Chambers and its crazy barrels, ridable maybe six times a season. Crowds gather on the jetty at Crash-boat Beach, near Aguadilla, to cheer and jeer — the "Quien es más macho?" mentality rules. Only very capable visitors should paddle out on a good day, and pity the poor gringo who is in position for a set wave and either doesn't go or fluffs the takeoff. He won't get another chance.

That's in the far northwest, around the town of Aguadilla. The coastline takes a 90-degree bend to the south here, and that makes all the difference as the prevailing northeast trade winds blow side-offshore for the many reef breaks in the area. It gets packed with local and visiting surfers, as you'd expect, but there are enough spots to spread the crowd — usually.

1 Chatarras

The Puerto Rican "Pipeline," this wave is a serious barrel that can provide the tube of a lifetime. It could also end your surf trip, as it breaks in shallow water over reef. Patience, skill, and respect are required to catch a wave, because when Chatarras is firing, the island's best surfers will be out in force, and foreign surfers start at the bottom of the pecking order.

WAVE TYPE Left

WAVE HEIGHT 4–12 ft (1.2–3.7 m)

BREAK TYPE Reef

BEST SWELL NW

BEST WIND SE

BEST TIDE Low–mid

BEST TIME August–April

HAZARDS Rips, urchins, rocks, territorial locals

DIRECTIONS Head east from San Juan on Los Governadores Ave (Route 187). Cross the river and continue for another 2 miles (3.2 km). The wave is on a long stretch of sandy beach — you'll see a straight, rocky reef close to shore.

2 El Cocal

The fun peaks along this ⅔-mile (1-km) stretch of beach are an ideal warm-up for, or wind-down from, the island's abundance of serious waves. It gets clean and punchy, offering good-length rides. There are also potential reef waves here because of the sporadic patches of reef. The rocky outcrop in the middle of the beach, in particular, can really come alive under the right conditions.

WAVE TYPE Left and right

WAVE HEIGHT 3–10 ft (0.9–3.1 m)

BREAK TYPE Beach-reef

BEST SWELL SE–S

BEST WIND NW

BEST TIDE All

BEST TIME August–April

HAZARDS Rips, reef

DIRECTIONS From the coastal town of Emajagua, El Cocal beach is 2 miles (3.2 km) northeast on Route 901.

3 El Domo

Consistent and reasonably powerful, El Domo is a fun wave, with barrels and ledging sections that you can cut loose on. Given the right combination of swell and wind, shorter, good-quality lefts will also break. It gets crowded.

WAVE TYPE Right

WAVE HEIGHT 3–10 ft (0.9–3.1 m)

BREAK TYPE Point

BEST SWELL N

BEST WIND SE

BEST TIDE All

BEST TIME August–April

HAZARDS Rips, rocks, urchins

DIRECTIONS From Rincon, head northwest on Route 413. Keep going straight through Tres Palmas and pass the lighthouse. The wave is in front of the dome-shaped nuclear reactor — hence the name.

4 Wilderness

This is a popular spot due to its scenic location and the overall quality of the wave. Usually hollow, Wilderness has abundant power and can handle big swells, which create ideal conditions for breaking out the big-wave gun. You can expect lots of paddling and long, memorable rides.

WAVE TYPE Left and right

WAVE HEIGHT 3–18 ft (0.9–5.5 m)

BREAK TYPE Reef

BEST SWELL NW–NE

BEST WIND E–SE

BEST TIDE All

BEST TIME August–April

HAZARDS Urchins, rocks, rips, cleanup sets

DIRECTIONS From the western end of Borinquen airstrip, head west down the road off Borinquen Ave. After 1 mile (1.6 km) you come to Punta Borinquen. The wave is about 500 yards (500 m) south along the coast.

Barbados

Barbados has been popular with visiting surfers since the 1960s. With a unique Afro-Caribbean–British "Bajan" culture, a vast choice of accommodation and entertainment, and easy access to a significant number of quality waves, it's not hard to see why.

It receives the most swell of any island in the eastern Caribbean. But the main factor for determining good waves here is not the swell, it's the wind — the trade winds deliver near-constant nor'easters of 10 to 25 knots. Some of the best waves, like Soup Bowl and Parlors, on the exposed east coast, are often blown out and unridable. Early mornings are best because there's less wind. Wind changes are frequent and unpredictable, so be vigilant and you may be rewarded with great waves when the wind stops or shifts direction for a few hours.

The south coast gets the northeast wind too, but less than the east coast. It also gets most of the prevailing windswell, which probably makes it the most popular and consistent area on the island. Surfers Point nearly always has ridable waves. The variety of peaks and takeoff spots at the main spot, South Point, can handle the regular crew of hot locals and courteous visitors.

The west coast of Barbados has the most tourist development. A single, narrow road makes for nightmarish traffic and parking. But it does have some of the best surfing reefs on the island, with flawless, peeling tubes and constant offshore winds. A lack of swell energy means reefs like Tropicana, Mullins Bay, and Church Point rarely break — until the northerly ground-swells of winter (November to March) arrive.

Mount Gay rum

One of the Caribbean's most famous products is rum, distilled from the ubiquitous sugar cane. The Mount Gay Distilleries of Barbados is one of the oldest brands. It's been in continuous production since 1703. You can take a tour of the distillery from Monday to Friday — this includes a taste of the legendary product.

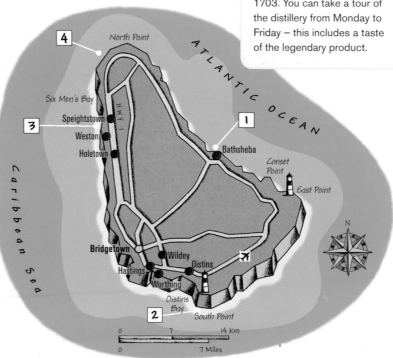

1 Soup Bowl

Soup Bowl in Bathsheba has been the venue for all the major surfing events in Barbados in the last 25 years. Eight-time World Champion Kelly Slater names the "Bowl" in his Top 10 breaks. Being on the east coast of the island, it catches any swell coming across the Atlantic Ocean. A fun, powerful wave, it can be ridden by both shortboarders and longboarders.

WAVE TYPE Right

WAVE HEIGHT 3–20+ ft (0.9–6.1+ m)

BREAK TYPE Reef

BEST SWELL NW–N

BEST WIND SE–SW

BEST TIDE All

BEST TIME July–March

HAZARDS Weekend crowds

DIRECTIONS From Worthing, head north up Rendezvous Hill to Wildey. Take ABC Hwy to Belle Junction and turn right. Follow to Lears Roundabout and head east. At the next junction, turn left and follow the road into Bathsheba.

2 Freights

Named after a local surfer, David "Freight" Allen, Freights is a long, perfectly shaped left in a protected bay – an ideal spot for beginners. Larger waves attract more crowds and usually develop from a high pressure or strong wind swell. With an easy entry and exit spot, Freights is excellent for shortboarding or longboarding. South Point is within walking distance and is usually 1–2 feet (0.3–0.6 m) bigger.

WAVE TYPE Left

WAVE HEIGHT 1–5 ft (0.3–1.5 m)

BREAK TYPE Reef

BEST SWELL SE–S

BEST WIND N–NE

BEST TIDE All

BEST TIME December–March

HAZARDS Crowds, sea urchins

DIRECTIONS In Oistins, turn right after the police station, then take the next right. At the next junction, turn left and then right onto Atlantic Shores. Freights is 50 yards (50 m) on the right.

3 Tropicana

Tropicana is a steep, hollow, and very fast barreling left. It rarely breaks, but when it does, it is known as the "Pipeline of Barbados." And it's worth the wait. It should only be surfed on a high tide and it is mostly frequented by shortboarders and bodyboarders. Nearby breaks include Miramar and Gibbes.

WAVE TYPE Left

WAVE HEIGHT 2–8 ft (0.6–2.4 m)

BREAK TYPE Reef

BEST SWELL NW–N

BEST WIND E–SE

BEST TIDE High

BEST TIME December–March

HAZARDS Fire coral, sea urchins

DIRECTIONS From Holetown, head north along Hwy 1 (the coast road) until you get to the town of Weston. The break is located in front of Reid's House Condos.

4 Duppies

Duppies is capable of producing some of the largest, longest surfable waves in Barbados. When it's 20 ft (6.1 m) plus, you can ride waves more than 200 yards (200 m) and they won't close out on you. You'll have to negotiate treacherous cliffs, and a long paddle through deep and dark water, to reach the break. Big-wave boards are a must on the larger days.

WAVE TYPE Right

WAVE HEIGHT 5–20+ ft (1.5–6.1+ m)

BREAK TYPE Reef

BEST SWELL N

BEST WIND E–SE

BEST TIDE All

BEST TIME December–March

HAZARDS Cliffs, currents

DIRECTIONS From Speightstown, head north on Hwy 1. Go through Six Men's Bay, up Sutherland Hill, and turn left at Four Crossings. Head north, past Maycock's Bay, then turn left on Cart Road. Proceed to Duppies Point.

Introduction

surf the Amazon

The Pororoca is a tidal bore that forms in the Atlantic Ocean and travels up the Amazon and surrounding rivers for almost 200 miles (320 km). March and April, the end of the dry season, are the best times to surf it. Surfers Picuruta Salazar and Serginho Laus have both surfed the Araguari River Pororoca in Amapá State, Brazil, for more than 6¼ miles (10 km). Hazards include crocodiles, snakes, piranhas, and floating logs.

Almir Salazar rides Joaquina, the most famous break on the island of Santa Catarina, in Brazil.

South America is the fourth largest continent on Earth, and arguably the most diverse. It reaches from the humid tropics in the north to the icebergs of Patagonia's Furious Fifties. Triangular in shape, it has over 19,000 miles (30,580 km) of coastline and is virtually surrounded by the Pacific and Atlantic Oceans and the Caribbean Sea.

Power on the Pacific

The west coast stretches for 6,620 miles (10,650 km) and receives southwest swells from the mighty Pacific. These originate southwest of New Zealand in the Southern Ocean, and Chile and Peru get their full brunt. They're typically at their biggest from March to November. The winds are usually southerlies blowing up this coast. They provide constant offshore winds for the copious number of mystically long, left points that the region is renowned for. Between November and March, northwest swells originating from the North Pacific Aleutian lows break on the north-facing coasts of Ecuador, Peru, and even parts of Chile and Colombia. They bring some of the continent's most hollow and perfect waves, particularly at Cabo Blanco, where Peru's tube maestros anxiously await their arrival.

The Humboldt Current's frigid water hugs this coast, so wetsuits are essential from Chile to tropical north Peru. But the shark threat is minimal, including in the Galapagos Islands (part of Ecuador), where the sharks are well fed and so aren't a problem.

South America's Pacific coast offers the most surfing possibilities on this continent. Brazil has the best spots on the Atlantic coast.

During El Niño years, heavy rains and flooding can cause mudslides and other problems, especially in Peru. However, this can also temporarily improve some waves, thanks to silt deposits from the otherwise dry rivers. Bordering this entire coast are the Nazca and the South American oceanic plates, which give the region its ongoing seismic activity — earthquakes and tsunamis are a constant risk.

The other side of the continent isn't as fortunate with waves because it receives only infrequent groundswell. The tropical northeast from Colombia to South America's easternmost point at Recife, in Brazil, receives high-pressure east and northeast windswells. Swell from North Atlantic lows between November and March make this the best time to surf this part of the coast. The southeast coast from Recife to Argentina gets its swell from south-to-southeast windswell, whipped up off the back of Antarctic lows moving east. The best time to surf this part of the coast is from March to November. The water is chilly in Uruguay and Argentina, but north of Florianópolis in Brazil, it's warm enough for boardshorts year-round.

Brazil's 4,600 miles (7,400 km) of coastline have the best surf on the east coast. There are plenty of powerful, quality beach breaks along its white-sand, palm-fringed beaches, interspersed by points. The large coastal cities mean that Brazil's surfing population has proliferated — it's now into the hundreds of thousands. Crowded lineups are a problem, and the fierce competition helps explain why Brazil churns out pro surfers on the World Championship Tour.

The other countries on the eastern seaboard all suffer the effects of a shallow continental shelf. Combine this with the average swell and the result is typically small waves that have limited power. Everywhere has its moments though, especially around Mar del Plata in Argentina, with its plentiful wave setups.

Brazil has problems with violent crime, particularly in the cities. Elsewhere, theft is common, although coastal regions are usually safe. Uruguay and Chile are the most stable and least corrupt countries and consequently the safest for travelers. There are plenty of sharks on the east coast, while malaria is a threat throughout tropical South America. So is the widespread pollution, not only from the coastal cities but also from industry discharging waste into rivers. Check travel advisories, and get any necessary inoculations and medicines before leaving. Despite these issues, the combination of varied, quality surf, vibrant cultures, and laid-back people make it well worth exploring the waves of this beautiful, diverse, and slightly mysterious continent.

Map labels:
Caribbean Sea
SOUTH ATLANTIC OCEAN
Ecuador pp.68–71
COLOMBIA
ECUADOR
Quito
Guayaquil
GALAPAGOS ISLANDS
Cabo Blanco
AMAPÁ
Equator
Amazon
BRAZIL
Trujillo
Lima
PERU
Peru pp.72–75
Brasilia
SOUTH PACIFIC OCEAN
Tropic of Capricorn
CHILE
São Paulo
Rio de Janeiro
Brazil pp.82–85
Florianópolis
Valparaíso
Santiago
ARGENTINA
Buenos Aires
URUGUAY
Concepción
Mar del Plata
Chile pp.76–79
Argentina pp.80–81
Valdes Peninsula
PATAGONIA
Cape Horn
Recife
N
0 900 1800 km
0 900 Miles

Ecuador

Warm, tropical Ecuador has 1,280 miles (2,060 km) of coastline, including the Galapagos Islands, with a variety of reefs, points, and beaches that offer year-round surfing opportunities. The mainland coast is a flat plain formed by mud and sand deposits from the Esmeraldas and Guayas Rivers. It gets both north swell (November to March) and south swell (March to October), but solid swell is inconsistent. Montañita's board-snapping rights break in north and south swells, making it the most popular wave in Ecuador. Farther north in Esmeraldas State, you'll find numerous north-facing waves, including Mompiche, a world-class left point set in lush, tropical surroundings.

The Galapagos Islands are full of unearthed surf potential that you'd need a boat to explore. San Cristóbal is the main surf island, and most of its powerful lava-reef waves can be accessed by taxi or on foot from the main town of Puerto Baquerizo Moreno. South and north swells give consistent waves – Punta Carola is the finest. Note that the archipelago is a national park; its rule that you hire a guide is designed to protect the many nesting birds from poachers.

Both Quito and Guayaquil have international airports, and offer daily flights to the Galapagos. There are also buses to all parts of the country. Temperatures are in the mid 70s°F (20s°C) year-round, with a rainy season from December to May. The water is cool by tropical standards, but boardshorts or springsuits should be adequate.

This is the place to enjoy quality waves in a tropical location with a very relaxed coastal vibe.

diving the Galapagos

The Galapagos Islands make a worthy surf trip, but it would be a missed opportunity if you didn't also explore the islands' famed wildlife. Abundant marine life creates amazing diving and snorkeling opportunities, where close encounters with eagle rays, hammerhead sharks, turtles, and sea lions are the norm. On land, there are colonies of primeval marine iguanas and nesting birds.

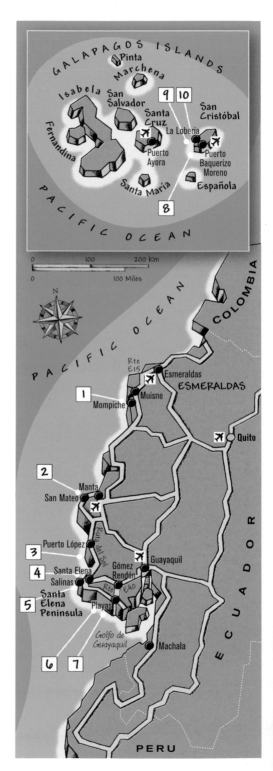

1 Mompiche

Mompiche is a quality wave, strong, fast, and consistent, up to 400 yards (400 m) long. It breaks on a rocky bottom. It is located in the "verde," or green, province of Esmeraldas in northwest Ecuador, amid a lush, equatorial landscape, and it's an adventure in itself just getting there.

WAVE TYPE Left

WAVE HEIGHT 3–12 ft (0.9–3.7 m)

BREAK TYPE Point

BEST SWELL NW–N

BEST WIND NE

BEST TIDE Low–mid

BEST TIME October–March

HAZARDS Rocks

DIRECTIONS From Esmeraldas, take Route E15 southwest along the coast for about 30 miles (48 km) to the village of Mompiche. You'll need a four-wheel-drive, especially in the rainy season (December–May).

2 San Mateo

This is the second-longest left break in South America after Chicama in Peru. It's ideal for longboards when it's small. When it gets big, it has three well-defined sections – the middle section gets big, hollow, and powerful. It runs from 300–450 yards (300–450 m) long and breaks on a rocky bottom. It's a great spot for practicing all the maneuvers in your repertoire.

WAVE TYPE Left

WAVE HEIGHT 3–12 ft (0.9–3.7 m)

BREAK TYPE Point

BEST SWELL NW–N

BEST WIND NE

BEST TIDE Low–mid

BEST TIME October–March

HAZARDS None

DIRECTIONS From Manta, take the road west for about 9 miles (15 km) to the fishing village of San Mateo. Walk along the beach to the point.

3 Montañita

The most famous right break in Ecuador, Montañita has size, form, and consistency. This is a world-class tube ride, with three distinct sections, when the swell and wind direction are right. The Latin American Championships and the Ecuadorean national tournament are both held here.

WAVE TYPE Right

WAVE HEIGHT 3–12 ft (0.9–3.7 m)

BREAK TYPE Point

BEST SWELL NW–N

BEST WIND NE

BEST TIDE Low–mid

BEST TIME December–May

HAZARDS Crowds, sea urchins

DIRECTIONS Drive west from Guayaquil on the Via a la Costa (Route E40) for 75 miles (120 km) to Santa Elena on the Santa Elena Peninsula. Turn right at the sign for the start of the Ruta del Sol and travel about 37 miles (60 km) north until you reach Montañita.

4 Ballenita

Ballenita is located at the start of the "Ruta del Sol," which is famous for its many surfing spots and variety of waves. These include Chuyuype, El Castillo, Pico Loco, La Bajada del Diablo, and Capaes. Ballenita has waves of average shape and force, which break on a rocky bottom. It doesn't get too crowded.

WAVE TYPE Left and right

WAVE HEIGHT 3–8 ft (0.9–2.4 m)

BREAK TYPE Point

BEST SWELL NW–N

BEST WIND NE

BEST TIDE Low–mid

BEST TIME October–April

HAZARDS Rocks

DIRECTIONS Drive west from Guayaquil on the Via a la Costa (Route E40) for 75 miles (120 km) to Santa Elena on the Santa Elena Peninsula. Turn right at the sign for the start of the Ruta del Sol and travel 2 miles (3.2 km) to Ballenita.

5 La FAE

At the westernmost tip of Ecuador, you'll find La FAE, named for the air force base, La Fuerza Aérea Equatoriana, where it's located. La FAE is a nicely shaped left point break that offers fast, powerful rides for most of the year. It breaks on a rocky bottom. Because you have to travel through the base, you'll need to get a special permit first. Ask local surfers in Salinas.

WAVE TYPE Left

WAVE HEIGHT 3–10 ft (1.0–3.1 m)

BREAK TYPE Point

BEST SWELL All

BEST WIND NE

BEST TIDE Low–mid

BEST TIME Year-round

HAZARDS Strong current, whirlpools

DIRECTIONS Travel west from Guayaquil on the Via a la Costa (Route E40) for 80 miles (130 km) to Salinas. Take the road to La Fuerza Aérea Equatoriana (Ecuadorean Air Force Base). In the base, head for the point near the runway end.

6 Engabao

This right point break is very consistent for most of the year. When there's enough wind, the wave has a nice shape, with a definite hollow section offering tube rides. It breaks on a rocky and sandy bottom, and there's almost no one out during the week.

WAVE TYPE Right

WAVE HEIGHT 3–8 ft (0.9–2.4 m)

BREAK TYPE Point

BEST SWELL S–SW

BEST WIND SW

BEST TIDE Low

BEST TIME April–October

HAZARDS Anglers

DIRECTIONS Travel west on the Via a la Costa (Route E40) from Guayaquil to Gómez Rendón, then turn left at the Playas (General Villamil) turnoff. Once at Playas, turn right on the road to Engabao, also known as Punta de Piedra. Drive for about 30 minutes until you reach the lighthouse. A four-wheel-drive is best.

7 El Pelado

This right point break reaches a good size when swells are coming from the south. It breaks on a rocky bottom, and has a hollow section with great shape that can offer long tube rides. There are no crowds during the week.

WAVE TYPE Right

WAVE HEIGHT 4–10 ft (1.2–3.1 m)

BREAK TYPE Point

BEST SWELL S–SW

BEST WIND SW

BEST TIDE Low

BEST TIME May–September

HAZARDS Rocks

DIRECTIONS Head west on the Via a la Costa (Route E40) from Guayaquil to Gómez Rendón, then take the Playas (General Villamil) turnoff on the left. Once at Playas, turn right on the road to Engabao. It's about 10½ miles (17 km) to El Pelado, and a four-wheel-drive is recommended.

8 Punta Carola

This spectacular, world-class right is on San Cristóbal, one of the islands of the famous Galapagos Islands. It's a big, fast, tubular wave of medium length in very clear, deep water. With so much speed and power, it's definitely not for beginners. It breaks on a rocky bottom.

WAVE TYPE Right

WAVE HEIGHT 5–17 ft (1.5–5.2 m)

BREAK TYPE Point

BEST SWELL NW–N

BEST WIND NE

BEST TIDE Mid

BEST TIME October–March

HAZARDS Rocks, strong currents

DIRECTIONS Fly into Puerto Baquerizo Moreno, on San Cristóbal in the Galapagos Islands. It's about a ten-minute taxi trip (all taxis are pickup trucks) from the town to Punta Carola. Or walk to the north side of Puerto Baquerizo and look for the harbor entrance and the point. You are supposed to get a guide.

Mompiche is a perfectly shaped left that just keeps on running – a great wave for practicing your maneuvers.

9 La Loberia

La Loberia is another big wave on the Galapagos Islands. The fast, powerful right breaks on rocks covered with very sharp sea urchins. The powerful left has a simple but spectacular tube section. It breaks on a rocky wall, so is not for beginners. La Loberia's name comes from the colony of sea lions that lives there – they may ride the waves with surfers.

WAVE TYPE Left and right

WAVE HEIGHT 5–17 ft (1.5–5.2 m)

BREAK TYPE Center peak

BEST SWELL S–SW

BEST WIND SW

BEST TIDE Mid

BEST TIME March–October

HAZARDS Rocks, sea urchins, strong currents, sea lions

DIRECTIONS Fly into Puerto Baquerizo Moreno on San Cristóbal. It's about a 20-minute taxi ride (all taxis are pickup trucks) from the town to La Loberia. You are supposed to get a guide.

10 Tongo Reef

Also on the Galapagos Island of San Cristóbal, Tongo Reef is a left point break with very good form. From a deep, hollow takeoff, it gains size and power in the middle section, then breaks over rocks in a small bay. This is a fun, problem-free wave, with no crowds. It's a great place to perfect your repertoire.

WAVE TYPE Left

WAVE HEIGHT 5–12 ft (1.5–3.7 m)

BREAK TYPE Point

BEST SWELL S–SW

BEST WIND SW

BEST TIDE Mid

BEST TIME March–October

HAZARDS Rocks, sea lions

DIRECTIONS Fly into Puerto Baquerizo Moreno on San Cristóbal. Get a taxi (a pickup truck) to the cemetery. Walk for about 20 minutes. Or walk through the naval base (you must leave your passport at the gate) and head south for about ⅔ mile (1 km). You are supposed to get a guide.

1 Pacasmayo

A world-class left point break, Pacasmayo can break up to 1,000 yards (1 km) long. It catches more swell than the more famous Chicama, farther south, too. So if Chicama's flat, head to Pacasmayo. It's a long, powerful wave with a sharp bottom.

WAVE TYPE Left

WAVE HEIGHT 3–12 ft (0.9–3.7 m)

BREAK TYPE Point

BEST SWELL S–SW

BEST WIND NE

BEST TIDE Low–mid

BEST TIME April–October

HAZARDS Rocks, rips

DIRECTIONS Travel north from Trujillo on the North Pan-American Hwy. Take the exit at Km 663 to the town of Pacasmayo (also known as El Faro). Head south out of town along the coast to find the wave.

2 Chicama

Chicama is widely known as the world's longest wave. It's a left point break that, given the right swell, can run for a mind-blowing 1 ¼ miles (2 km), with the section in front of the village barreling for hundreds of yards (meters). The break is very swell-dependent — it needs to be at least 6 ft (1.8 m) elsewhere to be working here. On smaller swells, it breaks into sections.

WAVE TYPE Left

WAVE HEIGHT 3–8 ft (0.9–2.4 m)

BREAK TYPE Point

BEST SWELL S–SW

BEST WIND NE

BEST TIDE Low–mid

BEST TIME April–October

HAZARDS Rock and coral bottom, rips, fatigue

DIRECTIONS Travel north from Trujillo on the North Pan-American Hwy. At Paiján (at Km 614 on the highway), take the road left to Puerto Chicama (also called Puerto Malabrigo), a small fishing village where you'll find the point.

Peru

Peru has a bleak desert coast, with a fog called *la garúa* from April to November. You should persevere though, because while the land might look unappealing, the ocean from Pacasmayo to San Bartolo holds abundant, quality breaks that receive constant swell and favorable winds. This region hosted the World Championships back in 1965, won by Peruvian Felipe Pomar, and local surfer Sofia Mulanovich was the women's world champion in 2004.

The continual south-to-southwest swell and light south-to-southeast winds make this stretch of coast a surfing playground. Around Lima, you'll find powerful waves such as Punta Rocas and La Herradura — and crowds. The locals are vocal and adept at dropping in, yet they make accommodating and willing hosts. Farther north are several long lefts — the longest, Chicama, is 1 ¼ miles (2 km) from point to pier. Many stoked surfers travel this distance with a single ride.

Lima has an airport and bus services to most parts of the country. However, driving can be pretty crazy — at night, avoid anything but short local trips because of booby traps and *banditos* attacks on the roads. Although Peru is in the tropics, the Humboldt Current keeps winter air temperatures around 64°F (18°C), and summer temperatures around 75°F (24°C). You'll need a full wetsuit from April to November, and a springsuit from December to March.

reed boat fishermen

In the northern coastal villages of Pimentel and Huanchaco, fishermen have used reed boats, called *caballitos de totora,* for more than 3,000 years. These boats weigh over 220 pounds (100 kg) when wet. Local fishermen can still be seen today, standing up in their boats, surfing back to the beach after a day's fishing.

3 Huanchaco

With enough swell, this left point break links up to give waves up to 300 yards (300 m) long. Usually, however, the wave breaks up into a few individual sections, which vary depending on where the sandbars are. A fun wave, it's often overlooked because of its proximity to the flashy northern opposition, Chicama.

WAVE TYPE Left

WAVE HEIGHT 3–8 ft (0.3–2.4 m)

BREAK TYPE Point, beach

BEST SWELL S–W

BEST WIND E–SE

BEST TIDE All

BEST TIME April–October

HAZARDS Pollution

DIRECTIONS From Trujillo, travel northwest on the road to the airport. After 6 miles (10 km), you'll have passed the airport and reached the coastal town of Huanchaco. Punta Huanchaco, where this wave is located, is the main point to the south along the coast.

4 Playa Grande

Playa Grande is a fast, barreling left with a heavy takeoff. Make the drop, pull in, and you're set. One of the hollowest waves in Peru, it's rarely crowded. The coral bottom is pretty sharp though, so consider wearing booties. And get out early before the wind blows too strong.

WAVE TYPE Left

WAVE HEIGHT 5–12 ft (1.5–3.7 m)

BREAK TYPE Point

BEST SWELL S–SW

BEST WIND NE

BEST TIDE Mid–high

BEST TIME April–October

HAZARDS Rock and coral bottom, heaving lip

DIRECTIONS Head south from Chimbote on the North Pan-American Hwy. At Km 336 you can see the break about 100 yards (100 m) from the highway.

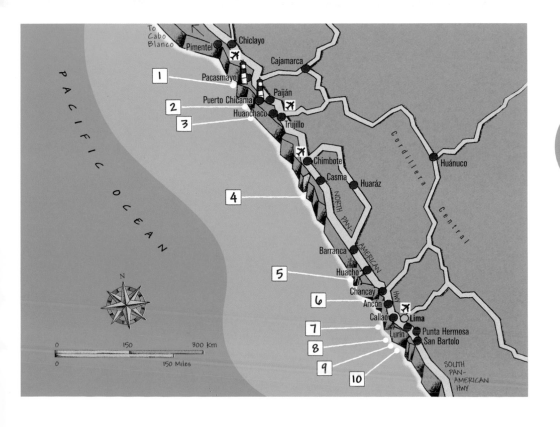

5 Centinela

Centinela has waves to satisfy most appetites. It's a heaving takeoff, with some nasty rock piles just below the surface on the section farthest out. If you make the drop, you will be rewarded with a fantastically rippable wall for up to 150 yards (150 m). The inside section is far more playful.

WAVE TYPE Left

WAVE HEIGHT 3–8 ft (0.9–2.4 m)

BREAK TYPE Point

BEST SWELL S–SW

BEST WIND E–SE

BEST TIDE Mid

BEST TIME April–October

HAZARDS Rocks, backwash on takeoff, rips, thieves, violent crime

DIRECTIONS Centinela is in Huacho, a city at Km 152 on the North Pan-American Hwy. To actually find the break, get a guide and a four-wheel-drive because the route is rough and local knowledge is essential. Be careful around here.

6 Pasamayo

This is a super-consistent right and left peak. It catches all available swell, so if it's shoulder-high elsewhere, Pasamayo will be overhead. If it's massive elsewhere, don't bother here. The wave can be really fun, with nice tubes on the peak, but it's very isolated and hard to get to.

WAVE TYPE Left and right

WAVE HEIGHT 3–12 ft (0.9–3.7 m)

BREAK TYPE Reef

BEST SWELL SW–NW

BEST WIND NE–SE

BEST TIDE All

BEST TIME November–March

HAZARDS Rocky bottom, isolated location, access

DIRECTIONS Buses on the old Pan-American Hwy go past the break (south of Chancay, north of Ancón) but may not stop. The new Pan-American Hwy runs farther away from the coast. Buses will let you off, for a 40-minute walk down steep dunes. Only commercial vehicles can use either road. Get plenty of local direction or a guide.

Chicama is the longest wave in the world – 1¼ miles (2 km) of perfection when conditions align.

7 La Herradura

This powerful left point break has three main sections: a ledging takeoff, a workable shoulder, and a racy inside section. It's a great wave when there's swell running, but given its proximity to Lima, it can get pretty crowded on a good day.

WAVE TYPE Left

WAVE HEIGHT 5–10 ft (1.5–3.1 m)

BREAK TYPE Point

BEST SWELL SW–W

BEST WIND E

BEST TIDE All

BEST TIME April–October

HAZARDS Crowds, rocks, sea urchins

DIRECTIONS La Herradura is just around the large headland of southern Lima. Travel south on the Circuito des Playas past the beaches of Lima until you come to the last beach.

8 Señoritas

Señoritas is a left point break at the southern end of the bay. It ranges from playful to pumping, depending on the swell. When it's on, the point can serve up some nice barrels and carvable walls. Another great spot 500 yards (500 m) away at the northern end of the bay is Caballeros. This fun right point break can be surfed on all tides; the best time is from April to October.

WAVE TYPE Left

WAVE HEIGHT 3–8 ft (0.9–2.4 m)

BREAK TYPE Point with rocky bottom

BEST SWELL SW–NW

BEST WIND E–SE

BEST TIDE Mid

BEST TIME November–May

HAZARDS Rocks, crowds

DIRECTIONS Head south from Lima on the South Pan-American Hwy. Past Lurín, turn right in the area of El Silencio and head for the coast.

9 Pico Alto

One of the world's best big-wave spots, Pico Alto holds ridable waves up to 20 ft (6.1 m). Avoid it unless you're experienced in really sizable surf, but if you are, you've found a gem. The break is about 700 yards (700 m) offshore, which adds to the intensity. When it's on, it is a real display of nature's ferocity, and a real find for those talented (or insane) enough to surf it.

WAVE TYPE Left and right

WAVE HEIGHT 10–25 ft (3.1–7.6 m)

BREAK TYPE Reef

BEST SWELL SW–NW

BEST WIND NE–SE

BEST TIDE All

BEST TIME April–October

HAZARDS Long hold-downs, rips, crazy shore break on the way in

DIRECTIONS Drive south from Lima on the Pan-American Hwy for 25 miles (40 km) to Punta Hermosa. A few keen locals will take you out in their boat. Or paddle from Playa Norte beach.

10 Punta Rocas

The real value of this punchy left and much longer right peak is its consistency and variety. An A-frame setup (you can go left or right), it gets plenty of swell and can handle big waves, but is still fun when the swell subsides. About 500 yards (500 m) south, there's a punchy left and right beach break called Explosivos.

WAVE TYPE Left (generally punchier) and right

WAVE HEIGHT 3–12 ft (0.9–3.7 m)

BREAK TYPE Reef

BEST SWELL SW–NW

BEST WIND NE–SE

BEST TIDE Low–mid

BEST TIME April–October

HAZARDS Rocky bottom (often exposed on smaller swells), rips

DIRECTIONS Travel south from Lima on the South Pan-American Highway for about 30 miles (48 km). Turn at the Punta Rocas sign and head toward the coast.

Chile

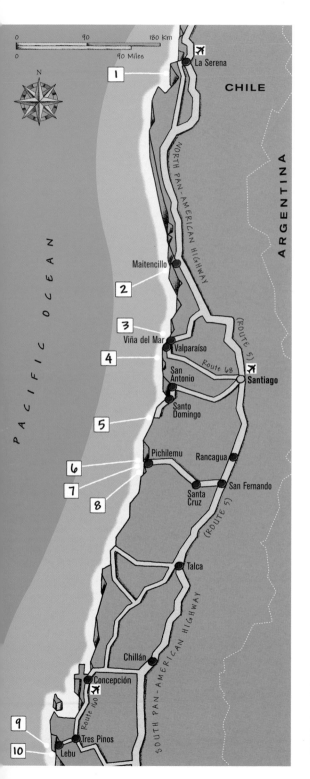

There's so much swell on the Chilean coast between Viña del Mar and Lebu that waiting for the swell to drop a little is just as common as waiting for it to pick up. Southwest swells up to 23 ft (7 m) can bring the Punta de Lobos big-wave arena to life – here, getting off the rocks into the waves demands as much bravado as surfing them. Left points typify this coast, interspersed with various reef and beach breaks. Surfing the points can be energy-sapping, because you need to paddle hard just to maintain your position against the current.

Southerly winds predominate, and are reasonably favorable for many spots, although mornings and evenings will often be glassy. Travelers often head straight for Pichilemu and its three quality breaks, including one of the longest waves in Chile, La Puntilla. And given that few Chileans venture into the water before 10 AM, dawn waves are a free-for-all for traveling surfers.

Santiago has an international airport and bus terminals with services to all parts of the country. This surf region is green and rustic, with a relaxed vibe. The Mediterranean climate means warm summers and chilly winters. But the water temperature rarely gets above 62°F (17°C), so full wetsuits are needed year-round, with booties optional. And during the winter months, from June to November, hoods and even gloves are common.

Chile has so much coastline and so many waves. And from a surfing point of view, it's still something of a last frontier.

Pichilemu's big waves

When Pichilemu's La Puntilla receives a solid swell, the major problem is getting out and catching a wave before you're swept down the point by the powerful current. After a couple of these cold-water circuits, most surfers retreat to warm up. Local professionals Diego Medina and Ramón Navarro overcome this problem by using their jet ski to tow each other into waves for hours, much to the envy of paddling surfers.

1 Totoralillo

The main wave in the northern part of Totoralillo Bay is a left and right point break. The left holds 13-ft (4-m) waves and runs more than 70 yards (70 m) long. The powerful, tubular right breaks over a sand and rock bottom, and tends to be short and deep. With its permanent swell, Totoralillo is a good place for beginners. It can get crowded on holidays and long weekends.

WAVE TYPE Left and right

WAVE HEIGHT 5–13 ft (1.5–4 m)

BREAK TYPE Point on rocky reef

BEST SWELL NW

BEST WIND S

BEST TIDE Low

BEST TIME March–June, November–February

HAZARDS Rocks in front, holiday crowds

DIRECTIONS Head south from La Serena on the North Pan-American Hwy for about 18 km. Take the road for Totoralillo and travel about 1¼ miles (2 km) to the town and beach.

2 El Abanico

At the extreme southern end of Maitencillo Bay is El Abanico, named for the perfect fan-shaped bay where it's located. El Abanico is a crowded beach that runs in different swell conditions with left and right beach breaks. The best power line is 100 yards (100 m) north of a rocky outcrop at the southern end of the beach, where you'll find a nicely shaped right peak.

WAVE TYPE Left and right

WAVE HEIGHT 4–10 ft (1.2–3.1 m)

BREAK TYPE Beach

BEST SWELL W–NW

BEST WIND S

BEST TIDE High

BEST TIME March–October

HAZARDS Very low sand bottom, weekend crowds

DIRECTIONS Head north from Santiago on the North Pan-American Hwy. After about 100 miles (160 km), take the turnoff for Playa Maitencillo. El Abanico is at the southern end of the bay.

3 Reñaca

Reñaca serves up moderately shaped right and left breaks on a long, white-sand beach. It's best in an offshore north wind, which allows for tube rides and strong drops, although sometimes it closes out. It's always crowded because it's so close to Viña del Mar, the most popular beach holiday resort in Chile.

WAVE TYPE Left and right

WAVE HEIGHT 3–12 ft (0.9–3.7 m)

BREAK TYPE Beach

BEST SWELL Depends on sandbar

BEST WIND N

BEST TIDE High, low

BEST TIME April–August

HAZARDS Thieves, territorial locals, crowds

DIRECTIONS Head north from Viña del Mar along the coast for about 4 miles (6.4 km) to Reñaca. The wave is at the far northern end of the beach. There's parking at the point.

4 El Mejoral

This left point break is on the north side of a small rocky island, one of Las Islas Bajas, which are in the middle of Algarrobo Bay. About 150 yards (150 m) from the shore, El Mejoral is a short, intense wave up to 7 ft (2.1 m). In big swells, it can reach more than 13 ft (4 m) and start breaking from a reef called Detroit, and when it runs right, it forms a big tube.

WAVE TYPE Left and right

WAVE HEIGHT 5–16 ft (1.5–4.9 m)

BREAK TYPE Point

BEST SWELL SW

BEST WIND S–SW

BEST TIDE High

BEST TIME March–April, August–October

HAZARDS Rocks

DIRECTIONS Head west from Santiago on Route 68 to Algarrobo Bay. Park at Playa del Pejerrey, near the Yacht Club. About 50 yards (50 m) south of the marina, jump in from the rocks and paddle out 200 yards (200 m) to the point.

5 Puertecillo

A secret spot for many years, Puertecillo is a big left break, with deep, perfect tubes similar to Chicama in Peru. It has four waves: Tumán, Topocalma, Secreto, and El Falso. This place is a paradise worth caring for, and it's on private property – a farm called Hacienda Topocalma. You'll need to get permission to gain access. Ask friendly locals the best way to do this.

WAVE TYPE Left

WAVE HEIGHT 3–15 ft (0.9–4.6 m)

BREAK TYPE Beach

BEST SWELL SE

BEST WIND S

BEST TIDE Low

BEST TIME Year-round

HAZARDS Territorial locals

DIRECTIONS Head south from San Antonio to Santo Domingo. Take Route 66 south, then turn onto G-50 and look for the gate for Hacienda Topocalma. You'll need a four-wheel-drive.

6 La Puntilla (Pichilemu)

Pichilemu is a classic, mystical place that is renowned for La Puntilla, a fast, powerful left break over long, sandy depths. Almost every important Chilean surfing contest takes place here. But be prepared for a long paddle and for the crowds, mostly on the weekends. Consider getting in with friendly locals.

WAVE TYPE Left

WAVE HEIGHT 3–15 ft (0.9–4.6 m)

BREAK TYPE Point, beach

BEST SWELL S

BEST WIND S

BEST TIDE Low

BEST TIME Year-round

HAZARDS Pollution

DIRECTIONS Head south from Santiago on the South Pan-American Hwy (Route 5) to San Fernando. Turn right and head west to Santa Cruz. Follow the signs to the town of Pichilemu. La Puntilla is about 400 yards (400 m) south of downtown Pichilemu.

7 Infiernillo

About 500 yards (500 m) south of La Puntilla is Infiernillo – Spanish for "little hell." But instead of flames, you get big waves with strong currents breaking over a mixture of black sand and rocks. This powerful left gets dangerous in swells over 15 ft (4.6 m). It's only for big-wave riders and experts, but it offers amazing and perfect barrels.

WAVE TYPE Left

WAVE HEIGHT 3–13 ft (0.9–4 m)

BREAK TYPE Point, beach

BEST SWELL S

BEST WIND S

BEST TIDE Low

BEST TIME December

HAZARDS Breaks in front of big rocks

DIRECTIONS Head to the southern end of the bay at Pichilemu.

8 Punta de Lobos

This ultra-powerful, ultra-long left break is considered one of the world's best waves. It forms three sections, runs all year, and can hold up to 30 ft (9.1 m), although it needs a medium to big swell to reach that size. It's hard to get in and out – beware of caves on the rock platforms. This wave is only for big-wave riders and experts looking for excitement. Never get in alone.

WAVE TYPE Left

WAVE HEIGHT 3–30 ft (0.9–9.1 m)

BREAK TYPE Point

BEST SWELL S

BEST WIND S

BEST TIDE Low

BEST TIME May–July, October–November

HAZARDS Rocks

DIRECTIONS Punta de Lobos is about 2 miles (3.2 km) south of Pichilemu.

9 Cueva del Toro

On a sandy beach at the northern end of Lebu Bay, surrounded by rocky walls, there's a wave that, when it strikes two holes in the rocks, produces a sound like a bull's roar – *toro* means "bull" in Spanish. This short, powerful wave has fun tubes. It runs with no wind, or with a moderate north wind.

WAVE TYPE Left and right

WAVE HEIGHT 3–10 ft (0.9–3.1 m)

BREAK TYPE Beach

BEST SWELL Depends on sandbar

BEST WIND N

BEST TIDE High

BEST TIME April–August

HAZARDS Thieves

DIRECTIONS Head south from Concepción on Route 160 to Tres Pinos. Turn right for Lebu. From downtown Lebu, cross the bridge over the river. Follow the coast to the northern point of Lebu Bay. Here you'll find some caves. Drive through two short tunnels to the small beach.

10 El Faro

El Faro is located at Boca Lebu, on the southern side of Lebu Bay. It's a short, intense left, with big tube rides up to 30–50 yards (30–50 m) long over a colorful reef bottom. It works perfectly in a moderate swell, and can stand up to 13 ft (4 m) in the right wind. And it's not crowded – you might even surf it alone. If this wave isn't working because the winds are unfavorable, try Cueva del Toro.

WAVE TYPE Left

WAVE HEIGHT 3–13 ft (0.9–4 m)

BREAK TYPE Point on rocky reef bottom

BEST SWELL NW

BEST WIND S

BEST TIDE Low

BEST TIME March–June

HAZARDS Seaweed, thieves

DIRECTIONS From downtown Lebu, follow the coast south to an old wharf at the southern end of Lebu Bay. Jump from the wharf and paddle out 200 yards (200 m) to the break.

The afternoon sun lights up the La Puntilla sets as they roll in at Pichilemu.

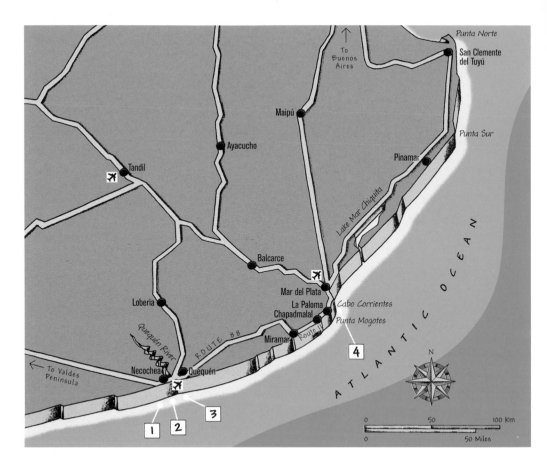

Argentina

Although Argentina has 2,940 miles (4,730 km) of coastline, most surfable waves are in an 80-mile (130-km) stretch between the resort city of Mar del Plata and Necochea. Beach breaks, and waves breaking off piers and breakwaters, make up the bulk of spots. Some right points add quality, as they offer the biggest swell and the longest rides.

Small south-to-southeast swells arrive throughout the year, much of it windswell. May to October are the biggest months, when some much-anticipated groundswells may roll through. It's often best to get out in the early morning to avoid onshore winds, and the day after swells arrive can also be good, when onshore winds can switch offshore. Local knowledge helps around here, as tides and winds affect many spots significantly. There's so much small, mushy surf, it pays to be vigilant — make the most of

decent swells as soon as they arrive because they usually only last for a couple of days.

Buenos Aires has an international airport, and several buses depart daily for Mar del Plata. Summer air temperatures average 59°–77°F (15°–25°C); winters are 41°–59°F (5°–15°C). Full suits are required all year, and from April to October, 50°F (10°C) waters mean that surfers wear every surf accessory they have.

orcas out to lunch

If you're visiting between March and May, it's worth making a trip farther south to the Valdes Peninsula. If you're organized, patient, and lucky, you may get to see orcas, also known as killer whales, launch up the beach to prey on unwary sea lion and elephant seal pups.

1 Cueva del Tigre

Cueva del Tigre is a quality wave with long walls offering rides of 150 yards (150 m) or more. It doesn't get particularly hollow, and is therefore more of a fun hot-dog wave, ideal for busting out your bag of tricks. It's worth checking when a big swell hits the coast because, like most points, this wave can handle the size. Being relatively remote, it's a good spot to camp and chill.

WAVE TYPE Right

WAVE HEIGHT 3–15 ft (0.9–4.6 m)

BREAK TYPE Point

BEST SWELL SE–S

BEST WIND NW–N

BEST TIDE Low–mid

BEST TIME March–November

HAZARDS Rocks

DIRECTIONS Take the coast road southwest from Necochea for 15½ miles (25 km) to the small point, Cueva del Tigre.

2 Escollera

This is a manmade wave, caused by the breakwater built on the southern side of the Quequén River. Waves jack up off the break wall and can provide very long rides. Escollera gets hollow on solid swells, offering tube rides. Otherwise, it's a carving wave. It can get very crowded, and it has a tight takeoff spot. There's always the alternative option of surfing the peaks farther south along the beach.

WAVE TYPE Left

WAVE HEIGHT 3–12 ft (0.9–3.7 m)

BREAK TYPE Breakwater-beach

BEST SWELL E–SE

BEST WIND NW–N

BEST TIDE All

BEST TIME March–November

HAZARDS Rips

DIRECTIONS In Necochea, head for the southern side of the mouth of the Quequén River. Look for the breakwater.

3 La Virazon

Quality peaks are found all along this stretch of coast. Usually a fun wave with the possibility of long rides, La Virazon in Quequén can get hollow and powerful on occasion. Also look out for fast, hollow lefts breaking off the shipwreck 2½ miles (4 km) north of the river mouth.

WAVE TYPE Left and right

WAVE HEIGHT 3–12 ft (0.9–3.7 m)

BREAK TYPE Beach-reef

BEST SWELL NW

BEST WIND SW

BEST TIDE High

BEST TIME March–November

HAZARDS The shipwreck, if you surf next to it

DIRECTIONS Head east on Route 88 from Necochea across the Quequén River. Turn right for the town of Quequén and head for the river mouth. The wave is on a long stretch of beach just north of the river mouth.

4 La Paloma

Situated on one of the most exposed parts of the Argentinian coastline, La Paloma is a quality wave that has abundant power when a decent swell arrives. It can break for well over 100 yards (100 m) and tubes are common, making it one of the best waves in Argentina.

WAVE TYPE Mostly right but left also

WAVE HEIGHT 3–12 ft (0.9–3.7 m)

BREAK TYPE Beach-reef

BEST SWELL SE

BEST WIND NW

BEST TIDE Mid–high

BEST TIME March–November

HAZARDS Rocks, access down steep cliff face

DIRECTIONS From downtown Mar del Plata, head south along Route 11 for about 6 miles (10 km) to La Paloma.

Brazil

With the Serra do Mar mountain range running parallel to the lush coast, the stretch from Cabo Frio to Santos in Brazil is one of exceptional beauty. And it's blessed with an abundance of powerful, world-class beach breaks interspersed with left and right points. No surprises then that it's one of the most densely populated places on Earth, both on land and on the waves. Many beach breaks, such as Saquarema, get thick-lipped and hollow, while the points can hold serious size and power.

With the most south-facing coast of the eastern seaboard, this area is well positioned to receive the south-to-southeast swells tracking across the Atlantic. While these are seldom more than 10 ft (3.1 m), the continental shelf drops away close enough to the shore for only a small amount of energy to be lost by the time they hit the coast. Northeast winds predominate here, which is cross-shore for many waves. But the looming Serra do Mar mountains can offer protection from the wind at certain spots.

São Paulo and Rio de Janeiro both have international airports. The temperature is tropical and humid, with downpours likely at any time. The water here is warm, too, so boardshorts or springsuits are all you'll need.

summer lovin'

From the sensory overload that is Carnival to the scantily clad bodies on the white-sand beaches, Brazilian summers are all about embracing love. This applies just as much to the crowded waves, where a dispute with a surfer who doesn't know Brazilian jiu-jitsu (a very popular martial art here) will end up in a forcible introduction to a friend of his who does. Making the effort to get to know the locals is like getting a key to the waves.

1 Bananas Point

Bananas Point is a sheltered point that only comes to life a few times a year. But it's worth waiting for. When a giant east swell hits, this wave lights up, with stacked-up lines wrapping around the point. Long waves with lengthy sections break in front of the rocks all the way to the beach.

WAVE TYPE Left

WAVE HEIGHT 3–15 ft (0.9–4.6 m)

BREAK TYPE Point

BEST SWELL E–SE

BEST WIND NE

BEST TIDE All

BEST TIME April–October

HAZARDS Rocks

DIRECTIONS Head out of São Paulo to the coastal SP-055. Bananas Point is 12½ miles (20 km) east of Boraceia in the village of Sahy. Take Rua do Pontal until it hits the beach. The wave is at the northern end of the beach.

2 Maresias

This world-class beach break gets very big and powerful. In good swells, A-frame peaks break along the beach, throwing up heaving barrels for the hordes of tube-riding connoisseurs. There are open faces to carve, too. The size of the waves means that Maresias has become popular for tow-in surfing.

WAVE TYPE Left and right

WAVE HEIGHT 3–15 ft (0.9–4.6 m)

BREAK TYPE Beach

BEST SWELL S

BEST WIND N

BEST TIDE All

BEST TIME April–October

HAZARDS Crowds, territorial locals

DIRECTIONS The coastal town of Maresias is 60 miles (100 km) southeast of São Paulo. Head out of São Paulo to the coastal SP-055 at Santos and travel east to Maresias.

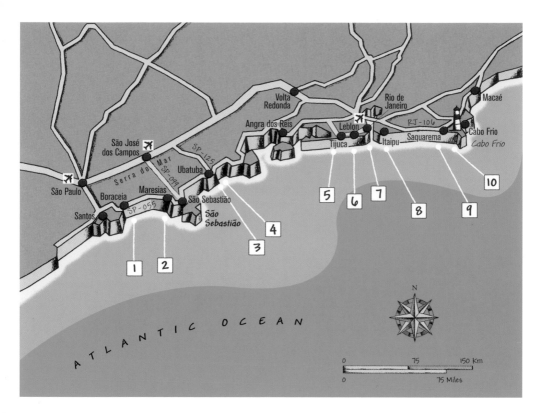

3 Vermelha Central

This long, scenic stretch of beach just north of Ubatuba has consistently good surf. More a hot-dog wave, Vermelha Central can turn it on and become hollow and powerful, and often has longish rides. This can be a good place to evade the crowds or to warm up for the more powerful beaches.

WAVE TYPE Left and right

WAVE HEIGHT 3–12 ft (0.9–3.7 m)

BREAK TYPE Beach

BEST SWELL SE

BEST WIND NW

BEST TIDE All

BEST TIME April–October

HAZARDS None

DIRECTIONS Vermelha Central is 102 miles (165 km) east of São Paulo and can be reached via SP-125 or SP-099. It's the first beach after the coastal town of Ubatuba, just 1 ¼ miles (2 km) east on Rodovia Rio Santos.

4 Praia do Felix

A small, scenic beach offers powerful, hollow waves. Sucky lefts break off the northern end of the beach, while well-formed peaks break farther south. This is a fun, high-performance wave with good tubes and plenty of opportunity for boosting airs or whacking lips. It gets crowded though, especially on weekends and in summer.

WAVE TYPE Left and right

WAVE HEIGHT 3–12 ft (0.9–3.7 m)

BREAK TYPE Beach

BEST SWELL E–SE

BEST WIND W–NW

BEST TIDE Low–mid

BEST TIME April–October

HAZARDS Crowds

DIRECTIONS Praia do Felix is 110 miles (175 km) east of São Paulo and can be reached via SP-125 or SP-099. The beach is the third beach after the coastal town of Ubatuba, 6 miles (10 km) northeast on Rodovia Rio Santos.

This long stretch of white sand is the location of the fast, powerful beach break of Maresias.

5 Reserva

Reserva is a high-quality beach break situated on a scenic stretch of coastline. With a large swell window, it's also something of a wave magnet. The waves here can have great shape, and offer fast, deep tube rides. It's worth checking out if you want to avoid the crowds.

WAVE TYPE Left and right

WAVE HEIGHT 3–10 ft (0.9–3.1 m)

BREAK TYPE Beach-reef

BEST SWELL SE–SW

BEST WIND NW–N

BEST TIDE Mid

BEST TIME April–October

HAZARDS Rocks

DIRECTIONS From Rio de Janeiro, head southwest on Avenida Paulo de Frontin to the coastal suburb of Tijuca, about 12 miles (20 km) away. Go west along Avenida do Pepé, which turns into Avenida Lúcio Costa. After 9 miles (15 km), you'll be at Praia da Reserva. If the reserve on your right becomes housing, you've gone too far.

6 Pontáo do Leblon

This classic point break offers a change from all the beach breaks in the Rio de Janeiro area. Although not particularly consistent, it's well worth waiting for. The takeoff is in front of the rocks, and long rides to the beach are possible. This wave is also a well-known big-wave spot that gets powerful and sometimes hollow. If the point isn't working, look out for peaks on the beach, which can also often be surfed.

WAVE TYPE Right

WAVE HEIGHT 3–18 ft (0.9–5.5 m)

BREAK TYPE Point

BEST SWELL S–SW

BEST WIND N

BEST TIDE All

BEST TIME April–October

HAZARDS Rocks, territorial locals, pollution

DIRECTIONS From Rio de Janeiro, head south to the coastal suburb of Leblon 6 miles (10 km) away. Pontáo do Leblon is at the southern end of Leblon Beach, on Avenida Delfim Moreira.

7 Leme

Leme is one of the closest surf breaks to downtown Rio. It's a relatively inconsistent wave that's popular with bodyboarders. When it's on, the lefts predominate, offering short, fast, hollow rides. It's often overlooked, but it does offer the possibility of escaping the crowds, especially when the swell is from the east.

WAVE TYPE Left and right

WAVE HEIGHT 2–8 ft (0.6–2.4 m)

BREAK TYPE Beach

BEST SWELL E–SE

BEST WIND NW–N

BEST TIDE All

BEST TIME March–October

HAZARDS None

DIRECTIONS From downtown Rio de Janeiro, head directly south to world-famous Copacabana Beach on Avenida Atlantica. Leme is at the northern end of the beach.

8 Itacoatiara

Fun when small, Itacoatiara becomes a heavy, board-snapping wave on a solid swell. Short, intense rides offer the opportunity of gaping barrels. You'll need commitment and speed to paddle into these thick waves, and a heavy beating awaits those who venture over the falls. Make a barrel here and you'll never forget it, but be ready for any punishment that it serves up.

WAVE TYPE Left and right

WAVE HEIGHT 3–15 ft (0.9–4.6 m)

BREAK TYPE Beach reef

BEST SWELL SW

BEST WIND N

BEST TIDE All

BEST TIME April–October

HAZARDS Crowds, territorial locals, rips, urchins, heavy waves

DIRECTIONS From Rio de Janeiro, head east over the Ponte Rio Niterói. Turn south anywhere off RJ-104 and head to the coastal town of Itaipu. Rua Matias Sandri leads to the beach.

9 Saquarema

This popular surf spot can get hollow, but it's more commonly a high-performance wave, ideal for top-to-bottom maneuvers on the open face. Because of its location near a town and its mellower waves compared to other, heavier spots, it gets very crowded. The lefts are generally longer than the rights, with rides of more than 100 yards (100 m) common.

WAVE TYPE Left and right

WAVE HEIGHT 3–10 ft (0.9–3.1 m)

BREAK TYPE Beach

BEST SWELL SE–S

BEST WIND N

BEST TIDE All

BEST TIME April–October

HAZARDS Crowds, territorial locals

DIRECTIONS From Rio de Janeiro, head east on RJ-106 for about 60 miles (100 km) to the coastal town of Saquarema. The wave is south of the town, on the southern side of the river and the headland.

10 Itaúna

One of the best waves in Brazil, this beach break gets hollow, fast, and powerful. Peaks are found all along the beach, but one of the best is close to the rocky outcrop at the northern end of the beach – it gets very crowded. The lefts generally offer longer rides, while the rights are rounder. This is a board-snapping wave where you're well advised to respect the locals.

WAVE TYPE Left and right

WAVE HEIGHT 3–15 ft (0.9–4.6 m)

BREAK TYPE Beach

BEST SWELL ESE–SE

BEST WIND NW–N

BEST TIDE Low–mid

BEST TIME April–October

HAZARDS Rocks, territorial locals, crowds

DIRECTIONS In Saquarema, the wave is just to the north of the river mouth on Avenida Oceanica.

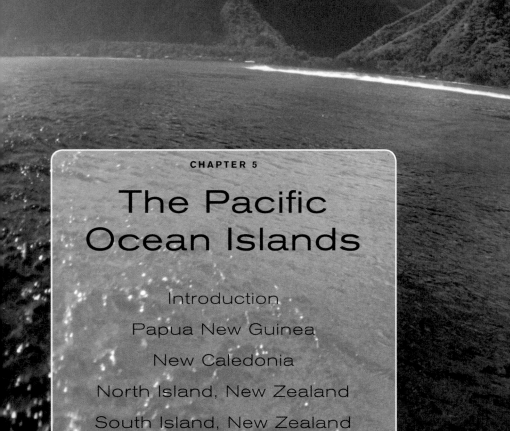

born of fire

Many of the islands in the Pacific, such as Hawaii and the Solomon Islands, are volcanic in origin. Huge, towering volcanic peaks – some higher than Everest when measured from the seafloor – thrust out of the ocean, thousands of miles from the nearest continental landmass. With little or no continental shelf to mitigate the ocean's energy, the Pacific region's surf is unrivaled in power and size.

The Pacific Ocean is home to thousands of islands, each one with many potential surf spots.

Introduction

The Pacific Ocean is, put simply, vast. Covering more than 63 million sq miles (165 million sq km), the Pacific is by far the largest ocean in the world, and covers just under one-third of the Earth's surface. Straddling both hemispheres – from the Bering Sea at latitude 60° north to Antarctica at latitude 60° south – the Pacific is larger than the total combined area of land on the planet. Named the "peaceful sea" (Latin: *mare pacificum*) by the Portuguese explorer Ferdinand Magellan, the Pacific Ocean is often quite the opposite, its sheer size giving rise to the biggest swells found anywhere in the world.

Scattered throughout this area are thousands of islands, home to some of the world's best-known surf spots – and to many less-publicized ones that are rarely surfed due to their remote location. There are three main island groups. The Polynesian triangle – connecting the three points of Hawaii in the north, Easter Island in the east, and New Zealand to the south – encompasses the island arcs and clusters of the

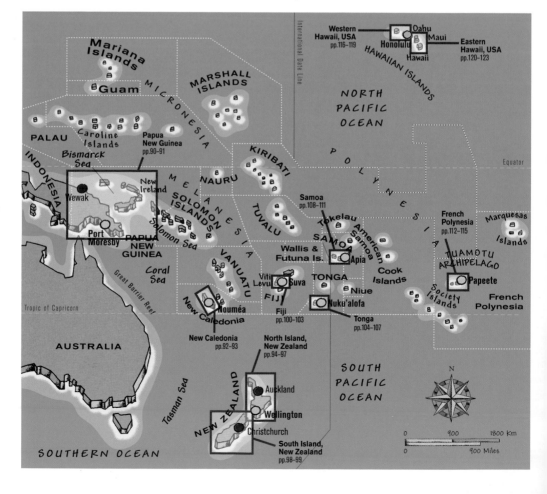

The sheer power of Pacific surf is nowhere more evident than at Jaws, Hawaii's monster wave.

Cook Islands, Tuvalu, Samoa, Tokelau, Tonga, Wallis and Futuna, and the islands of French Polynesia, including Tuamotu, the Marquesas, and Tahiti and Moorea. Micronesia is a collection of nations and territories comprising hundreds of small islands, scattered across an area north of the equator and west of the International Date Line. It encompasses the Caroline Islands (including Palau), the Marshall Islands, and the Mariana Islands. The Melanesian group in the southwestern Pacific is dominated by New Guinea, and includes the Bismarck Archipelago, Fiji, New Caledonia, the Solomon Islands, and Vanuatu.

With such a huge area for swell generation and very few significant landmasses to get in the way, many of the Pacific islands are exposed to swells from both the Northern and Southern hemispheres. Northern storms are generally more intense, which results in Hawaii seeing the most regular big swells.

The Pacific contains perhaps the greatest amount of untapped surfing potential in the world, particularly in the thinly populated outer island chains. The middle of the Pacific is an extremely long way from anywhere. To explore the most remote islands, a boat is the only way to travel, and it would be possible to spend months, if not years, charting the islands of Micronesia and Melanesia for surfing potential.

Hazards include the sheer size and power of the surf – especially in Hawaii – and the sharp coral or rocky reef lying not far below the surface in many places. Wearing a helmet may be a good idea. Sharks can also be a problem. The tropical sun is unforgiving, so don't forget sun protection. Malaria is present in a few places, including Papua New Guinea, Vanuatu and the Solomon Islands; consult a doctor before traveling.

The Birthplace of Surfing

The Pacific region is the place where surfing originated. The sport has been a part of Polynesian – particularly Hawaiian – culture since as early as 400 AD. On his arrival in Hawaii in the 1770s, Captain James Cook witnessed Hawaiians surfing at Kealakekua Bay, and found evidence that surfing had been a part of life for many generations; he also saw Tahitians catching waves in their outrigger canoes. Following the arrival of Christian missionaries in Hawaii, the practice of surfing declined until the sport was revived at Waikiki in the early twentieth century.

Today, it's something of a paradox that the region that is home to many of the world's best waves, has produced some of the world's finest surfers, and saw the birth of the sport itself is still one of the final frontiers for surf exploration.

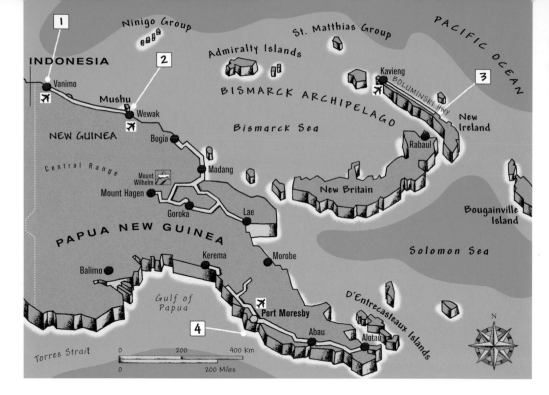

Papua New Guinea

Papua New Guinea (PNG) consists of the eastern half of the island of New Guinea, and a number of smaller, offshore islands, notably New Britain and New Ireland. PNG is just south of the equator, yet the highest peak, Mt. Wilhelm, at 14,793 ft (4,509 m), is often snow-capped.

The most consistent areas for surf are the north-facing coast of the main island, between Vanimo and Madang, and the area around Kavieng on New Ireland. The best time of year for surf is from November to late April, when consistent swells are generated in the Bismarck Sea and Pacific Ocean. The waves are typically in the 3–8 ft (0.9–2.4 m) range, and they break over coral reefs.

Kavieng is a very popular destination for traveling surfers, with a surf camp and surf charter boat operating in the area. New Ireland is part of the Bismarck Archipelago, a chain of islands with fringing coral reefs, making Kavieng a convenient base from which to surf the surrounding reefs. On the PNG mainland, the south coast picks up swell from the southeast, but there has to be plenty of size to get the breaks near Port Moresby and Alotau working.

International flights arrive at the capital city, Port Moresby, from where there are flights to Kavieng, Vanimo, and Madang. From Kavieng, most spots are accessed by boat.

Papua New Guinea's location just south of the equator makes for a generally humid and wet climate. Average daily temperatures range from 81°F (27°C) to 88°F (31°C), with the outer islands being slightly cooler and less humid.

Malaria is present in the area, so be sure to take medical advice before traveling. AIDS is also on the increase. Other hazards include sharks and the potentially deadly box jellyfish.

tread warily

In Papua New Guinea, the reefs and the ocean are the property of the traditional landowners. Therefore, you'll need to seek permission before you surf anywhere, even if there's no one around. The best idea is to stay at one of the resorts or guesthouses or have a local tour guide. For further information, contact the Surfing Association of Papua New Guinea (www.surfingpapuanewguinea.org.pg).

1 Vanimo (Lido), PNG mainland

This point break at Lido, near Vanimo, handles big swell. A right-hander in the morning, it becomes a left-hander in the afternoon when the winds change. When it's pumping up to 10 ft (3.1 m), it can be powerful, with long, 150-yard (150-m) rides. It's close to five other point breaks.

WAVE TYPE Left and right

WAVE HEIGHT 3–10 ft (0.9–3.1 m)

BREAK TYPE Point

BEST SWELL NW

BEST WIND SE, NW

BEST TIDE All

BEST TIME October–April

HAZARDS Crowds

DIRECTIONS From Port Moresby, fly to Vanimo. The break is a 4½-mile (7-km) drive west of Vanimo at the village of Lido. An increasingly popular route for surf travelers is to fly from Bali to Jayapura, just over the border in Indonesia, from where it's 28 miles (45 km) by road to Lido.

2 Sup Point, Mushu Island

Located on the eastern side of a small island called Mushu, north of Wewak town, Sup Point is a right- and backdoor left-hander breaking over reef. This challenging wave is short and fast, and gets shallow on the outgoing tides. Not for beginners.

WAVE TYPE Left and right

WAVE HEIGHT 3–8 ft (0.9–2.4 m)

BREAK TYPE Point

BEST SWELL NW–N

BEST WIND NW, SE

BEST TIDE All

BEST TIME October–April

HAZARDS Sharp reef, shallow water

DIRECTIONS Fly to Wewak from Port Moresby. Catch a dinghy to Sup Point from the Wewak town beach near the yacht club. It takes about 20 minutes to get there.

3 Dalom, New Ireland

Dalom, well south of Kavieng, is mostly a fast, hollow right, breaking over a reef and finishing on a sandbar. When the swell is a bit more out of the north, the left starts to work, but it ends over very shallow reef. Dalom is best on a medium-to-high tide due to the shallow nature of the inside section, although it's possible to surf at low tide on a big swell.

WAVE TYPE Right and occasional left

WAVE HEIGHT 3–10 ft (0.9–3.1 m)

BREAK TYPE Reef

BEST SWELL N–NE

BEST WIND W

BEST TIDE Mid–high

BEST TIME October–March

HAZARDS Shallow reef, long distance to medical help

DIRECTIONS Kavieng is a 90-minute flight from Port Moresby. To surf the break at Dalom, you must stay at the Dalom guesthouse, two hours from Kavieng on the Boluminski Hwy.

4 Titties, PNG mainland

This reef break off Sero Beach, West Taurama Point, is the best wave near Port Moresby. A right-hander, Titties jacks up on a reef ledge and gives a fast, fun 30-yard (30-m) ride. The other break just to the left of Titties is Hooters.

WAVE TYPE Left and right

WAVE HEIGHT 3–6 ft (0.9–1.8 m)

BREAK TYPE Reef

BEST SWELL E, SE

BEST WIND W, NW

BEST TIDE Outgoing

BEST TIME April–November

HAZARDS Box jellyfish, sharks, kitesurfers, windsurfers

DIRECTIONS Sero Beach is five minutes from Port Moresby. Drive through the Taurama military barracks (tell the guards you're going to the Sero Surf Club) and take the first right turn, which leads to the clubhouse. Let club members know you're surfing. Catch a dinghy to the break from here or paddle out 500 yards (500 m).

New Caledonia

New Caledonia, lying between Australia and Fiji, is an overseas territory of France, made up of a main island, Grande Terre, and several smaller islands. Grande Terre is 217 miles (350 km) long, and is encircled by the world's second-largest barrier reef, which runs for 895 miles (1,440 km).

With so much coral around, it's no surprise that New Caledonia is home to heaps of top-quality reef breaks, mostly scattered along the southwest-facing coast of Grande Terre. Breaks here include Dumbéa, Ténia, and Corvette (closest to Ténia). The sheer scale of the barrier reef, however, means that getting to some of the more distant breaks is time-consuming and expensive, but this is offset by the potential for discovering perfect, empty breaks.

May to September is the most consistent time for surf on the south-facing reefs, when swells generated in the Roaring Forties pulse up from the Tasman Sea. During this time, the swell rarely drops below 3 ft (0.9 m) and can get up to 10 ft (3.1 m) or bigger.

The water temperature ranges from 72°F (22°C) in July to 79°F (26°C) in January, but strong winds often make a shorty wetsuit more comfortable than boardshorts; a wetsuit also offers some protection from the shallow, sharp coral reefs. Average daily maximum temperatures range from a low of 74°F (23°C) in July to a high of 84°F (29°C) in January.

New Caledonia's international airport is about 30 miles (48 km) west of the capital, Nouméa. A rental car is the easiest way to get around the island.

if there's no swell …

Check out the sea life. Many of the boats that take surfers to the outer reefs also operate as diving boats. The world's biggest lagoon has some fantastic diving and snorkeling sites, and is home to turtles, sharks, dugongs, and colorful tropical fish galore.

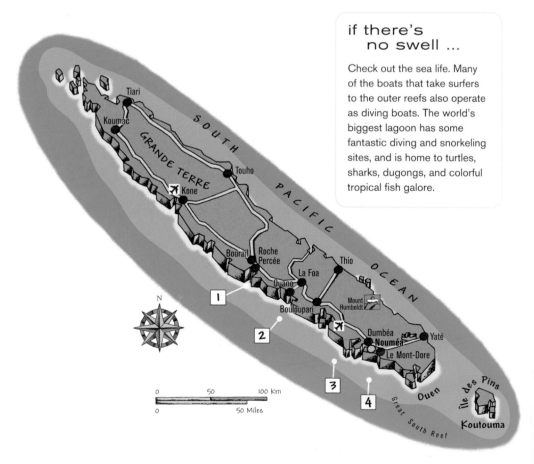

1 Roche Percée

The only beach break on the island is also the only wave on the mainland. A long left-hander that peels off a sandbar at the mouth of the Nera River, the wave is ideal for beginners because of its sheltered location. The reef offshore has excellent left and right breaks accessible by boat.

WAVE TYPE Left

WAVE HEIGHT 2–6 ft (0.6–1.8 m)

BREAK TYPE Beach

BEST SWELL S–SW

BEST WIND N–NE

BEST TIDE All

BEST TIME May–July

HAZARDS Crowds on weekends

DIRECTIONS From Bourail, drive south for 4 miles (6.5 km) to Roche Percée Beach. Offshore reefs are accessible only by boat — ask at the surf camp near the beach.

2 Ouano

On good days when all the sections link up, the left at Ouano gives 300-yard (300-m) rides, which alternate between speedy tube sections and workable walls. The right on the opposite side of the pass is a short, fast wave with a great barrel section, but is less consistent.

WAVE TYPE Left

WAVE HEIGHT 2–15 ft (0.6–4.6 m)

BREAK TYPE Reef

BEST SWELL SE–SW

BEST WIND E–SE

BEST TIDE Incoming

BEST TIME May–July

HAZARDS Shallow reef, coral

DIRECTIONS From Bouloupari, drive west for 6 miles (10 km) in the direction of La Foa. Just before La Foa, turn left at the sign to Ouano Beach. The reef pass is 6 miles (10 km) offshore and accessible only by boat. Jayak Surfari runs a speedboat service from the village of Ouano.

3 Dumbéa

The best wave at Dumbéa, the left, is long with a fast barrel section and a heavy takeoff. When big, the takeoff gets even heavier as water is sucked off the reef. The right is a long, steady wall, which offers the occasional tube in a big swell on low tide.

WAVE TYPE Left and right

WAVE HEIGHT 3–12 ft (0.9–3.7 m)

BREAK TYPE Reef

BEST SWELL SE–SW

BEST WIND NE–E

BEST TIDE Incoming

BEST TIME May–July

HAZARDS Shallow reef, coral, remote location

DIRECTIONS Dumbéa reef pass is accessible only by boat — a two-hour return trip from Nouméa.

4 Ténia

Ténia's three waves — two lefts and a right — offer something in almost all conditions. The best wave is the left at the reef pass, which works in just about any size, from waist-high waves to a seriously big swell. A very consistent spot in an idyllic location.

WAVE TYPE Left

WAVE HEIGHT 2–12 ft (0.6–3.7 m)

BREAK TYPE Reef

BEST SWELL SE–SW

BEST WIND NE–E

BEST TIDE Incoming

BEST TIME May–July

HAZARDS Shallow reef, coral, remote location

DIRECTIONS Ténia reef pass is accessible only by boat — a two-hour return trip from Nouméa.

a record breaker

On the North Island, a ridge 60 miles (97 km) south of Hastings has the longest place name in the world: Taumatawhakatangihanga-koauauotamateaturipuka-kapikimaungahoronukupo-kaiwhenuakitanatahu. The Maori translates roughly as "The brow of the hill where Tamatea, the man with the big knees who slid down, climbed up, and swallowed mountains, known as the land eater, played his nose flute to his loved one."

North Island, New Zealand

The North Island of New Zealand, with its largely subtropical climate, stunning scenery, and world-class waves, is a great destination for a surf trip. The North Island boasts over 4,600 miles (7,400 km) of coastline, much of it well placed to pick up the powerful south swells generated in the Roaring Forties. March to August is the most consistent time of year for waves, but it can get chilly, with water temperatures in July bottoming out at 54°F (12°C) and average daily maximum air temperatures also 54°F (12°C), making a 3/4 mm wetsuit and boots essential. January is a much more pleasant time of year, with water temperatures of 64°F (18°C) and a daily average of 75°F (24°C).

The North Island has two main surf areas. South of Auckland, the west coast picks up swell from the south and north, and is home to some incredible waves, including the renowned left point at Raglan. The area around the foot of Mt. Taranaki, 200 miles (320 km) south of Auckland, has a good range of quality breaks which work in a variety of conditions.

On the east coast, the area around Napier, Gisborne, and the Mahia Peninsula is stacked with waves and is much wilder and less developed than the west coast. Surf spots include Makarori Point and Waikanae Beach.

International flights arrive at Auckland airport. The best way to get around is to rent a car or motor home, or take internal flights.

1 Ahipara or Shipwreck Bay

Wild west coast swells are transformed into perfectly formed waves at Ahipara, making this one of New Zealand's surfing gems. The large headland at this bay provides a combination of points and reefs. The farther out along the point you go, the bigger it gets.

WAVE TYPE Left

WAVE HEIGHT 2–8 ft (0.9–2.4 m)

BREAK TYPE Point, reef

BEST SWELL SW

BEST WIND S–SW

BEST TIDE All

BEST TIME June–August

HAZARDS None

DIRECTIONS Ahipara is located at the southern end of Ninety Mile Beach on the west coast of the Northland region. Follow SH 1 north from Auckland, through Whangarei, to Kaitaia. Ahipara is 9 miles (14.5 km) to the west on the Kaitaia–Awaroa Rd.

2 Mangawhai Heads

A river bar and beach break combine to provide different breaks for different skill levels. The river bar suits the more experienced surfer and is best on the lower tide. The beach provides easy-to-handle waves for all levels of expertise.

WAVE TYPE Left and right

WAVE HEIGHT 2–4 ft (0.6–1.2 m)

BREAK TYPE Beach, river bar

BEST SWELL NE

BEST WIND SW

BEST TIDE Mid

BEST TIME February–September

HAZARDS None

DIRECTIONS Head north on SH 1 from Auckland, and turn right at Kaiwaka (north of Wellsford) onto the Kaiwaka–Mangawhai Rd for Mangawhai Heads.

3 North Piha

At Piha, a long strip of sand is divided into North and South Piha beaches by Lion Rock. Open to swell from the southwest, North Piha Beach is best when it's 2–4 ft (0.6–1.2 m). The northern end is sheltered from the north wind, while the southern end has a wave more suited to learners on the higher tide.

WAVE TYPE Left and right

WAVE HEIGHT 2–10 ft (0.6–3.1 m)

BREAK TYPE Beach

BEST SWELL SW

BEST WIND NE–E

BEST TIDE Mid–high

BEST TIME November–March

HAZARDS Strong rips and undertows when bigger

DIRECTIONS Take the Northwestern Motorway (SH 16) from Auckland to Henderson. From there, follow signs to the west coast and Piha.

4 South Piha

South Piha has a left-hand-breaking river bar at the southern end and usually good sandbanks in the middle. The rips can get bad when it starts to max out. Of the two Piha beaches, South Piha provides the more consistent surf.

WAVE TYPE Left and right

WAVE HEIGHT 2–10 ft (0.6–3.1 m)

BREAK TYPE Beach, river bar

BEST SWELL SW

BEST WIND NE–E

BEST TIDE Mid–high

BEST TIME November–March

HAZARDS Strong rips and undertows when bigger

DIRECTIONS Take the Northwestern Motorway (SH 16) from Auckland to Henderson. From there, follow signs to the west coast and Piha.

5 Raglan

This is New Zealand's surfing icon. There are three points, starting with Manu Bay, then Whale Bay, and finally Indicators, a left that links three sections to provide a long and challenging ride. A difficult entry and exit, plus a rocky bottom, make Raglan's points unsuitable for novices.

WAVE TYPE Left

WAVE HEIGHT 2–10 ft (0.6–3.1 m)

BREAK TYPE Point

BEST SWELL S

BEST WIND SE

BEST TIDE All

BEST TIME March–September

HAZARDS Rocks, rips, difficult entry and exit

DIRECTIONS From Hamilton, take SH 23 to Raglan township, then keep heading west on Wainui Rd toward Whale Bay for 9 miles (14.5 km) and you'll get to Manu Bay, the first point.

6 Ngaranui Beach

When the points at Raglan are too small, this beach break swings into action. Sandbars and banks partly determine surf quality, but generally Ngaranui is best on an incoming mid-to-high tide. Check conditions from the top of the hill before going down to the beach.

WAVE TYPE Left and right

WAVE HEIGHT 2–6 ft (0.6–1.8 m)

BREAK TYPE Beach

BEST SWELL SW

BEST WIND NE–E

BEST TIDE Mid–high

BEST TIME January–March

HAZARDS Rips

DIRECTIONS Take SH 23 from Hamilton to Raglan township. Head west on Wainui Rd for 3 miles (4.8 km) and turn right at the sign for Wainui Reserve and beach access.

7 Fitzroy Beach

A coarse sand bottom with a rock base keeps the banks at this beach in good shape. It can handle 2–8 ft (0.6–2.4 m) of swell and is best with an offshore wind. When bigger and on a lower tide, Fitzroy gets quite hollow.

WAVE TYPE Left and right

WAVE HEIGHT 2–10 ft (0.6–3.1 m)

BREAK TYPE Beach

BEST SWELL SW–W

BEST WIND E

BEST TIDE All

BEST TIME March–September

HAZARDS None

DIRECTIONS Fitzroy Beach is located in the northern suburbs of New Plymouth. Just follow the main street north until you get to a small shopping area in the suburb of Devon. You'll see a sign directing you left to Fitzroy Beach.

8 Stent Road

Stent Road is a powerful wave that starts at a reef with a steep takeoff, then fires off through a bowl section, and finishes along a shallow point. The surrounding area is full of waves – follow virtually any road to the coast and you'll find a break.

WAVE TYPE Left and right

WAVE HEIGHT 2–12 ft (0.6–3.7 m)

BREAK TYPE Reef, point

BEST SWELL SW

BEST WIND NE–E

BEST TIDE All

BEST TIME March–September

HAZARDS Rocks

DIRECTIONS From New Plymouth, take Surf Highway 45 south for 10 miles (16 km) to Oakura. About 2 miles (3.2 km) farther on, turn onto Stent Rd.

9 Pipe (Waikanae Beach)

What can look like any old beach break when it's small really starts to shine when the south swell pumps in through the winter. Many of Gisborne's best surfers have honed their skills on The Pipe's barrels.

WAVE TYPE Left and right

WAVE HEIGHT 2–6 ft (0.6–3.1 m)

BREAK TYPE Beach

BEST SWELL SE

BEST WIND NW

BEST TIDE All

BEST TIME March–September

HAZARDS None

DIRECTIONS From Gisborne's main street, turn east at the clock tower and head to Salisbury Rd. This will bring you to the northern end of Waikanae Beach. Turn right, follow the road a short distance, and park in the grassy area.

10 Makarori Point

Breaking out in deep water off the point at the southern end of Makarori Beach, this wave starts off a peak that soon bends itself into a downline point wave. It's perfect for longboarders. The beach also provides good peaks and is one of the most consistent breaks in the region.

WAVE TYPE Right

WAVE HEIGHT 2–8 ft (0.6–2.4 m)

BREAK TYPE Point, beach

BEST SWELL E–SE

BEST WIND NW

BEST TIDE All

BEST TIME March–September

HAZARDS None

DIRECTIONS Head north on SH 35 from Gisborne to Wainui. Continue, and as you come down a hill at the northern end of Wainui, you'll see Makarori Point to your right.

Putting in a few turns at Raglan, the wave that put New Zealand on the international surfing map.

South Island, New Zealand

New Zealand's South Island is dominated geographically — and climatically — by the Southern Alps. This mountain range runs along the length of South Island, with a string of 18 peaks over 9,800 ft (3,000 m) high dividing the northwest- and southeast-facing coasts. Like the surf spots of the North Island, the South Island's spots are mainly points, beaches, and rocky reefs — but the water's colder.

The climate is distinctly cooler than on the North Island, with the average daily maximum temperatures in Christchurch ranging from 44°F (7°C) in July to 70°F (21°C) in January. Water temperatures are 52°F (11°C) in July to 61°F (16°C) in January, making wetsuits necessary year-round.

The South Island's two largest cities, Christchurch and Dunedin, are both on the southeast coast, and are well placed to pick up the dominant south swells, which are most consistent from March to August. Both cities have a vast array of breaks nearby and a sizable — and talented — local surf community.

Westport, on the northwest-facing coast, is another surf hotspot, exposed to both south and north swells. It is much milder and wetter here, and the variety of breaks makes the area a good destination at all times of the year.

Home to some of the world's most beautiful scenery, the South Island is very much on the tourist map. Most international flights to New Zealand arrive in Auckland, and internal flights to Christchurch and Dunedin are regular and affordable. A rental car or motor home is recommended, as public transport is not extensive.

world-class wines

The Marlborough region in the north of the South Island is famous for producing some of the world's best wine — particularly sauvignon blanc, which thrives in the cool climate. Many of the wineries around Blenheim run tours and tastings, with Cloudy Bay, Villa Maria, and Montana being among the best known.

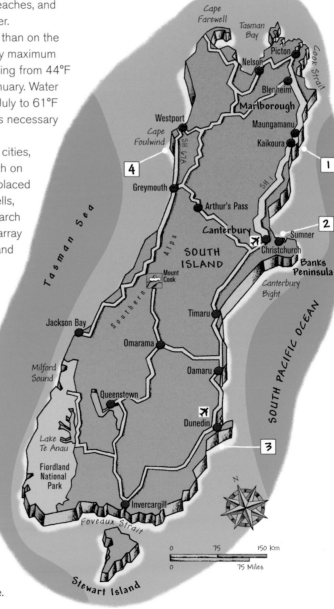

1 Maungamanu

This right-hand point break at Maungamanu, in the Kaikoura region, suits all levels of expertise. A couple of nearby breaks are for advanced surfers. If you want a day off surfing, try a whale-watching trip from Kaikoura, or go for a hike in the foothills of the Southern Alps.

WAVE TYPE Right

WAVE HEIGHT 2–8 ft (0.6–2.4 m)

BREAK TYPE Point

BEST SWELL SE

BEST WIND W

BEST TIDE All

BEST TIME March–September

HAZARDS Crossing the train line and state highway to get to the waves

DIRECTIONS The port of Kaikoura is 115 miles (184 km) north of Christchurch on SH 1, and 98 miles (157 km) south of Picton, also on SH 1. Maungamanu is about 10 miles (16 km) to the north of Kaikoura on SH 1.

2 Sumner

Located near Christchurch, this is not the most consistent spot, but when waves arrive it's a great place to be. The pier or the estuary provides good waves in a south swell, while Taylors Mistake, a horseshoe-shaped bay on the other side of the hill from Sumner, will make a north swell punchy and hollow at one end and gentle at the other.

WAVE TYPE Left and right

WAVE HEIGHT 2–4 ft (0.6–1.2 m)

BREAK TYPE Beach

BEST SWELL E

BEST WIND W

BEST TIDE All

BEST TIME February–August

HAZARDS None

DIRECTIONS Sumner is 7½ miles (12 km) from Christchurch. From central Christchurch, head east and follow Linwood Ave, which turns southeast and eventually becomes Main Rd. This runs beside an estuary into Sumner.

3 St. Clair

Dunedin's St. Clair is a beach break that receives swell from the north and south. In offshore wind conditions, the beach can offer nice clean peaks, breaking left and right, while the more sheltered southern end has a right-hand point setup next to a swimming pool.

WAVE TYPE Left and right

WAVE HEIGHT 2–6 ft (0.6–1.8 m)

BREAK TYPE Point, beach

BEST SWELL S

BEST WIND SE

BEST TIDE All

BEST TIME March–September

HAZARDS Rocks, rips

DIRECTIONS From central Dunedin, follow the signs south to St. Clair.

4 Tauranga Bay

Although the west coast gets masses of swell, most of the breaks are not very good, except for Tauranga Bay, which has an offshore wind in a southwest swell. In the summer months, when the westerlies are gone, this coastline can provide a surf experience like no other. And mountains plunging into the sea provide a backdrop straight out of *Lord of the Rings*.

WAVE TYPE Left and right

WAVE HEIGHT 2–8 ft (0.6–2.4 m)

BREAK TYPE Point, beach

BEST SWELL SW

BEST WIND SW

BEST TIDE All

BEST TIME March–September

HAZARDS Rocks, rips

DIRECTIONS From Westport, drive southwest on SH 67A to Cape Foulwind. Tauranga Bay is a short distance to the south.

Fiji

The Fijian archipelago is extensive, comprising 322 islands and 522 islets, spread over an area 700 miles (1,120 km) across. Unsurprisingly, the surf potential in Fiji is vast, with most of the smaller islands and islets being either coral cays, or surrounded by coral reefs, and many well positioned to receive swell from all directions. According to *Surfer* magazine, Fiji is home to two of the planet's best waves, Cloudbreak and Restaurants.

The two major islands are Viti Levu and Vanua Levu. Both are volcanic in origin, and have peaks over 4,000 ft (1,200 m) high and coastlines fringed by coral reefs punctuated by numerous reef-pass breaks.

Viti Levu, with an area of about 4,000 sq miles (10,360 sq km) is the largest of the islands. It's also the most densely populated: three-quarters of the country's population live here in the capital city, Suva.

Also on Viti Levu is Fiji's international airport, located close to the main area of hotels and resorts around Nadi, on the west coast 125 miles (201 km) from Suva. Many resorts offer free transfers from the airport. Car rental is expensive and usually unnecessary as most of the surf spots are within easy reach of the tourist resorts. The south coast of Viti Levu and the nearby Mamanuca Group of islands are easily accessible from Nadi, and offer some world-class waves.

The prime surf season runs from April to October when swells generated in the Southern Ocean pulse up to the south-facing coast. The water temperature at this time of year averages 79°F (26°C), making boardshorts extremely comfortable, although protection from the tropical sun is essential. Fiji is warm year-round, with average daily maximum temperatures of 79°F (26°C) in July and 86°F (30°C) in January.

1 Restaurants

Located off Tavarua Island, this is one of the top ten waves in the world, as judged by *Surfer* magazine. It breaks only in a large groundswell, although when it does break it's perfection in motion: very hollow, 150 yards (150 m) long, and barreling all the way.

WAVE TYPE Left

WAVE HEIGHT 3–12 ft (0.9–3.7 m)

BREAK TYPE Reef

BEST SWELL SW

BEST WIND SE

BEST TIDE High

BEST TIME Year-round

HAZARDS Shallow reef, aggressive locals

DIRECTIONS Restaurants is "owned" by the people who run the resort on Tavarua Island, off the coast of Viti Levu, west of Nadi, and non-guests need permission to surf here. The break is within paddling distance of the island. You can also take a boat from the mainland and anchor on the inside of the reef.

2 Cloudbreak

Another top-ten wave, according to *Surfer* magazine, for consistency, length (200 yards/ 200 m or so), and the way it holds big swells. At the moment, the wave, like its neighbor, Restaurants, is "owned" by Tavarua Island Resort, but this situation may change soon.

WAVE TYPE Left

WAVE HEIGHT 3–20 ft (0.9–6.1 m)

BREAK TYPE Reef

BEST SWELL S–SW

BEST WIND SE

BEST TIDE All

BEST TIME Year-round

HAZARDS Shallow reef, aggressive locals

DIRECTIONS Cloudbreak lies about 1¼ miles (2 km) south of Tavarua Island. The break is accessible by boat from Tavarua Island Resort (for guests only), or from the mainland from Sonaisali Resort (by arrangement with the Fiji Surf shop in Nadi) or Seashell Cove Resort.

Cloudbreak open for business?

The luxurious island resort of Tavarua sparked strong debate in the surfing world when it purchased exclusive surfing "rights" for the waves at Cloudbreak and Restaurants. For many years, only paying guests at the resort were able to surf the world-class lefts. Since the military coup in December 2006, however, this situation seems likely to change, with the government expected to open up access to the waves to everyone.

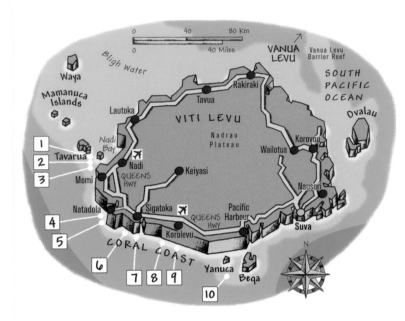

3 Tavarua Rights

Tavarua Rights is a gentle right-hander on the back of Tavarua Island. It's a fun, playful alternative to the two world-class powerful lefts off the island, Restaurants and Cloudbreak, and will accommodate all levels of experience. Like those other waves, Tavarua Rights is "owned" by Tavarua Island Resort.

WAVE TYPE Right

WAVE HEIGHT 3–12 ft (0.9–3.7 m)

BREAK TYPE Reef

BEST SWELL SE, SW

BEST WIND SE

BEST TIDE High

BEST TIME Year-round

HAZARDS Shallow reef, aggressive locals

DIRECTIONS Paddle out from the back side of Tavarua Island or take a boat from the mainland.

4 Natadola Main Reef Left

This very challenging left is a 20-minute paddle out from the famous (and gorgeous) Natadola Beach. It's peaky, and can be very hollow and powerful. Natadola Beach was voted one of the 25 sexiest beaches in the world by *Forbes Traveler* magazine in 2006.

WAVE TYPE Left

WAVE HEIGHT 3–12 ft (0.9–3.7 m)

BREAK TYPE Reef

BEST SWELL S–SW

BEST WIND N, SE

BEST TIDE Low

BEST TIME November–February

HAZARDS Sharks, sea urchins, long distance from shore

DIRECTIONS The Natadola Beach turnoff is a 30-minute drive from Nadi town heading south on the Queens Highway. A major resort and golf course development opens soon, so access to the beach will be controlled through the proposed parking lot.

5 Natadola Beach Break

This inner reef left breaks only when there's a large groundswell around. It's great for beginners at high tide as the trade winds blow offshore here and the wave is only 50 yards (50 m) from the beach. Natadola Beach Break is normally very well protected and has a great fun wave on most days, even if it is small.

WAVE TYPE Left

WAVE HEIGHT 1–3 ft (0.3–0.9 m)

BREAK TYPE Reef

BEST SWELL S–SW

BEST WIND SE, N

BEST TIDE High

BEST TIME Year-round

HAZARDS Shallow reef at low tide

DIRECTIONS The Natadola Beach turnoff is a 30-minute drive from Nadi town heading south on the Queens Highway. A major resort and golf course development opens soon, so access to the beach will be controlled through the proposed parking lot.

6 Fijian Hotel

This right-hander on the main reef in front of the Shangri-La Fijian Resort is short and steep, and can be hollow at times, becoming heavy when the swell picks up. It's at its best in calm conditions, usually in the morning.

WAVE TYPE Right

WAVE HEIGHT 3–10 ft (0.9–3.1 m)

BREAK TYPE Reef

BEST SWELL SW

BEST WIND N

BEST TIDE Mid–high

BEST TIME Year-round

HAZARDS Sea urchins, barracudas

DIRECTIONS From Nadi, follow the Queens Highway south and east in the direction of Suva for about 40 minutes to the Shangri-La Fijian Resort, on Yanuca Island (not to be confused with the Yanuca Island where Frigates Pass is located), which is accessible via a causeway. Paddle to the break from the resort side of Yanuca Beach or go by boat from the resort.

Champion Australian surfer Melanie Redman-Carr gets set for a barrel ride at Cloudbreak.

7 Sigatoka River Mouth

The Sigatoka sand dunes stretch for just over 4 miles (7 km) west from the mouth of the Sigatoka River, with waves breaking along their length. The river mouth is considered more consistent than the dunes as it's better protected from the trade winds and the sandbanks are more stable.

WAVE TYPE Left and right

WAVE HEIGHT 3–15 ft (0.9–4.6 m)

BREAK TYPE Beach, river mouth

BEST SWELL SW

BEST WIND N

BEST TIDE Low

BEST TIME November–February

HAZARDS Sharks, rips

DIRECTIONS From Nadi, follow the Queens Highway south and east toward Sigatoka. About 1 mile (1.6 km) before the town, look for the large Club Masa surf resort sign on the left. Follow the signs to the resort, and from there walk to the river mouth.

8 Naviti Hotel Right

This is a powerful and fast, typically South Sea island reef break, a 15-minute paddle from the resort that gives it its name. It's very rarely surfed. The break is at its best when the wind is light in the morning, and an hour either side of high tide.

WAVE TYPE Right

WAVE HEIGHT 3–10 ft (0.9–3.1 m)

BREAK TYPE Reef

BEST SWELL SE–S

BEST WIND N

BEST TIDE High

BEST TIME June–August

HAZARDS Shallow reef at low tide, sea urchins

DIRECTIONS Follow the Queens Highway south and east from Nadi to the Naviti Resort on the Coral Coast, east of Sigatoka. Park at the resort, walk to the beach, and paddle out to the break.

9 Korolevu

Korolevu is a right-hand shallow reef break that's semiconsistent. It's normally surfed by the local surfers of Korolevu. You can sometimes get local villagers to take you out in a boat; otherwise it's a 15-minute paddle out to the mouth of the bay.

WAVE TYPE Right

WAVE HEIGHT 3–10 ft (0.9–3.1 m)

BREAK TYPE Reef

BEST SWELL S–SW

BEST WIND N

BEST TIDE High

BEST TIME Year-round

HAZARDS Shallow reef at low tide

DIRECTIONS Take the Queens Highway south and east from Nadi to the Korolevu Resort on the Coral Coast, east of Sigatoka. Paddle out to the break from the resort.

10 Frigates Pass

A minimum 40-minute boat trip from the mainland, this wave is exposed and picks up every ounce of energy in the Southern Ocean. When it's lining up properly, Frigates is one of the longest waves in Fiji, breaking for more than 100 yards (100 m). It's a world-class wave that rivals Cloudbreak.

WAVE TYPE Left

WAVE HEIGHT 3–20 ft (0.9–6.1 m)

BREAK TYPE Reef

BEST SWELL SW

BEST WIND SW

BEST TIDE All

BEST TIME Year-round

HAZARDS Reef when shallow, jelly legs after long ride

DIRECTIONS Frigates Pass lies off Viti Levu's south coast, but is much closer to Yanuca Island. It's accessible only by boat, either from Yanuca Island or the mainland at Pacific Harbour, about midway between Sigatoka and Suva.

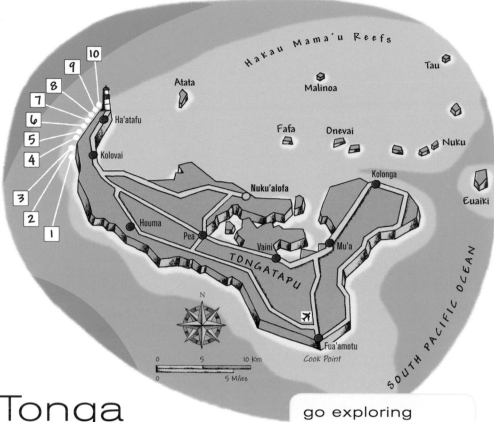

Tonga

The Tongan archipelago's 169 islands lie scattered about 500 miles (804 km) southeast of Fiji. Tongatapu, the largest and most heavily populated of the group, is the focus for most surfers visiting the nation. Practically all of the surf spots on Tongatapu are condensed on a 5-mile (8-km) stretch of coastal reef at the western end of the island. Trade winds blow consistently offshore year-round, ensuring that whenever the island receives swell, the waves are on here.

Tonga picks up less swell than its location in the middle of the Pacific Ocean would suggest. With the breaks all facing northwest, swells originating in the Roaring Forties of the Southern Ocean lose some of their size as they wrap in from the southwest, while east swells are blocked altogether. That said, the south swell season, which runs from April to October, is the most consistent time of year for waves. It's also cooler than other times, with average daily maximum temperatures of 79°F (26°C)

go exploring

A short boat ride to the outer reefs north of Tongatapu opens up a whole new world of possibilities. The Hakau Mama'u Reefs are home to some classic spots, such as ET's, Loonies, Razors, and Sharkie's. These waves work most often in the north swell season, which extends from November to February.

and water temperature at 72°F (22°C) allowing the use of a springsuit.

North swells dominate from November to February. The climate is warmer and wetter at this time, with air temperatures often exceeding 86°F (30°C), and the water comfortable for board shorts at 79°F (26°C).

The international airport is located at Fua'amotu in the southwest of the island, 14 miles (24 km) from the capital, Nuku'alofa. After a transfer to Ha'atafu village on the west coast, all breaks can be reached on foot, or by boat.

1 Pass Lefts

Ideal for beginners, Pass Lefts is a mellow, easy-going wave that wraps steadily around the coral reef into a well-defined channel. In ideal conditions, the wave does get hollow, but it's still one of the least challenging in the region. Best in a swell under 4 ft (1.2 m).

WAVE TYPE Left

WAVE HEIGHT 2–4 ft (0.6–1.2 m)

BREAK TYPE Reef

BEST SWELL S–SW

BEST WIND SE

BEST TIDE Mid–high

BEST TIME May–September

HAZARDS Sharp coral

DIRECTIONS From Ha'atafu village, take one of the many public paths to the beach. Pass Lefts is at the south end, near the Otuhaka Beach Resort.

2 Pass Rights

Pass Rights breaks in two sections: a barreling takeoff that runs for 20 yards (20 m) or so, and a more mellow shoulder that breaks in deeper water and is perfect for putting in a few turns. Both sections are good for beginners when small (under 3 ft/0.9 m). Pass Rights needs a direct north swell or it closes out.

WAVE TYPE Right

WAVE HEIGHT 2–6 ft (0.6–1.8 m)

BREAK TYPE Reef

BEST SWELL N

BEST WIND SE

BEST TIDE Mid–high

BEST TIME November–March

HAZARDS Sharp coral, strong current over a 4-ft (1.2-m) swell

DIRECTIONS Pass Rights is opposite Pass Lefts on the other side of the channel.

3 Leftovers

This left-hander breaks off the same peak as Pass Rights, across the channel from Pass Lefts. It's one of the least crowded waves in the area, largely due to the number of better waves nearby. Leftovers is a fast wave, but it rarely breaks with any quality or power.

WAVE TYPE Left

WAVE HEIGHT 2–6 ft (0.6–1.8 m)

BREAK TYPE Reef

BEST SWELL S–SW

BEST WIND SE

BEST TIDE Mid–high

BEST TIME May–September

HAZARDS Sharp coral

DIRECTIONS Leftovers is opposite Pass Lefts on the other side of the channel.

4 Motels

A fast, long left, Motels is one of the most consistent waves in the region. After a fast, tubing takeoff section, the wave slows just enough to jam in a cutback before setting up for the inside barrel section. The wave has good shape, even in very small conditions.

WAVE TYPE Left

WAVE HEIGHT 1–6 ft (0.3–1.8 m)

BREAK TYPE Reef

BEST SWELL S–SW

BEST WIND SE

BEST TIDE Mid–high

BEST TIME May–September

HAZARDS Sharp coral

DIRECTIONS Motels is a 100-yard (100-m) paddle across the lagoon from Ha'atafu Beach.

5 Kamikazes

As the name suggests, this wave is not for the fainthearted. On its day, Kamikazes can give perfect, peeling lefts with incredible barrels; more often, it's a lethally fast closeout breaking over very shallow coral. It is therefore only for experts, and a wetsuit, boots, and helmet are recommended for protection against the coral.

WAVE TYPE Left

WAVE HEIGHT 2–6 ft (0.6–1.8 m)

BREAK TYPE Reef

BEST SWELL S–SW

BEST WIND SE

BEST TIDE Mid–high

BEST TIME May–September

HAZARDS Very shallow, sharp coral

DIRECTIONS Kamikazes is 150 yards (150 m) north of Motels.

6 The Peak

This right-hander, which breaks off the same peak as Kamikazes, is a great small-wave setup that can close out dangerously above about 4 ft (1.2 m). The wave peels mechanically along the reef for around 50 yards (50 m) before closing out in the channel. Because the wave is very shallow, boots are essential.

WAVE TYPE Right

WAVE HEIGHT 2–4 ft (0.6–1.2 m)

BREAK TYPE Reef

BEST SWELL N

BEST WIND SE

BEST TIDE Mid–high

BEST TIME November–March

HAZARDS Shallow, sharp coral

DIRECTIONS The Peak is 150 yards (150 m) north of Motels.

7 Corners

In a strong south swell, Corners is a thick, intense, barreling left that rifles across the reef into a defined channel. It's fast and shallow, so a wetsuit is recommended for protection from the reef. Corners also works in north swells when it's a more approachable wave for the less experienced surfer.

WAVE TYPE Left

WAVE HEIGHT 2–6 ft (0.6–1.8 m)

BREAK TYPE Reef

BEST SWELL S

BEST WIND SE

BEST TIDE Mid–high

BEST TIME May–September

HAZARDS Very shallow, sharp coral

DIRECTIONS Corners is next to Kamikazes and The Peak.

8 The Bowl

The Bowl is a short, powerful, intense right that gives perfect barrels when conditions come together. It's a fickle spot requiring a strong south swell to break at its best. Deep tubes are possible here, so as with other shallow spots a wetsuit and boots are recommended for protection against the reef.

WAVE TYPE Right

WAVE HEIGHT 3–8 ft (0.9–2.4 m)

BREAK TYPE Reef

BEST SWELL S

BEST WIND SE

BEST TIDE All

BEST TIME May–September

HAZARDS Very shallow, sharp coral

DIRECTIONS The Bowl is a 100-yard (100-m) paddle across the lagoon from Ha'atafu Beach.

9 Fishtraps

A long left, Fishtraps starts working at around 3 ft (0.9 m), and, as the swell size increases, the wave gets progressively better and longer. Rides of up to 200 yards (200 m) are a regular occurrence, and can take in tubes, long walls, racy sections, and slower, whackable shoulders. Gets very shallow at low tide.

WAVE TYPE Left

WAVE HEIGHT 2–6 ft (0.6–1.8 m)

BREAK TYPE Reef

BEST SWELL S–SW

BEST WIND SE

BEST TIDE Mid–high

BEST TIME May–September

HAZARDS Very shallow, sharp coral

DIRECTIONS Fishtraps is 500 yards (500 m) north of The Bowl.

10 Lighthouse

Two right-hand waves, Outside Lighthouse and Inside Lighthouse, break on the same reef divided by a long closeout section. Outside Lighthouse is a fast, barreling right working on all tides, and is often best – and most dangerous – on low tide. Inside Lighthouse is an intense barreling wave with a heavy takeoff.

WAVE TYPE Right

WAVE HEIGHT 2–8 ft (0.6–2.4 m)

BREAK TYPE Reef

BEST SWELL S

BEST WIND SE

BEST TIDE All

BEST TIME May–September

HAZARDS Shallow, sharp coral

DIRECTIONS Lighthouse is next to the lighthouse at the far northwest tip of the island.

A surfer settles down for a fast ride at Pass Rights. Note the shallowness of the water.

Samoa

Samoa is located to the northeast of Fiji, about 1,800 miles (2,900 km) from Auckland and 5,200 miles (8,400 km) from Los Angeles. It's made up of two major volcanic islands, Upolu and Savaii, and a further eight small islets.

Upolu is the location of the nation's capital and largest city, Apia, which has Samoa's only international airport. Upolu is the more developed of the two islands: about 75 percent of the country's population live here and the transport infrastructure is better than that of Savaii. Savaii is a quieter, more laid-back, and less touristy place. What both islands have in common is some incredible surf spots. Most of the waves break over coral or lava reefs relatively close to the shore, but some spots are only accessible by boat.

Samoa experiences two distinct surf seasons. From late March to November, the south coasts of Upolu and Savaii are pounded by consistent swells generated in the Southern Ocean, which can last up to a week as the lows track across the Tasman Sea beneath New Zealand. Then from December to March, north swells from the North Pacific can be ridden on the north coasts of both islands. These swells generally reach Samoa around five days after hitting the Hawaiian Islands.

The climate is tropical, with average daily maximum temperatures of 84°F (29°C) year-round, while water temperature rarely fluctuates from a boardshort-friendly 82°F (28°C). The reefs are generally shallow and the coral often sharp, and the sun can be fiercely hot, so adequate protection from both is recommended.

no surfing on Sunday

With 98 percent of the Samoan people identifying themselves as Christians, Sunday is universally held as a day of rest – no work or play is allowed, and that includes surfing. Attendance at church services is very high. Usually, the only people who don't go to church on Sunday are those preparing the family meal, called a *toanai*.

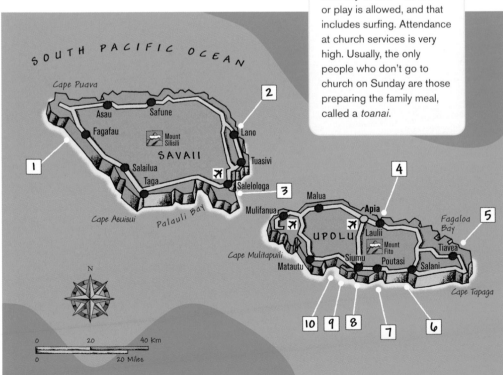

1 The Leap, Savaii

This is a big, round, dangerous beast of a wave that picks up just about any south swell, and dishes it out with ferocity. It is one of the squarest, most intense waves on Savaii: after a heavy takeoff the wave barrels off the peak followed by a short, whackable section.

WAVE TYPE Left

WAVE HEIGHT 3–10 ft (0.9–3.1 m)

BREAK TYPE Reef

BEST SWELL S–SW

BEST WIND NE

BEST TIDE Mid–high

BEST TIME May–September

HAZARDS Shallow, very heavy

DIRECTIONS Drive northwest for 3 miles (5 km) from Fagafau along the coast road. The Leap is close to the Lovers Leap lookout point. From there, it's a short paddle out.

2 Malama Lefts, Savaii

On a north swell, waves wrap around this left-hand point to give long, workable walls peeling close to the shore. Malama doesn't throw up any nasty surprises, and gets hollower and faster in bigger swells. There's a fairly easy paddle out from the top of the point.

WAVE TYPE Left

WAVE HEIGHT 2–10 ft (0.6–3.1 m)

BREAK TYPE Point

BEST SWELL N

BEST WIND SW

BEST TIDE Mid–high

BEST TIME November–January

HAZARDS Strong currents when big

DIRECTIONS From Lano, drive north for 6 miles (10 km) on the coast road to Malama village.

3 The Wharf, Savaii

It takes a moderately big swell to get The Wharf firing, but it can be a very worthwhile option when the rest of the south coast is maxed out. Usually the wave offers clean, fun rights breaking over coral, and it has a degree of protection from the southeast trade winds.

WAVE TYPE Right

WAVE HEIGHT 2–8 ft (0.6–2.4 m)

BREAK TYPE Reef

BEST SWELL S

BEST WIND W–NW

BEST TIDE Mid–high

BEST TIME May–September

HAZARDS Sharp coral

DIRECTIONS From Salelologa, drive south for 1¼ miles (2 km) toward the harbor. The Wharf is at the southern end of the bay.

4 Laulii, Upolu

One of the best waves on the north coast of Upolu, Laulii is a right-hand point that breaks close to the shore and as a result is sheltered from most winds. A fun point when small, it will barrel when it gets bigger. It needs a big swell to fire up.

WAVE TYPE Right

WAVE HEIGHT 3–10 ft (0.9–3.1 m)

BREAK TYPE Point

BEST SWELL N

BEST WIND S–SW

BEST TIDE Low–mid

BEST TIME November–January

HAZARDS Powerful in bigger swells

DIRECTIONS Drive east from Apia for 5 miles (8 km) on the coast road to the village of Laulii.

5 Tiavea Bay, Upolu

There's plenty of choice in this expansive bay, with multiple lefts and rights on offer. Highlights include a right-hand peak that dishes out heavy tubes and can hold huge swells; a more mellow option can be found at the river mouth, where fun lefts and rights break off a central peak.

WAVE TYPE Left and right

WAVE HEIGHT 3–15+ ft (0.9–4.6+ m)

BREAK TYPE Reef

BEST SWELL N

BEST WIND SW

BEST TIDE All

BEST TIME November–January

HAZARDS Powerful in bigger swells

DIRECTIONS From Apia, drive east for about 25 miles (40 km) on the coast road to the village of Tiavea.

6 Salani, Upolu

Two waves break either side of a reef pass created by the Salani River. The right is a short but very powerful wave that throws out gaping tubes. The other one, a left-hander, is longer with some open-face sections, but it needs a large swell and light winds to be good.

WAVE TYPE Left and right

WAVE HEIGHT 2–8 ft (0.6–2.4 m)

BREAK TYPE Reef

BEST SWELL SE–SW

BEST WIND N

BEST TIDE Mid–high

BEST TIME May–September

HAZARDS Shallow reef

DIRECTIONS From Apia, drive south to the coast at the village of Salani. The reef is directly in front of the Salani Surf Resort, from where it's a ten-minute paddle or short boat ride.

7 Nuusafee Island (Devil's Island), Upolu

A world-class left on an outer reef, Nuusafee Island (Devil's Island) is one of the best waves on Upolu. When the swell is over 8 ft (2.4 m), the three separate sections link up to create a wave that delivers incredibly long barrels. This is a very consistent break that is offshore in the southeast trade winds.

WAVE TYPE Left

WAVE HEIGHT 6–15 ft (1.8–4.6 m)

BREAK TYPE Reef

BEST SWELL SE–SW

BEST WIND SE

BEST TIDE Mid–high

BEST TIME May–September

HAZARDS Very powerful, remote location

DIRECTIONS The island lies about 1 mile (1.6 km) off the south coast of Upolu, and is accessible only by boat — usually from Poutasi.

8 Boulders, Upolu

This is a classic left-hand point break that requires a decent amount of swell to start working, but then it comfortably holds up to 15 ft (4.6 m) or even more. It is a very powerful, hollow wave giving long rides. The sheltered location affords protection from the southeast trade winds.

WAVE TYPE Left

WAVE HEIGHT 6–15 ft (1.8–4.6 m)

BREAK TYPE Point

BEST SWELL SE–SW

BEST WIND N–NE

BEST TIDE Low

BEST TIME May–September

HAZARDS Very powerful, remote location

DIRECTIONS From Apia, drive south to the coast at Siumu village. Guests of nearby resorts or surf camps can get to Boulders by boat. Otherwise, you'll need a four-wheel-drive vehicle for land access on a poorly signed, unsealed road that runs south from Siumu village.

The view from the tube at Salani, which is home to two impressive waves, a left and a right.

9 Siumu, Upolu

Siumu has two waves. Both are lefts, but that's where the similarities end. Inside Siumu is a short, fun wave with whackable walls. Outside Siumu is much longer and hollower, and the wave bowls as it wraps around the reef. Both waves can be classic given the right swell direction.

WAVE TYPE Left

WAVE HEIGHT 2–8 ft (0.6–2.4 m)

BREAK TYPE Reef

BEST SWELL SE–SW

BEST WIND NE

BEST TIDE Mid–high

BEST TIME May–September

HAZARDS Shallow, powerful

DIRECTIONS From Apia, drive south to the coast at Siumu village. The reef is a ten-minute paddle out or a short boat ride.

10 Coconuts, Upolu

One of the few right-handers on the island of Upolu, Coconuts is a truly world-class setup. The wave is fast, seriously hollow, and breaks with almost mechanical precision. The peak throws out a thick lip on takeoff and horseshoes around the reef. Tubes are guaranteed. It can cope with a swell of up to 10 ft (3.1 m).

WAVE TYPE Right

WAVE HEIGHT 3–10 ft (0.9–3.1 m)

BREAK TYPE Reef

BEST SWELL SE–SW

BEST WIND N

BEST TIDE Mid–high

BEST TIME May–September

HAZARDS Shallow, very powerful

DIRECTIONS From Apia, drive south to the coast at Coconuts Resort, near Siumu village. The reef is a 20-minute paddle from the resort, or a short boat ride.

1 Hauru Point (Club Med), Moorea

This excellent right-hand reef pass can produce very decent waves on a north swell. The offshore reef is a long paddle, but outrigger canoes can be hired from the beach to take you out to the wave. The wave is sometimes known as Club Med, after a now defunct resort here.

WAVE TYPE Right

WAVE HEIGHT 3–10 ft (0.9–3.1 m)

BREAK TYPE Reef

BEST SWELL NW

BEST WIND S

BEST TIDE Mid–high

BEST TIME November–February

HAZARDS Sharp coral

DIRECTIONS Hauru Point is a short distance west of Papetoai. The reef pass is a 45-minute paddle out, so most people take a boat from the resort area.

2 Temae, Moorea

Temae offers a top-quality wave highly prized by the local surfers. There are excellent rights, but there needs to be a big southeast-to-south swell – as a rule, if Taapuna on Tahiiti is closing out, it will be working here. On its day, this long, sweeping wave is one of Polynesia's best.

WAVE TYPE Right

WAVE HEIGHT 3–8 ft (0.9–2.4 m)

BREAK TYPE Reef

BEST SWELL SE–S

BEST WIND W

BEST TIDE Mid–high

BEST TIME April–October

HAZARDS Shallow, sharp coral, aggressive locals

DIRECTIONS The reef is within walking distance of Moorea's airport.

French Polynesia

The 118 islands that make up French Polynesia are spread over 950,000 sq miles (2,470,000 sq km) of ocean. They offer vast potential for waves; much of the area is uncharted surfing territory.

For those who really want to get away from the crowds, a boat charter can open up an array of quality breaks in the outer islands that are seldom — if ever — surfed. The surf in these places is often extremely powerful and this, together with the remote nature of these waves, makes injuries a serious concern. Most surfers, however, find the Society Islands of Tahiti and Moorea offer more than enough in the way of world-class surf.

Surf in Tahiti has become synonymous with one break in particular, the fearsome left at Teahupoo (pronounced *cho-pu*). The monster swells at "Chopes," as it's known, familiar to avid surf magazine readers and suited to only the most expert surfers, do occur several times a year. But for the most part, surfing in Tahiti and Moorea is also possible for mere mortals.

March to October is the most consistent time for waves, with regular swells generated from low-pressure systems in the Southern Ocean. The south-facing breaks receive swell in the 4–15 ft (1.2–4.6 m) range, and water temperature is close to the average of 79°F (26°C) throughout the year. During the wet season (November to February), long-distance north swells are common but are typically smaller and less intense.

At 28 miles (45 km) long at the widest point, Tahiti is easy to navigate by rental car. International flights arrive at the capital, Papeete, where the most affordable lodgings can be found. Papeete is also the departure point for the passenger ferry to Moorea, 10½ miles (17 km) away.

3 Haapiti, Moorea

The reef pass at Haapiti is home to a quality left-hander which is well positioned to pick up south swells. Under 10 ft (3.1 m), it is a good, fun wave, not too shallow or heavy; in big swells it is spectacular. There are very strong currents running out to sea through the pass.

WAVE TYPE Left

WAVE HEIGHT 3–15+ ft (0.9–4.6+ m)

BREAK TYPE Reef

BEST SWELL SW

BEST WIND NE

BEST TIDE All

BEST TIME April–October

HAZARDS Strong currents, sharp coral

DIRECTIONS From Afareaitu, drive south and west on the coast road for 7½ miles (12 km) to Haapiti village. The reef pass is a long paddle out from Haapiti village, and the paddle back is even longer.

4 Taapuna, Tahiti

Taapuna is a world-class left that's fast, hollow, and technically challenging. Timing on the takeoff has to be just right to give enough time to set up for the barrel section. Make that and you'll be rewarded with a workable wall and perhaps another tube in the end section.

WAVE TYPE Left

WAVE HEIGHT 3–8 ft (0.9–2.4 m)

BREAK TYPE Reef

BEST SWELL SW

BEST WIND NE

BEST TIDE Mid–high

BEST TIME April–October

HAZARDS Shallow, sharp coral, occasionally crowded

DIRECTIONS Follow the coast road south from Papeete to Taapuna. It's a 15-minute paddle out from the boat ramp.

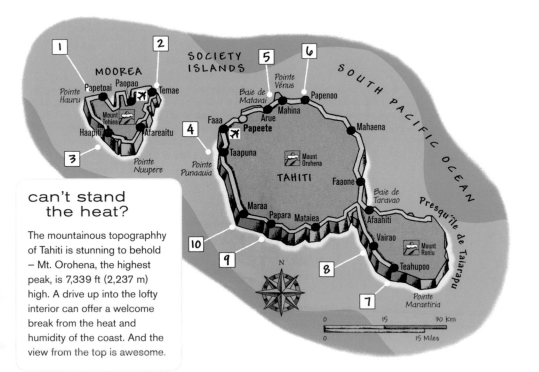

can't stand the heat?

The mountainous topograpghy of Tahiti is stunning to behold – Mt. Orohena, the highest peak, is 7,339 ft (2,237 m) high. A drive up into the lofty interior can offer a welcome break from the heat and humidity of the coast. And the view from the top is awesome.

5 Pointe Vénus, Tahiti

An extremely hollow right-hander breaks off the western end of the barrier reef at Pointe Vénus. This is a very intense wave with a heaving takeoff and bowling tube section right off the peak. It's very shallow, so protection from the coral is a good idea.

WAVE TYPE Right

WAVE HEIGHT 3–10 ft (0.9–3.1 m)

BREAK TYPE Reef

BEST SWELL NE

BEST WIND S

BEST TIDE Mid–high

BEST TIME November–February

HAZARDS Shallow, sharp coral

DIRECTIONS From Papeete, drive east on the coast road to Mahina and turn right to Pointe Vénus Beach. It's a ten-minute paddle to the western end of the reef.

6 Papenoo, Tahiti

Papenoo is home to two waves: a beach break and an excellent river-mouth sandbar, both of which work in any north swell. Papenoo Beach's long, fun waves are very popular with beginners. The river mouth is often good, gets very hollow in offshores, and can hold big swell.

WAVE TYPE Left and right

WAVE HEIGHT 3–10 ft (0.9–3.1 m)

BREAK TYPE Beach

BEST SWELL N

BEST WIND S

BEST TIDE Low

BEST TIME November–February

HAZARDS After heavy rain, the river mouth can be both sharky and polluted

DIRECTIONS From Papeete, drive east on the coast road to Papenoo. Turn left after the bridge and continue for about 400 yards (400 m) to the parking lot.

With its huge waves, Teahupoo blew minds when the first WQS contest was held there in 1998.

7 Teahupoo, Tahiti

This world-famous left is an incredibly thick-lipped beast of a wave. It dredges water off the reef before throwing out the widest barrel in surfing. The annual WCT in May always seems to have epic swell.

WAVE TYPE Left

WAVE HEIGHT 4–20+ ft (1.2–6.1+ m)

BREAK TYPE Reef

BEST SWELL S–SW

BEST WIND N

BEST TIDE Mid

BEST TIME April–October

HAZARDS Extremely powerful, very shallow

DIRECTIONS Teahupoo village is located at the end of the coast road on the south of Presqu'île de Taiarapu.

8 Vairao, Tahiti

Another of Tahiti's world-class waves, Vairao is a left-hand reef break that holds just about any amount of swell the southern Pacific can throw at it. The wave is characterized by long, perfect walls punctuated by hollow sections. Only for the most competent surfers.

WAVE TYPE Left

WAVE HEIGHT 4–20 ft (1.2–6.1 m)

BREAK TYPE Reef

BEST SWELL S

BEST WIND NE

BEST TIDE Mid–high

BEST TIME April–October

HAZARDS Shallow, heavy wave

DIRECTIONS Vairao is halfway to Teahupoo on the coast road on the south of Presqu'île de Taiarapu.

9 Papara, Tahiti

This is a cracking beach break that can provide a welcome change from the fierce and uncompromising reefs. It offers varied conditions; it's generally an ideal spot for beginners, but can occasionally produce barreling peaks for more experienced surfers. Popular with local surfers and travelers alike.

WAVE TYPE Left and right

WAVE HEIGHT 2–6 ft (0.6–1.8 m)

BREAK TYPE Beach

BEST SWELL S–SW

BEST WIND N

BEST TIDE All

BEST TIME April–October

HAZARDS Occasional crowds

DIRECTIONS From Papeete, drive south on the coast road to Papara. You can't miss the beach.

10 Maraa, Tahiti

This left-hand reef break can be excellent: thick, fast, and very hollow. Breaking over shallow coral, Maraa is actually easier to surf than first impressions suggest, and deeper takeoffs are rewarded with more speed for the inside bowl section. The long paddle out is worth it as Maraa is usually uncrowded.

WAVE TYPE Left

WAVE HEIGHT 3–10 ft (0.9–3.1 m)

BREAK TYPE Reef

BEST SWELL SW

BEST WIND NE

BEST TIDE Mid–high

BEST TIME April–October

HAZARDS Shallow, sharp coral

DIRECTIONS From Papeete, drive south on the coast road to Maraa.

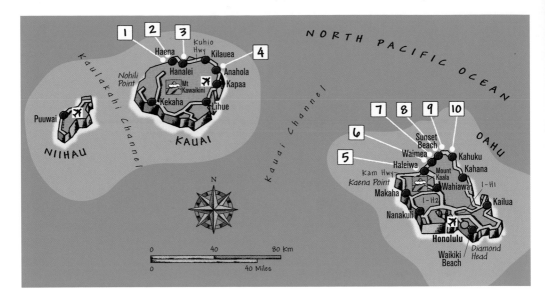

Western Hawaii, USA

Hawaii, and in particular the North Shore of Oahu, is dripping in surfing history and culture. For generations, the North Shore has been the proving ground for new surfboard designs and a place where reputations have been made and legends created. The 7-mile (11-km) stretch of coastline is home to a trio of world-famous breaks: Pipeline, where the ASP's World Championship Tour reaches its finale; Waimea Bay, the venue for the original big-wave contest held in memory of lifeguard and waterman Eddie Aikau; and Sunset, where some of pro surfing's greatest battles have been fought.

The "season" runs from October to March, when the north-facing coasts of Oahu, Kauai, and Niihau feel the full impact of winter storms in the North Pacific. Swells can hit rapidly, turning a relatively calm ocean into a seething mass within hours, and creating some of the biggest and best surf on the planet. The surf is very powerful, and the sheer number of professional surfers in the water can make Oahu a difficult place for the average surfer to get a wave.

Kauai is, by contrast, much quieter. The surf is every bit as powerful and critical as on Oahu, but the level of competition for the waves is a notch or two lower.

surfing's greatest ambassador

Known as the Father of Surfing, Duke Kahanamoku (1890–1968) fell in love with the ocean as a Waikiki beach boy. An Olympic swimming gold medalist, Duke traveled the world giving swimming exhibitions and surfing demonstrations, introducing the sport to both mainland USA and Australia in 1914. Kahanamoku also performed in Hollywood movies. He is remembered by a statue at Waikiki Beach in Honolulu.

Water temperature bottoms out at 75°F (24°C) in February, reaching a high of 81°F (27°C) in October, with daily maximum air temperatures typically around 5°F (2°C) higher.

International flights arrive at Honolulu, and domestic flights run to Kauai and Niihau. Car rental and accommodation are expensive, but the buses are cheap and frequent.

1 Cannons, Kauai

This jacking, tubing left breaks over an offshore lava ledge. Some say Cannons is named for the thundering noise of the lip detonating; others put it down to the explosive burst of spray that accompanies the lucky surfers who exit one of these seriously heavy tubes. Both explanations are valid.

WAVE TYPE Left

WAVE HEIGHT 4–15 ft (1.2–4.6 m)

BREAK TYPE Reef

BEST SWELL W–NW

BEST WIND SE

BEST TIDE All

BEST TIME November–February

HAZARDS Currents, sharks, long paddle

DIRECTIONS From Hanalei, drive west on the Kuhio Hwy to Haena Beach Park. The wave is 400 yards (400 m) offshore.

2 Tunnels, Kauai

An offshore reef that can handle plenty of swell, Tunnels is well known for its gaping, wide barrels. Historically, this spot has been the focus for big-wave surfing on Kauai, and the outside reef, Dumptrucks, has become very popular with tow-in surfers in recent years.

WAVE TYPE Right

WAVE HEIGHT 4–20 ft (1.2–6.1 m)

BREAK TYPE Reef

BEST SWELL W–NW

BEST WIND SE

BEST TIDE All

BEST TIME November–February

HAZARDS Currents, sharks

DIRECTIONS From Hanalei, drive west on the Kuhio Hwy to Haena Beach Park. Tunnels is next to Cannons.

3 Hanalei, Kauai

The expansive Hanalei Bay is home to no less than seven breaks. Hanalei, a right point, breaks in swells up to 20 ft (6.1 m). The 200-yard (200-m) wave starts offshore at The Point and connects through to the busy bowl section. Also in the bay are Hideaway's, Waikoko's, Middles, and Pinetrees.

WAVE TYPE Right

WAVE HEIGHT 4–20 ft (1.2–6.1 m)

BREAK TYPE Point

BEST SWELL N

BEST WIND SE

BEST TIDE Mid

BEST TIME November–February

HAZARDS Rocks, crowds

DIRECTIONS Hanalei, on Hanalei Bay, is a short drive west of Kilauea by the coast road. Hanalei Point is at the northeastern end of the bay.

4 Anahola, Kauai

This right-hand point breaks over a shallow rock bottom at Kahala Point. It is a relatively easy, fun wave, which can cope with plenty of size, and also works in a range of swell directions. There are several beach breaks nearby within Kahala Beach Park that are ideal for novice surfers.

WAVE TYPE Right

WAVE HEIGHT 4–15 ft (1.2–4.6 m)

BREAK TYPE Point

BEST SWELL NW–NE

BEST WIND S

BEST TIDE Mid–high

BEST TIME November–February

HAZARDS Shallow reef on the point

DIRECTIONS From Anahola town (north of Kapaa), take the road a short distance east to Kahala Point at the southern end of Anahola Bay.

5 Haleiwa, Oahu

This incredibly fast, hollow, heavy wave gets seriously busy. Haleiwa is a real performance wave, with long workable walls and heaving barrel sections, ending in a shallow Toilet Bowl section. A WQS/Triple Crown contest is held here in November. Avalanche, an outside reef, breaks in huge swells.

WAVE TYPE Right

WAVE HEIGHT 6–20+ ft (1.8–6.1+ m)

BREAK TYPE Reef

BEST SWELL W

BEST WIND E

BEST TIDE All

BEST TIME November–February

HAZARDS Crowds, currents

DIRECTIONS Haleiwa is about 30 miles (48 km) northwest of Honolulu via I-H1, I-H2, and Hwy 803. Park near Haleiwa Harbor. The main peak is 300 yards (300 m) offshore from Alii Beach Park.

6 Waimea Bay, Oahu

The spiritual home of big-wave surfing, Waimea is only for the very experienced. A fearsome drop is followed by a huge wall section and a race to avoid being swallowed by the mass of white water. This is the venue for the big-wave contest held in memory of Eddie Aikau.

WAVE TYPE Right

WAVE HEIGHT 6–30+ ft (1.8–9.1+ m)

BREAK TYPE Reef

BEST SWELL NW–N

BEST WIND E

BEST TIDE All

BEST TIME November–February

HAZARDS Crowds, drop-ins, difficult entry and exit

DIRECTIONS Drive north from Haleiwa on the Kam Hwy, and park just before the bridge at Waimea Bay.

7 Pipeline/Backdoor, Oahu

This is the most famous wave in the world, legendary for the biggest, squarest tubes in the islands. First Reef Pipe starts working at around 4 ft (1.2 m), Second Reef at 10 ft (3.1 m); both give very heavy tubes right off the peak. Backdoor, the right off the same peak, is even heavier. Critical takeoff, insane crowds.

WAVE TYPE Left and right

WAVE HEIGHT 4–25 ft (1.2–7.6 m)

BREAK TYPE Reef

BEST SWELL W–NW

BEST WIND E

BEST TIDE Mid

BEST TIME November–February

HAZARDS Extremely powerful, heavily crowded

DIRECTIONS From Waimea, drive north for about 2 miles (3.2 km) to the southern end of Ehukai Beach Park.

8 Rocky Point, Oahu

Rocky Point is best known for its quality right-hander, which in north swells gives long rides and long tubes. West swells set off the left, which breaks at lightning speed and can get very hollow. This spot is a real swell magnet and so attracts crowds.

WAVE TYPE Left and right

WAVE HEIGHT 3–8 ft (0.9–2.4 m)

BREAK TYPE Reef

BEST SWELL NW

BEST WIND E

BEST TIDE All

BEST TIME November–February

HAZARDS Crowds, rocks

DIRECTIONS Follow the Kam Hwy north from Pipeline for ⅔ mile (1 km).

9 Sunset Beach, Oahu

The multiple reefs here work in a range of swell sizes and directions. On a big west swell, Sunset is a heavy, pitching peak that gets very hollow on the inside. Sunset Point works in smaller conditions, while Outside Sunset is a tow-in spot breaking in massive swells.

WAVE TYPE Right

WAVE HEIGHT 4–15+ ft (1.2–4.6+ m)

BREAK TYPE Reef

BEST SWELL W

BEST WIND E

BEST TIDE Mid

BEST TIME November–February

HAZARDS Powerful currents, crowds

DIRECTIONS From Waimea, drive north for 4 miles (6.4 km) and park just after Kammieland.

10 Turtle Bay, Oahu

Oahu is not the best place to learn to surf, but Turtle Bay is just about the safest place for beginners on the North Shore. On smaller days, lefts and rights break over a sand-and-reef bottom with relatively few hazards. Crowds are manageable and generally more relaxed.

WAVE TYPE Left and right

WAVE HEIGHT 3–6 ft (0.9–1.8 m)

BREAK TYPE Reef

BEST SWELL NW–N

BEST WIND SE

BEST TIDE Mid

BEST TIME November–February

HAZARDS Rocks

DIRECTIONS From Waimea, drive north on the Kam Hwy for about 6 miles (10 km). Park near Turtle Bay golf course. A footpath through the golf course gives access to the beach.

A crew of adrenaline junkies hurl themselves down a wall of water at Waimea Bay.

Eastern Hawaii, USA

Hawaii's three largest eastern islands, Hawaii (aka the Big Island), Maui, and Molokai, all pick up plenty of north and south swell, but their proximity to each other does mean swell from certain directions is blocked.

The small islands of Lanai and Kahoolawe, lying directly to the south of Molokai and Maui, are protected from the north swells of the prime surf season, which runs from October to March. In turn, they reduce the size of south swells, which are most common from May to August, reaching the south coasts of Maui and Molokai. Similarly, the northwest-facing coast of Maui is blocked by Molokai, and Hawaii by Maui, making swells originating from the north or northeast the biggest on the north-facing coasts.

Maui can be great at any time of year, but the biggest waves are found on the north coast from October to March. The best time of year for surfing on the Big Island is between May and August, when southerly swells light up the island's west and southwest coasts.

Molokai is a world away from the hectic bustle of Maui and the Big Island (or, for that matter, Oahu, in the western islands). It's often compared to the Oahu of 50 years ago. Here, the pace of life is slow, tourism is far less developed than elsewhere, and uncrowded surf can be found.

From May to August, water temperatures average 79°F (26°C), with typical daily maximum air temperatures of 84°F (29°C). October to March is slightly cooler in the water at 75°F (24°C) and air temperatures peak around 81°F (27°C). Northeast trade winds blow all year, but are strongest between May and August, although Kona winds from the south or southwest can occur at any time, and often bring stormy and humid conditions.

International flights arrive at Honolulu on Oahu, and internal flights to Kahului on Maui, Hilo on Hawaii, and Molokai are frequent and reasonably priced. Rental cars are the best way to get around.

the jet-ski revolution

Maui, being more exposed to the trade winds than other Hawaiian islands, has traditionally been better known for windsurfing than surfing, but the advent of jet-skis and tow-in surfing has given the island fresh notoriety. Truly massive waves have been ridden at Peahi, known as Jaws, by a pioneering crew of Hawaiian and international big-wave specialists.

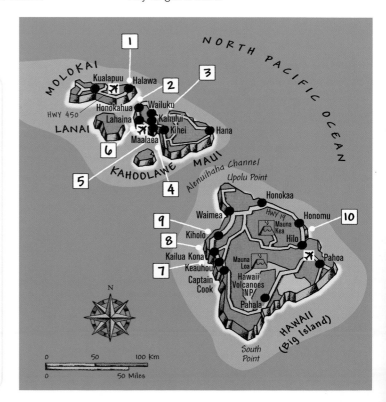

1 Halawa Bay, Molokai

A rocky boulder point divides two beaches within Halawa Bay: protected Kamaalaea Beach to the west and more exposed Kawilli Beach to the east. A right-hander breaks off the point in a big north swell, and can be extremely good. This is a beautiful and remote spot that rarely gets crowded.

WAVE TYPE Right

WAVE HEIGHT 3–10 ft (0.9–3.1 m)

BREAK TYPE Reef

BEST SWELL NE

BEST WIND SW

BEST TIDE Mid

BEST TIME November–February

HAZARDS Rocks, isolated location

DIRECTIONS Take Hwy 450 to the end of the road at Halawa. Cross the bridge and follow the rough road to the gravel parking area. The two beaches are about 100 yards (100 m) ahead.

2 Honolua Bay, Maui

A series of right-hand reefs is laid out around the point at the eastern end of Honolua Bay. Right outside, Subs often links up with Coconuts farther in. The Cave and then Keiki Bowl on the inside also connect together. All the sections are fast, hollow, and powerful; a truly world-class wave.

WAVE TYPE Right

WAVE HEIGHT 3–18 ft (0.9–5.5 m)

BREAK TYPE Reef and point

BEST SWELL W–N

BEST WIND NE

BEST TIDE All

BEST TIME November–February

HAZARDS Strong currents, rocks, crowds

DIRECTIONS From Lahaina, drive north on the coast road through Honokahua and Honolua village to the parking lot on the top of the cliffs, then use the footpaths.

3 Jaws/Peahi, Maui

The scene of some of the biggest waves ridden anywhere in the world, this offshore reef has become synonymous with tow-in surfing (Jaws was the venue for the first ever tow-in surfing competition). House-sized lumps of water hit the deep outer reef, breaking left and right.

WAVE TYPE Left and right

WAVE HEIGHT Up to 60+ ft (18+ m)

BREAK TYPE Reef

BEST SWELL NW

BEST WIND SE

BEST TIDE All

BEST TIME November–February

HAZARDS Can get dangerously busy

DIRECTIONS From Kahului, drive east on the coast road to Hookipa, then turn left to Maliko Gulch. Jet-skis are launched from here.

4 Kalama Park, Maui

The Point, a left-hand reef break at the southern end of Kalama Beach Park, is a fairly long, barreling wave, and is often smaller than many other spots on Maui. Farther up the beach there are lefts and rights breaking over a rock-and-sand bottom; these are popular with beginners.

WAVE TYPE Left and right

WAVE HEIGHT 3–8 ft (0.9–2.4 m)

BREAK TYPE Reef

BEST SWELL S–W

BEST WIND NE

BEST TIDE Mid

BEST TIME May–August

HAZARDS Rocks, crowds

DIRECTIONS Drive south on the coast road from Lahaina and then to Kihei to Kalama Beach Park; The Point is at the beach's southern end.

5 Maalaea, Maui

A world-class right, Maalaea is one of the fastest waves in the world. Breaking off a man-made harbor breakwater, this spot needs a big southwest swell to work; then it gives extremely long, barely makable tube rides, and always attracts a large crowd.

WAVE TYPE Right

WAVE HEIGHT 4–10 ft (1.2–3.1 m)

BREAK TYPE Reef

BEST SWELL SW

BEST WIND NW

BEST TIDE Mid

BEST TIME May–August

HAZARDS Crowds, shallow bottom

DIRECTIONS From Lahaina, take Hwy 30 and drive south to Maalaea breakwater. The wave breaks off the southwest end of the eastern arm of the breakwater.

6 Lahaina, Maui

There are two breaks here. One of Maui's best waves, Lahaina Breakwater is an excellent barreling left that gets very hollow and is suitable only for very experienced surfers. Lahaina Harbor, breaking just north of the harbor, is a better option for intermediate surfers, with a left and right A-frame peak breaking over reef.

WAVE TYPE Left and right

WAVE HEIGHT 3–10 ft (0.9–3.1 m)

BREAK TYPE Reef

BEST SWELL S

BEST WIND NE

BEST TIDE Mid

BEST TIME May–August

HAZARDS Crowds, shallow bottom

DIRECTIONS From Kahului, take Hwy 380 south for a few miles and turn onto Hwy 30, heading south. Follow the highway along the coast to Lahaina. Lahaina Breakwater is right in front of Lahaina Harbor.

7 Lymans/Banyans, Hawaii

Lymans, a great left-hand point, is a popular spot with locals, who love its long walls and sucking tube sections. Banyans, just ⅔ mile (1 km) to the north, is a reef breaking both ways with the lefts better in south swells. A square-barreling wave, Banyans is a heavy spot and comes with locals to match.

WAVE TYPE Left and right

WAVE HEIGHT 3–10 ft (0.9–3.1 m)

BREAK TYPE Reef

BEST SWELL SW

BEST WIND NE

BEST TIDE Mid

BEST TIME May–August

HAZARDS Rocks, crowds

DIRECTIONS Banyans is near the Bali Kai Hotel on Alii Drive, between Kailua Kona and Keauhou; Lymans is ⅔ mile (1 km) south of Banyans, off Kamoa Point.

8 Pinetrees, Hawaii

Best known for the long lefts that break on the reef in front of Kaloko Point, Pinetrees also has a decent right on occasions. This is one of the most consistent spots on the Big Island. Honokohau, just south of Pinetrees, is another good location, with lefts and rights breaking over sandy reef.

WAVE TYPE Left and occasional right

WAVE HEIGHT 3–10 ft (0.9–3.1 m)

BREAK TYPE Reef

BEST SWELL SW–W

BEST WIND NE

BEST TIDE High or Mid

BEST TIME May–August

HAZARDS Rocks, crowds

DIRECTIONS Head north from Kailua Kona on Hwy 19. Pinetrees breaks in front of Kaloko Point, just off the highway.

Only expert tow-in surfers should attempt Jaws' incredible waves, which can be over 60 ft (18 m) high.

9 Kiholo Bay, Hawaii

Lefts and rights break in the middle of this stunning 2-mile (3.2-km) black-sand bay. On offer are good fun waves with no major hazards (except the occasional turtle), and it's generally uncrowded. There's also a right-hand point at the eastern end of the bay that's sometimes good.

WAVE TYPE Left and right

WAVE HEIGHT 3–10 ft (0.9–3.1 m)

BREAK TYPE Reef

BEST SWELL W–N

BEST WIND E

BEST TIDE All

BEST TIME November–February

HAZARDS Heavy at low tide in big swells

DIRECTIONS Drive north from Kailua Kona on Hwy 19 and take the turning for Kiholo. Footpath access.

10 Honolii, Hawaii

A beach break with left and right peaks, Honolii is a pretty consistent spot and that, combined with its proximity to Hilo, means it's often crowded. The river mouth at the northern end of the beach is home to a good, long left breaking over lava pebbles and sand.

WAVE TYPE Left and right

WAVE HEIGHT 3–8 ft (0.9–2.4 m)

BREAK TYPE Beach

BEST SWELL N–NE

BEST WIND SW

BEST TIDE Mid

BEST TIME November–February

HAZARDS Rocks, crowds

DIRECTIONS Drive north from Hilo on Hwy 19 and turn right before the bridge to Honolii Cove.

Australia

Introduction

Bordering three oceans and four seas, the coastline of Australia (Tasmania included) stretches for 22,293 miles (35,877 km), with its islands offering an additional 14,825 miles (23,859 km) of shore. The mainland coastline is basically one long beach, broken up by dramatic cliffs, headlands, inlets, rivers, and waterways. Its climatic and geographical diversity combine to churn out waves suitable for surfers of all levels of expertise.

Most surfing takes place in the south. Along these shores, reefs, beach breaks, and peeling point breaks abound, and are the source of

Australia's well-deserved reputation for its great diversity of magnificent waves.

Distances here are vast. The trip from Sydney to Perth, for example, at 2,554 miles (4,110 km), is longer than the 2,462 miles (3,962 km) between New York and Los Angeles. The population of this, the sixth biggest country by area, is, however, relatively small, at about 21 million. The vast majority of people live within 50 miles (80 km) of the coast, mainly on the eastern seaboard, and this results in some very busy beaches — two-time world surfing champion Tom Carroll reckons The

Australia's prime surfing spots are in the south, running from North West Cape around Cape Leeuwin, across South Australia and Victoria, and north to Bundaberg in Queensland.

Southern Ocean swells

The Roaring Forties winds that provide Australia's big waves are the same weather systems that run west from South Africa to Australia. These systems also send long fetch swells into Indonesia and across to New Zealand. They can even cross the Pacific, eventually hitting Hawaii's southern shores during the Northern Hemisphere summer.

Superbank on the Gold Coast is the world's most crowded break.

If you want to surf perfect barrels with smaller numbers of like-minded souls, you will have to be ready to get off the beaten track and be prepared to cope with cold water, spend time in remote camping grounds where local wildlife can bite, sting, and poison, and not be spooked by true stories recounted by locals about sharks as big as a school bus. Those small matters aside, the rewards of getting off the well-trodden path may provide you and your companions with priceless surfing memories that will last for the rest of your lives. In the far south, there are remote breaks where swells originating from frigid Antarctic waters mechanically pound the desert coastline, and the air temperature is a blazing 113°F (45°C) while the water temperature hovers around 54°F (12°C). The splendid isolation of these areas remains largely intact because of the often well-deserved reputations of massive sharks and very powerful waves.

The extremely powerful waves found along Australia's south coast result from the combination of big westerly swells and a narrow continental shelf.

Seasonal Patterns

Australia receives waves year-round. The tropical cyclone season from December to April is the best time to catch the world-famous right-hand point breaks from north of Newcastle in New South Wales up to the Queensland coast's northernmost surf break at Agnes Water, near Bundaberg. In recent years, March has proven itself a reliable provider of the low-pressure systems that form over the warm water in the Coral Sea and whip up northeasterly and easterly swells, accompanied by southeast winds that can see the points pump for days on end. But the Southern Hemisphere fall and winter, from March to August, is more consistent for the surfer not deterred by having to wear thick rubber or by big "noah's arks" (as the locals refer to sharks). It is then that the storms from the Roaring Forties — the area between latitude 40° south and 50° south — fire up and send long fetch waves along the Western Australian coast, into South Australia, Victoria, and Tasmania and up the New South Wales coast, with some even reaching right into Queensland.

So, point breaks, board shorts, an abundance of nightlife, accommodation, and insane crowds; or fetch waves, full rubber, camping, tranquility, and big sharks. It's your call.

Western Australia

The focus of surfing in Western Australia is the far southwest coast, particularly the stretch of rugged shore between Cape Naturaliste in the north and Cape Leeuwin, 84 miles (135 km) to the south (the most southwesterly point on the Australian mainland). The region's relative proximity to the state capital Perth, about 145 miles (233 km) away, makes it a popular weekend destination.

Looking right down the throat of one of the world's longest and most consistent swell fetches, which runs all the way from South Africa and is fueled by the almost constant westerly winds of the Roaring Forties, this coastline offers some of the biggest ridable waves in the country. In particular, there are scores of very good to excellent waves in the 31-mile (49-km) stretch of coast centered on the town of Margaret River.

The southwest is exposed to dramatic wind shifts and sudden weather changes, and weeks of blasting onshore gales occur through the winter months. February through to June provides the most stable weather. Water temperatures are affected by regular upwelling and rarely rise above 72°F (22°C), even in midsummer, despite land temperatures rocketing beyond 100°F (38°C). There is only one tide a day, and the ranges are not large.

what's in a name?

With breaks called Surgeon's Table, Suicides, The Gallows, and The Guillotine along this section of coast, as well as unnamed slabs of reef that can suck nearly dry before offering gaping barrels, even experienced surfers should be prepared for long hold-downs and a solid working over when the swell is over 6 ft (1.8 m). But there are also many spots along the coast suitable for beginners.

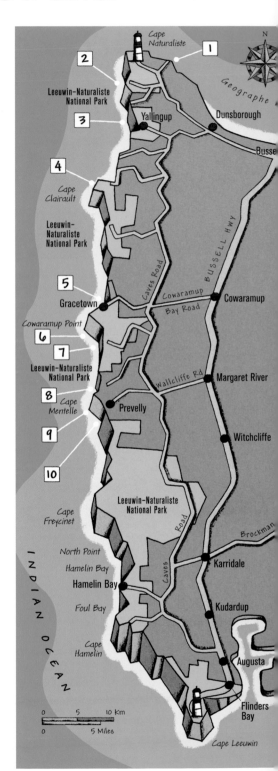

1 The Farm

Tucked in behind Cape Naturaliste, The Farm requires a very large swell to break, but offers shelter from strong south to southwest winds. Unfortunately, as it is one of very few places here that do that, it is usually crowded. The beach breaks are good quality, though, and are worth the walk, as are a number of nearby reefs such as Rocky Point and Boneyards.

WAVE TYPE Left and right

WAVE HEIGHT 1–4 ft (0.3–1.2 m)

BREAK TYPE Sand and reef

BEST SWELL SW–W

BEST WIND S–SW

BEST TIDE Mid

BEST TIME March–October

HAZARDS Sharks, crowds

DIRECTIONS Take the Cape Naturaliste Rd from Dunsborough, and then turn off on the Bunkers Bay Rd. It's a short stroll from there.

2 The Three Bears

The Three Bears are three separate left-handers: Papa Bear, Mama Bear, and Baby Bear, of which Mama Bear is arguably the best. Hard-hitting waves, they offer excellent barrels for experienced surfers, and deliver the best conditions during small to moderate swells.

WAVE TYPE Left

WAVE HEIGHT Baby Bear: 1–4 ft (0.3–1.2 m); Mama Bear: 3–8 ft (0.9–2.4 m); Papa Bear: 6–10 ft (1.8–3.1 m)

BREAK TYPE Reef

BEST SWELL SW–W

BEST WIND NE–E

BEST TIDE Mid

BEST TIME October–April

HAZARDS Sharks, rocks, crowds

DIRECTIONS A four-wheel-drive vehicle is essential. Take the Cape Naturaliste Rd from Dunsborough, turn onto Sugarloaf Rd, then follow the rough track for about half an hour.

3 Yallingup

The beautiful coastal town of Yallingup has a fine variety of waves. Main Break offers very good lefts and rights, and is popular with long-boarders and as a competition venue. To the south, The Bubble is a fast left-hander over a shallow reef, more suited to shortboarders; to the north, Rabbit Hill offers hollow, peaky waves that are often heavier than they look from shore.

WAVE TYPE Left and right

WAVE HEIGHT 2–8 ft (0.6–2.4 m)

BREAK TYPE Reef

BEST SWELL SW–W

BEST WIND NE–E

BEST TIDE Mid

BEST TIME October–April

HAZARDS Sharks, rocks, crowds

DIRECTIONS From Dunsborough, follow the signs from Caves Rd into Yallingup Beach Rd. There is convenient beach access from the main parking lot, just past the Yallingup Beach Holiday Park.

4 Injidup

Several quality waves are available around Cape Clairault. A quality right-hander known as Pea Break offers excellent waves on small to medium swells. Injidup Car Park can produce good quality lefts and rights under similar conditions. Injidup Point is a long left-hander requiring a large swell and a lengthy walk from the parking lot, but provides protection from fresh afternoon sea breezes.

WAVE TYPE Left and right

WAVE HEIGHT 2–8 ft (0.6–2.4 m)

BREAK TYPE Reef

BEST SWELL SW

BEST WIND Pea Break: NE–SE; Injidup Car Park NE–SE; Injidup Point SE–SW

BEST TIDE Mid

BEST TIME October–April

HAZARDS Sharks, rocks, crowds

DIRECTIONS From Yallingup, follow Caves Rd, turn off into Wyadup Rd, and then onto Cape Clairault Rd. You can't miss the parking lot.

5 North Point

One of the region's classic waves, North Point delivers some of the heaviest drops available, with a memorable barrel (or hideous wipeout) to follow. It's always crowded with finely tuned locals, so you'll really have your work cut out for you here. There is great viewing off the point, too.

WAVE TYPE Right

WAVE HEIGHT 3–10 ft (0.9–3.1 m)

BREAK TYPE Reef

BEST SWELL SW–W

BEST WIND NE–E

BEST TIDE Mid–high

BEST TIME March–October

HAZARDS Sharks, rocks, crowds

DIRECTIONS Take Caves Rd south from Yallingup, then turn right into Cowaramup Bay Rd. North Point is on the right just before you get to the holiday village of Gracetown.

6 South Point

Though it's a long walk from the parking lot and can be very crowded at times, this long left-hander breaking inside Cowaramup Point offers good waves for intermediate surfers as well as protection from gusty southerly winds. South Point is also a popular competition venue. Watch out for the rocks!

WAVE TYPE Left

WAVE HEIGHT 3–8 ft (0.9–2.4 m)

BREAK TYPE Reef

BEST SWELL SW–W

BEST WIND SE–SW

BEST TIDE Mid–high

BEST TIME March–October

HAZARDS Sharks, rocks, crowds

DIRECTIONS Take Caves Rd south from Yallingup, then turn right into Cowaramup Bay Rd. Continue through Gracetown to the South Point parking lot.

7 Lefthanders

A popular wave that delivers hollow barrels under small to moderate swells and easterly winds. A number of nearby reefs offer similarly high-quality waves, which helps to disperse the crowds. Lefthanders is a popular choice for midweek surfers looking for some isolation.

WAVE TYPE Left

WAVE HEIGHT 2–6 ft (0.6–1.8 m)

BREAK TYPE Reef

BEST SWELL SW–W

BEST WIND NE–SE

BEST TIDE Mid–high

BEST TIME November–April

HAZARDS Sharks, rocks, crowds

DIRECTIONS From Gracetown, take the dirt road running south to the parking lot. Lefthanders is a long walk from the parking lot, so pack the water and sunscreen.

8 The Box

Probably the most photogenic wave in the southwest, The Box is frequented by surfers and bodyboarders with a penchant for danger. Even if you survive the drop, you'll then need to negotiate the sharp rocks that lie just below the surface. A wipeout here can have serious consequences.

WAVE TYPE Right

WAVE HEIGHT 4–8 ft (1.2–2.4 m)

BREAK TYPE Reef

BEST SWELL SW–W

BEST WIND NE–E

BEST TIDE Mid–high

BEST TIME March–October

HAZARDS Sharks, submerged rocks

DIRECTIONS From Margaret River, take Wallcliffe Rd, cross over Caves Rd, then turn right into Surfers Point Rd. A final right-hand turn into Rivermouth Rd will take you to a small parking lot. The Box can also be viewed from the Main Break parking lot at Margaret River.

Rides at Injidup are normally short, but in favorable conditions they can run for up to 500 yards (500 m).

9 Margaret River

One of Australia's top spots, Margaret River has several fine waves. Main Break (or The Point) is a shifty left-hander offering heart-in-the-mouth drops of over 15 ft (4.6 m). To the south Suicides is a good indicator for impending swell activity at Main Break. The Bommie breaks well offshore and is capable of holding some of the biggest waves in the area. Beginners are catered for at the River Mouth.

WAVE TYPE Left and right

WAVE HEIGHT 3–18 ft (0.9–5.5 m)

BREAK TYPE Reef

BEST SWELL SW–W

BEST WIND NE–E

BEST TIDE Mid

BEST TIME March–October

HAZARDS Rogue waves, sharks, crowds

DIRECTIONS From Margaret River, take Wallcliffe Rd, cross over Caves Rd, then turn right into Surfers Point Rd. There is parking at Main Break and on Rivermouth Rd.

10 Gas Bay

Another popular location for barrel aficionados, Gas Bay delivers excellent-quality waves during a moderate swell and an easterly airstream. However, the locals have this place wired and you may have difficulty snaring a set wave when it's cooking. Grunter, another terrific wave close by, can produce long and heavy right-handers during powerful groundswells.

WAVE TYPE Right

WAVE HEIGHT 2–8 ft (0.6–2.4 m)

BREAK TYPE Sand on reef

BEST SWELL SW–W

BEST WIND NE–SE

BEST TIDE High

BEST TIME November–April

HAZARDS Sharks

DIRECTIONS From Margaret River, take Wallcliffe Rd, cross over Caves Rd (still on Wallcliffe Rd), and follow until the road turns to gravel. The parking lot is at the end of this road.

South Australia

South Australia is blessed with clean, cold water and reasonable weather for much of the year. The coast receives its best swells from March to June, directly from the Southern Ocean, when wetsuits are necessary. Acceptable surf can be found fairly close to the state capital, Adelaide, but for those prepared to travel farther afield, fantastic setups are available not far away.

Three hours' drive from Adelaide, the Yorke Peninsula has some of the best setups in the state and is one of Australia's great surfing drawcards for the committed surfer. The coastline inside Innes National Park, near Stenhouse Bay, is rugged and exposed to strong Southern Ocean swells. To the north lies west-facing coastline characterized by rugged limestone cliffs and long, white, sandy beaches. The Fleurieu Peninsula has a long and varied shoreline that includes secluded beaches rarely visited by anyone, as well as fiercely weathered limestone cliffs and headlands that take the full force of the Southern Ocean.

cold water, big sharks

South Australia has had more shark fatalities than any other place in Australia in the last 20 years. Furthermore, 20 out of 46 attacks have been fatal – an unusually high proportion. In 2000, two surfers were taken within 48 hours: one at Cactus on the Great Australian Bight and the other at Black Point near Elliston, on the Eyre Peninsula, some 155 miles (250 km) away.

Located just off the Fleurieu Peninsula, Kangaroo Island is seven times the size of Singapore, bigger than Long Island, New York, and teeming with wildlife. Half the native vegetation on the island remains just as it was when British navigator Matthew Flinders put a name to this untamed wilderness in 1802, and more than one-third of the island is national or conservation park. Ferries operate between Cape Jervis on the mainland and Penneshaw, a journey of about 45 minutes.

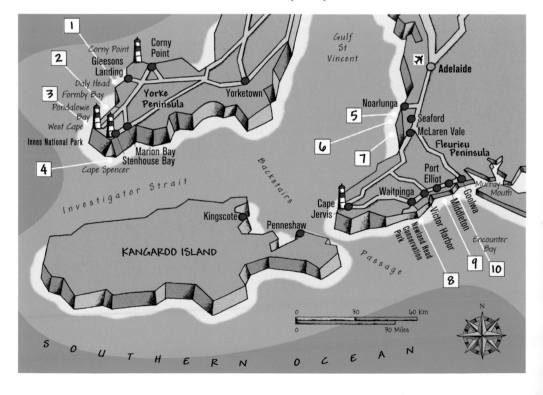

1 Daly Head

A series of reefs just south of Gleesons Landing pick up large swells and offer some of the biggest surfable waves on the Yorke Peninsula. Daly Head is a good location to access the swell, as there are several quality waves nearby that work under different wind directions. Daly Head is generally not a high-performance wave, but is still a very popular location when the wind and swell are favorable.

WAVE TYPE Left and right

WAVE HEIGHT 3–12 ft (0.9–3.6 m)

BREAK TYPE Reef

BEST SWELL SW

BEST WIND E–SE

BEST TIDE Low

BEST TIME November–April

HAZARDS Sharks, currents

DIRECTIONS Take the Corny Point Rd from Marion Bay, and follow the signs to Daly Head.

2 Baby Lizard Bay

The southern end of Dustbowl Beach has a permanent right-hand wave breaking into a small outcrop of rocks. Baby Lizard is a good option for intermediate surfers, and good quality beach breaks can be found to the north when the swell is small. A fickle left-hander sometimes delivers good waves at the base of the cliff below the parking lot, but access is tricky. Watch out for exposed rocks at low tide.

WAVE TYPE Right

WAVE HEIGHT 1–5 ft (0.3–1.5 m)

BREAK TYPE Sand over reef

BEST SWELL SW

BEST WIND E–SE

BEST TIDE Low

BEST TIME November–April

HAZARDS Sharks, rocks, rips

DIRECTIONS Take Corny Point Rd from Marion Bay, and follow the signs to Baby Lizard Bay.

3 Pondalowie Bay

"Pondi" is a favorite destination for traveling Adelaide surfers, and offers a well-shaped left up to 4 ft (1.2 m), and a high-quality right-hander up to 8 ft (2.4 m). Richards is an excellent-quality right-hander located a short stroll to the north, and is usually less crowded than Pondi. Beware of the sudden shore break, which has a habit of breaking surfboards in half.

WAVE TYPE Left and right

WAVE HEIGHT 1–8 ft (0.3–2.4 m)

BREAK TYPE Sand over reef

BEST SWELL SW–W

BEST WIND E–SE

BEST TIDE Low

BEST TIME November–April

HAZARDS Sharks

DIRECTIONS Follow the road inside Innes National Park until you reach the surfers campground (just past the Pondalowie Bay campground). A five-minute walk across the boardwalk will take you to the surf.

4 Chinamans

A heavy reef break offering excellent barrels, Chinamans is mainly a left, although good quality rights are also available. The ledge can create some difficulty in getting in and out of the water at low tide, and the break doesn't handle crowds very well, so only surf here if you have complete confidence in your ability.

WAVE TYPE Left and right

WAVE HEIGHT 3–8 ft (0.9–2.4 m)

BREAK TYPE Reef

BEST SWELL S–SW

BEST WIND NW–N

BEST TIDE Mid

BEST TIME March–October

HAZARDS Sharks, reef cuts

DIRECTIONS Chinamans is located inside Innes National Park at the bottom of Yorke Peninsula. Take the road west of Stenhouse Bay, and you'll see the break as you come over the rise, just to the right of Chinamans Hat Island.

5 Southport

This wide, sandy beach offers waves suitable for all levels of surfers. The Hump at the northern end attracts the largest surf, while the river mouth can deliver fast peeling left-handers when the sand is well positioned. A small reef in the southern corner provides short lefts and rights in larger swells.

WAVE TYPE Left and right

WAVE HEIGHT 1–5 ft (0.3–1.5 m)

BREAK TYPE Sand and reef

BEST SWELL SW

BEST WIND NE–SE

BEST TIDE All

BEST TIME March–October

HAZARDS Sharks, summer crowds

DIRECTIONS From Noarlunga, take Weatherald Tce and park near the footbridge which provides access to the beach. A second parking lot is located above the river mouth and has a staircase to the beach.

6 Triggs

Several reefs in close proximity comprise the surf breaks at Triggs. Triggs 1 is a double-peaked right-hander, while Triggs 2 is usually a little smaller and more appropriate for longboarders. U-turns (farther south) and Snakes (farther north) offer alternatives during crowded conditions.

WAVE TYPE Right

WAVE HEIGHT 2–5 ft (0.6–1.5 m)

BREAK TYPE Reef

BEST SWELL SW

BEST WIND NE–SE

BEST TIDE All

BEST TIME March–October

HAZARDS Sharks

DIRECTIONS Drive south from Port Noarlunga along the Esplanade. Triggs has a large dedicated parking lot with beach access via a ramp and staircase.

7 Seaford

A reliable sand-over-reef combination that performs well under all kinds of conditions, Seaford is a popular competition venue offering high-performance waves. A number of reefs farther south are less consistent but can deliver hollower waves when the swell is strong.

WAVE TYPE Right

WAVE HEIGHT 2–5 ft (0.6–1.5 m)

BREAK TYPE Sand and reef

BEST SWELL SW

BEST WIND NE–SE

BEST TIDE All

BEST TIME March–October

HAZARDS Sharks

DIRECTIONS From Seaford, take Seaford Rd to the Esplanade. There are several parking lots here, but the closest access is via the ramp next to the roundabout.

8 Waitpinga

Even when the surf is small, Waitpinga always has something to offer. Dangerous rips are very common though, so this beach should only be tackled by experienced surfers. Constantly shifting sands mean that the perfect waves you surfed today may not be there tomorrow. An abundance of marine life attracts the big men in grey suits (sharks, in other words), so keep your feet up and don't surf at dawn or dusk.

WAVE TYPE Left

WAVE HEIGHT 1–5 ft (0.3–1.5 m)

BREAK TYPE Sand

BEST SWELL S–SW

BEST WIND NW–NE

BEST TIDE Mid

BEST TIME March–October

HAZARDS Rips, sharks, rogue waves

DIRECTIONS Take the Waitpinga road west from Victor Harbor and follow the signs to Waitpinga. Dennis Rd will lead you to the main parking lot.

9 Knights

A broad outcrop of granite rock east of Boomer Beach reflects wave energy perpendicular to the shore, creating Knights' infamous wedge. This wave is very popular with bodyboarders and can offer a thrilling barrel, or the wipeout of a lifetime. The cliffs above the break offer great viewing for spectators.

WAVE TYPE Left

WAVE HEIGHT 1–5 ft (0.3–1.5 m)

BREAK TYPE Sand over rock

BEST SWELL S–SW

BEST WIND NE

BEST TIDE Low–mid

BEST TIME Year-round

HAZARDS Sharks, rocks, shallow water

DIRECTIONS In Port Elliot, turn right into The Strand and then right again into Merrilli Pl, and park on the side of the road just before the road veers right. Access is via a staircase.

10 Middleton

This infamously slow and average-quality wave is the result of a gradual incline in the ocean floor off the coast. Middleton Point (not a point at all) is best suited to beginners and longboarders; shortboarders can often find a short peaky left inside Middleton Bay. Less crowded options can be found farther east toward Goolwa.

WAVE TYPE Right, left and straight

WAVE HEIGHT 1–6 ft (0.3–1.8 m)

BREAK TYPE Sand and reef

BEST SWELL SW

BEST WIND NW–NE

BEST TIDE Mid–high

BEST TIME March–October

HAZARDS Sharks, seaweed

DIRECTIONS Heading east from Victor Harbor, turn off Goolwa Rd into Mindacowie Tce (at the Middleton pub), cross the railway line, and then turn right into Dover Rd. This will turn into Ocean Pde, which has a number of parking lots.

Waitpinga offers diverse, reliable surf, but as wave size increases so does the power of the ocean currents.

Victoria

The 800-mile (1,287-km) Victorian coast gets its best surf from March until October, when Roaring Forties storms are spinning around in the cold waters of the Southern Ocean. Occupying the bottom end of the Australian mainland, Victoria is well positioned to act as a magnet to those swells. The resulting consistency of good surfing conditions is matched by few other parts of Australia.

The Victorian coastline can be divided into four main surfing areas: the southeast coast from Mallacoota to Cape Patterson; the east coast (Point Leo to Portsea), including Phillip Island; the Surf Coast, which extends from Barwon Heads to Cape Otway; and the southwest coast from Cape Otway to Portland. Of these, the Surf Coast has the densest concentration of top surfing spots and, most famously, is home to Bells Beach, known around the globe as the home of the world's longest-running professional surfing contest.

if there's no swell ...

The 155-mile (249-km) trip along the Great Ocean Road, from Torquay to Allansford, is one of the world's great scenic drives, taking in stunning coastal scenery, including cliffs, sea stacks, and beaches. Surfworld at Torquay is the world's biggest surfing museum, and houses the Australian Surfing Hall of Fame.

When Bass Strait is angry, the Surf Coast is not for the fainthearted. Bodies, boards, and egos can all be smashed in the blink of an eye. Waiting for the wind and rain to mellow can be frustrating. But the rewards for the patient can be memorable.

Melbourne, 59 miles (95 km) north of Barwon Heads, has Victoria's only international airport. Summer's average maximum air temperature on the Surf Coast is 75°F (24°C), while the winter average maximum is 57°F (14°C). The average maximum ocean temperature ranges from 55°F (13°C) in winter to 64°F (18°C) in summer.

1 Kennett River

A well-defined peak shelters inside the headland here. There is a steep, fun takeoff allowing a laid-out bottom turn, then a climb and drop on the short but hollow face as it runs 100 yards (100 m) or so to the beach along the point. Either paddle out to the break from the beach or walk round the point, clamber over the rocks, and paddle across to the lineup.

WAVE TYPE Right from a peak

WAVE HEIGHT 3–5 ft (0.9–1.5 m)

BREAK TYPE Point

BEST SWELL SW

BEST WIND SW–W

BEST TIDE Low–mid

BEST TIME Year-round

HAZARDS Summer crowds

DIRECTIONS Follow the picturesque 25-minute drive west from Lorne along the Great Ocean Rd past Wye River, then turn off at the sign.

2 Lorne Point

The swell refracts around Point Grey and swings into the bay to hit the point a third of a mile (0.5 km) inside. Comes into its own in southerly times when it's glassy, or in full-throttle easterly conditions when the sea and wind push straight in to Lorne and wedge into the point, providing powerful but very uneven waves.

WAVE TYPE Right

WAVE HEIGHT 1–6 ft (0.3–1.8 m)

BREAK TYPE Point

BEST SWELL SW

BEST WIND SW–W, NE–E

BEST TIDE Low–mid

BEST TIME February–May

HAZARDS Shallow rock ledges, strong current, frustrating mix of shortboards and longboards

DIRECTIONS From the center of Lorne, go west along the beachfront to the surf-lifesaving club.

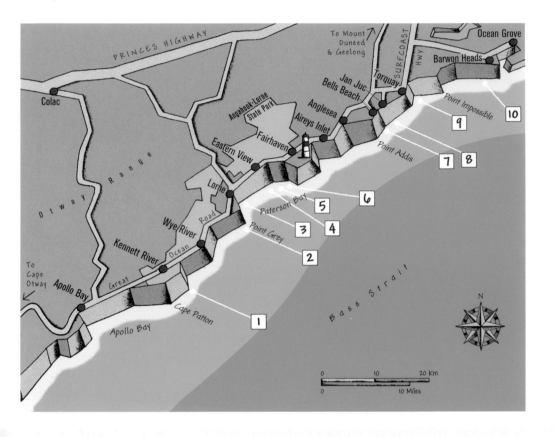

3 Cathedral Rock

This powerful wave has down-the-line speed and steepness to get the adrenaline going. In big seas, it's possible to surf right into the bay – a 300-yard (300-m) ride. Usually, the wave face and sections improve in shape as wave size increases.

WAVE TYPE Right

WAVE HEIGHT 3–15 ft (0.9–4.6 m)

BREAK TYPE Point

BEST SWELL SW

BEST WIND W

BEST TIDE Low–mid

BEST TIME March–September

HAZARDS Rock shelves, turbulent white water along the point in big seas

DIRECTIONS Cathedral Rock is halfway between Fairhaven and Lorne along the Great Ocean Rd, just off the south side of the major S-bend. Park above the point, and enter the water via a channel in the rocks west of the peak.

4 Spout Creek

A couple of outside reefs break up the swell into peaks on the inside. The surf tends to close out during a large swell, but the sand bottom sometimes provides an outside peak surprise. Reasonably protected from southwest winds, Spout Creek often has a ridable wave on otherwise flat summer days.

WAVE TYPE Left and right

WAVE HEIGHT 1–6 ft (0.3–1.8 m)

BREAK TYPE Beach

BEST SWELL SW

BEST WIND W

BEST TIDE Mid–high

BEST TIME All year

HAZARDS Longshore drift to the north, dumping shore break when waves are bigger

DIRECTIONS Drive west from Aireys Inlet on the Great Ocean Rd, past Fairhaven to Moggs Creek. "Spout" is at the westernmost end of this beach, just before the road winds into the hills.

5 Eastern View

Also known as The Spot, this has a sand bottom that turns up fun waves, usually on a couple of peaks. It is often better on the incoming tide. On "no swell" days over summer, it still draws waves, and it is also worth checking out in the calm period after easterly storms when it can throw up some nice peaks.

WAVE TYPE Left and right

WAVE HEIGHT 1–6 ft (0.3–1.8 m)

BREAK TYPE Beach

BEST SWELL SW

BEST WIND NW–N

BEST TIDE Incoming

BEST TIME December–June

HAZARDS Longshore drift to the south in easterly conditions

DIRECTIONS From Aireys Inlet, drive west through Fairhaven on the Great Ocean Rd. Just to the west of Moggs Creek you will find three parking lots overlooking the open beach.

6 Fairhaven

Fairhaven draws the summer swell, but is open to the wind. The waves can be powerful and are often best just after an easterly storm. A reef to the north of the surf club maintains a section during higher tides; a "hole" to the south helps form a bank usually best on lower tides.

WAVE TYPE Left and right

WAVE HEIGHT 1–8 ft (0.3–2.4 m)

BREAK TYPE Beach

BEST SWELL SW, E–SE

BEST WIND NW–N

BEST TIDE All

BEST TIME December–June

HAZARDS Strong currents in heavy E and SW conditions

DIRECTIONS From Aireys Inlet, drive west along the Great Ocean Rd past the lighthouse and the river flats, where you'll come to the sign for Fairhaven.

7 Bells Beach Surfing Recreation Reserve

The jewel in Victoria's crown has some world-class breaks: from west to east, Southside, Centreside, Rincon, Bells Bowl, and Winkipop (including Lower Winkipop). The most popular in heavy swells are Bells Bowl and Winkipop, which both also hold onshore conditions well.

WAVE TYPE Right (except Southside: left)

WAVE HEIGHT Southside: 3–6 ft (0.9–1.8 m); Centreside: 2–10 ft (0.6–3.1 m); Rincon: 2–8 ft (0.6–2.4 m); Bells Bowl: 2–20 ft (0.6–6.1 m); Winkipop: 2–20 ft (0.6–6.1 m)

BREAK TYPE Reef

BEST SWELL SW (except Southside: S)

BEST WIND W–NW

BEST TIDE Southside: High; Centreside: Mid–high; Rincon: Mid–high; Bells Bowl: All; Winkipop: Low–mid

BEST TIME March–October

HAZARDS Occasional sharks, strong currents

DIRECTIONS Take the Surfcoast Hwy west from Torquay and turn left at Bells Beach Rd.

8 Jan Juc

This long sand beach shelters under cliffs. The moving sandbanks provide variable waves, but it's Mecca for locals seeking a quick surf after work. To the east is Torquay Point, a flat but fun right-hander; to the west, other reefs pop up right-handers, mostly on higher tides.

WAVE TYPE Left and right

WAVE HEIGHT 1–6 ft (0.3–1.8 m)

BREAK TYPE Beach

BEST SWELL SW

BEST WIND W–NW

BEST TIDE Mid

BEST TIME Year-round

HAZARDS Crowds, occasional strong currents in heavy seas

DIRECTIONS Travel west from Torquay, past the golf club, then turn left to Jan Juc. Surfer parking is to the west of the surf club.

9 Point Impossible

It needs a solid swell back at Torquay Point to get "Possos" going; once running, it is usually a forgiving wave for long and shortboarders alike. Nearby Outside Reef Point Impossible offers a speedy and well-formed wave on higher tides. Farther east, Bancoora Point provides a protected break in a large swell.

WAVE TYPE Right

WAVE HEIGHT 2–6 ft (0.6–1.8 m)

BREAK TYPE Reef

BEST SWELL SW

BEST WIND W

BEST TIDE Mid–high

BEST TIME All year

HAZARDS Rock shelves under breaking waves at high tide

DIRECTIONS From Torquay, follow The Esplanade east along the beachfront to Point Impossible.

10 Thirteenth Beach

The beach stretches from The Bluff at Barwon Heads in the east to Black Rock; most surfing takes place at the eastern end. Experienced surfers love the power out front of The Beacon, a navigation sign on the clifftop here. To the west are variable beach breaks, which are best at higher tides.

WAVE TYPE Left and right

WAVE HEIGHT 2–10 ft (0.6–3.1 m)

BREAK TYPE Reef and beach

BEST SWELL SE–SW

BEST WIND NE

BEST TIDE All

BEST TIME November–May

HAZARDS Rock shelves under breaking waves at high tide; longshore drift in big surf conditions

DIRECTIONS Traveling from Geelong toward Torquay, turn left at Mount Duneed. Immediately before crossing the Barwon River, turn right and the ring road will take you along the beachfront.

Bells Beach is the venue for major surfing competitions, including the annual ASP WCT Rip Curl Pro.

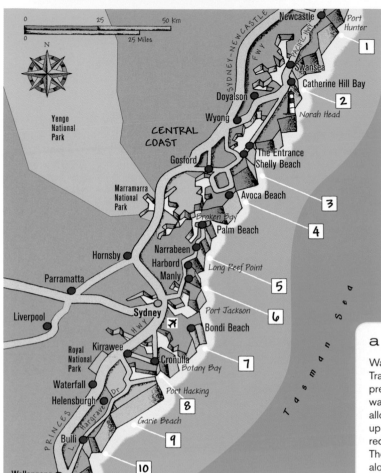

a sudden chill

Watch out for the "Ekman Transport" effect, whereby prevailing winds strip off a warm top layer of seawater, allowing cold water to rise up to the surface and reduce water temperatures. The phenomenon can occur along this coast in summer following a couple of days of northeast winds. In that time, the water temperature can drop from 68°F (20°C) to 57°F (14°C), and you'll need a steamer.

Central New South Wales

A 155-mile (250-km) "surf strip" extends down the central New South Wales coast, encompassing the state's three largest cities: Newcastle in the north; Sydney, the capital, in the center; and Wollongong in the south. April to October sees this region's best surf, generated by storms in the Tasman Sea and by lows passing north and south of Tasmania. February and March also see some big seas resulting from low-pressure systems close to the coast in the Tasman Sea. The coastline has numerous geographical nooks and crannies, with point, reef, and beach breaks.

Sydney has always been Australia's surf capital. Surfboard riding in Australia caught on following a surfing demonstration by Hawaiian surfer and gold medal Olympian Duke Kahanamoku at Sydney's Freshwater Beach in December 1914. In 1956, Duke brought a team of 22 Californian and Hawaiian surf-lifeguards to Sydney, who amazed around 300 locals by "hot dogging" their skegged malibus across the waves. Fittingly, a statue of Duke can be found at Harbord on Sydney's northern beaches.

Sydney has New South Wales's only international airport, and Newcastle has a domestic airport. Summer's average maximum air temperature is 79°F (26°C), while the winter average maximum is 61°F (16°C). The average maximum ocean temperature ranges from 61°F (16°C) to 68°F (20°C), with the highest temperatures occurring during March and April.

1 Merewether Beach

The area's talented surfers have helped make this Newcastle's best-known break. The Ladies' reef at the southern end is a right-hander that can hold big swells but is best at 7–10 ft (2.1–3.1 m), when it still packs a punch! The beach break is suited to all levels of surfers. A favorite of local legend Mark Richards.

WAVE TYPE Right on reef; left and right on beach

WAVE HEIGHT 3–15 ft (0.9–4.6 m)

BREAK TYPE Point and beach

BEST SWELL NE–SE

BEST WIND SW

BEST TIDE Mid–low

BEST TIME Winter

HAZARDS Rips, rocks, talented locals!

DIRECTIONS Heading north into Newcastle, turn right off the Pacific Hwy to Scenic Dr and follow this road to the beach.

2 Catherine Hill Bay

"Catho" is an old coal-mining town with historic miners' cottages. Its beach usually picks up most swells. The north end has a peaky beach break that produces excellent lefts and rights. The south end (near the pier) frequently has smaller waves. If you're up for a walk-in, South Moonee and Ghosties, nearby to the south, can provide some surprise waves.

WAVE TYPE Left and right

WAVE HEIGHT 3–6 ft (0.9–1.8 m)

BREAK TYPE Beach

BEST SWELL SE

BEST WIND SW–NW

BEST TIDE Mid–low

BEST TIME All year

HAZARDS Rips, shore dump

DIRECTIONS Take the Swansea turnoff from the freeway and follow the signs to Swansea. Past Doyalson, take the first turn right after the giant model prawn onto Colliery Rd, then turn left onto Flowers Dr past the pub to the beach.

3 Shelly Beach

Good beach breaks are found all along this beach near The Entrance. The north end often has an excellent left holding bigger swells from northeast to southeast. In the right conditions, the south end provides consistent waves. This can be a particularly good beach for beginners.

WAVE TYPE Left and right

WAVE HEIGHT 1–10 ft (0.3–3.1 m)

BREAK TYPE Beach

BEST SWELL NE–SE

BEST WIND S–SW

BEST TIDE Mid–low

BEST TIME All year

HAZARDS Rips

DIRECTIONS From the Sydney–Newcastle Freeway, take the Wyong turnoff to the Pacific Hwy. Then drive all the way along Wyong Rd and veer right onto Shelly Beach Rd. It leads to the south end of the beach.

4 Avoca Beach

One of the most consistent beaches on the Central Coast, Avoca picks up most swells. Avoca Point at the southern end breaks close to rocks and forms an excellent right-hander. Peaks form all along the beach to North Avoca and can line up perfectly with the right wind and swell.

WAVE TYPE Right-hand point; left and right on beach breaks

WAVE HEIGHT 3–10ft (0.9–3.1 m)

BREAK TYPE Point and beach

BEST SWELL NE–SE

BEST WIND SW–NW

BEST TIDE Mid–low

BEST TIME Year-round

HAZARDS Crowds, rips, rocks

DIRECTIONS Heading north on the freeway from Sydney toward Newcastle, take the first Gosford turnoff. Follow the signs to Avoca. Once there, follow Avoca Dr to the south end of the beach.

5 North Narrabeen

North Narrabeen is a surf break with a river mouth setup at Narrabeen Lagoon. One of Sydney's most consistent breaks and a world-class beach break, North Narrabeen picks up most swells to create an often-perfect left-hander. The peak can become crowded with great surfers; at such times it's worth checking out the breaks farther down the beach.

WAVE TYPE Left and right

WAVE HEIGHT 3–8 ft (0.9–2.4 m)

BREAK TYPE Beach

BEST SWELL NE–E

BEST WIND NW–NE

BEST TIDE Mid–low

BEST TIME Summer

HAZARDS Crowds, rips, rocks

DIRECTIONS From Sydney city center, head north over the Harbour Bridge, turn onto Military Rd, cross the Spit Bridge and continue straight ahead, following the signs to Narrabeen.

6 Manly Beach

Manly has several different areas. In the north, Queenscliff breaks on a rock-and-sand bottom and can produce some great lefts and rights. Queenscliff Bombie on the outside breaks on swells over 10 ft (3.1 m). North Steyne is a beach break; South Steyne offers clean conditions in big swells. Fairy Bower is Sydney's best point break, while Winkipop on the outside is for experienced surfers only.

WAVE TYPE Left and right

WAVE HEIGHT 1–10 ft (0.3–3.1 m) plus

BREAK TYPE Beach and point

BEST SWELL NE–E

BEST WIND NE

BEST TIDE Mid–high

BEST TIME Year-round

HAZARDS Crowds, rips, rocks (Fairy Bower)

DIRECTIONS From Sydney, head north over the Harbour Bridge, turn onto Military Rd, cross the Spit Bridge, turn right onto Sydney Rd and follow the signs; or catch a ferry from Circular Quay.

7 Bondi Beach

Australia's most famous beach attracts a diverse crowd and is always fun and funky. Facing southeast, it picks up all available south swells and has favorable winds blowing offshore in summer. South Bondi produces excellent beach breaks, while North Bondi is a haven for kids and learners on soft boards. Ben Buckler Point at the north end starts breaking over 7 feet (2.1 m) and is only for the experienced.

WAVE TYPE Left and right

WAVE HEIGHT 1–8 ft (0.3–2.4 m)

BREAK TYPE Beach

BEST SWELL SE

BEST WIND NE

BEST TIDE Mid–high

BEST TIME Year-round

HAZARDS Rips, weekend crowds, too much fun!

DIRECTIONS Follow the signs to Bondi from Sydney city center and take Bondi Rd to the beach.

8 Cronulla Beach

Divided into several areas, including Shark Island, Cronulla Point, Voodoos, The Wall, The Alley, Elouera, Wanda, and Green Hills, the beach faces southeast and so generally picks up most south swells. Shark Island is a heavy, barreling wave; Cronulla Point is a powerful wave breaking on a rocky bottom. The rest are beach breaks that can be fickle – or perfect!

WAVE TYPE Left and right

WAVE HEIGHT 3–10 ft (0.9–3.1 m)

BREAK TYPE Mainly beach (reef at Cronulla Point and Shark Island)

BEST SWELL SE

BEST WIND SW–NW

BEST TIDE Mid–low

BEST TIME Year-round

HAZARDS Rips, rocks, reef, crowds

DIRECTIONS From Sydney, drive south on Princes Hwy, turn left at Kirrawee and follow Kingsway and Denman Ave. There is also a train from Sydney Central Station almost to the beach.

Sydney's iconic surfing beach, Bondi, lies just a short bus or car ride from the city center.

9 Garie Beach

Situated in the Royal National Park, Garie provides consistent waves with beach and reef breaks. The northern end offers a great left in east–northeast swells, breaking on a sand-and-rock bottom. The rest of the beach is sand, with a rocky shelf at the south end. A 15-minute walk south leads through Little Garie to an excellent left point break, North Era.

WAVE TYPE Left and right

WAVE HEIGHT 1–8 ft (0.3–2.4 m)

BREAK TYPE Rock and sand (reef at North Era)

BEST SWELL NE–SE

BEST WIND SW–NW

BEST TIDE Mid–low

BEST TIME Year-round

HAZARDS Rips, rocks, reef

DIRECTIONS Drive south from Sydney on the Princes Hwy, turn left at Waterfall into the Royal National Park. Follow the signs to Garie Beach along 20 minutes of winding roads. Check out Captain Cook Lookout for great views.

10 Sandon Point

This world-class right-hand point break is known for its size and power. It is renowned as the place to go in big south swells, which can thunder over the rocky bottom like a freight train. But it can also provide a good intermediate wave in small east swells.

WAVE TYPE Right

WAVE HEIGHT 3–15 ft (0.9–4.6 m)

BREAK TYPE Rocky reef

BEST SWELL SE–S

BEST WIND S–SW

BEST TIDE Mid

BEST TIME May–September

HAZARDS Rocks, sea urchins, crowds (respect the locals!)

DIRECTIONS Drive south from Sydney on the Princes Hwy, take the Helensburgh turnoff and then go south on Lawrence Hargrave Dr. At Bulli, turn left onto Point St and drive to the end of the road.

North Coast, New South Wales

I n the 1960s, the North Coast region of New South Wales was the focus of burgeoning links between surfing and the alternative life-styles. During that period, the region's numerous sand-bottomed, right-hand playgrounds provided ideal conditions for shortboard pioneers including Bob McTavish and Nat Young, who were at the vanguard of a surfing revolution that fleetingly viewed surfing as a kind of art or dance rather than a competitive sport.

The region includes Australia's most easterly point, Cape Byron, a rocky promontory that rises 351 ft (107 m) above the town of Byron Bay. Site of a former whaling station and abattoir, the town is now one of the most popular and expensive resort towns on the east coast, attracting hordes of visitors ranging from backpackers to cashed-up Hollywood escapees. The population influx has seen environmental issues come to the forefront in an attempt to stem rampant development.

The closest international airport is Brisbane, which is around 112 miles (180 km) to the north. There is a large domestic air terminal, the Gold Coast Airport, situated at Bilinga, near Coolangatta, which is about 30 minutes away by road. Summer's maximum average air temperature is 75°F (24°C), and the maximum average winter temperature is 62°F (17°C). The maximum average ocean temperatures range from around 68°F (20°C) to 77°F (25°C) in summer.

best time to go

Generally, the best time for surfing northern New South Wales and southern Queensland, all the way north to the Sunshine Coast, is from February through to April. This is when swells and other undersea patterns in the Coral Sea result in numerous perfect days when the lines are stacked corduroy, all the way to the horizon.

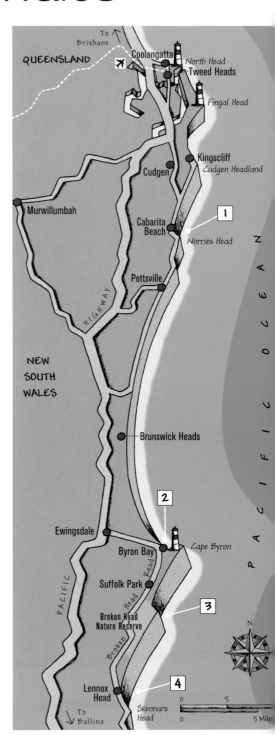

1 Cabarita

The south side of Norries Head offers a protected beach during northerlies. On the north side, a right-hand break runs across a small bay, past a rocky outcrop, and onto southern Cabarita Beach. Paddle out from the southern side of the bay against the headland and, if you get your timing right, you'll pop out between the sets and not get washed away.

WAVE TYPE Right

WAVE HEIGHT 2–15 ft (0.6–4.6 m)

BREAK TYPE Beach and point

BEST SWELL E–SE

BEST WIND W

BEST TIDE Low–mid

BEST TIME December–June

HAZARDS Longshore drift; difficult paddle out in big surf; waves breaking in front of rocks

DIRECTIONS From Tweed Heads, take the Pacific Hwy, then Tweed Heads Coast Rd past Cudgen and Casuarina Beach; you'll see the headland and parking lot south of Cabarita township.

2 Byron Bay

The town nestles on the north side of the cape by two protected bays: Wategos Beach and The Pass. From the boat ramp at The Pass, it's possible to surf more than 500 yards (up to 500 m) toward town if the banks and swell are right. Farther into the bay, it's a matter of racing the sections and following the flow of the wave. Near town, The Wreck is a high-tide speed track. To the south, Tallows offers classic lefts.

WAVE TYPE Right

WAVE HEIGHT 1–8 ft (0.3–2.4 m)

BREAK TYPE Point

BEST SWELL NE–SE

BEST WIND S–SW

BEST TIDE Low–mid

BEST TIME December–June

HAZARDS Crowds of novice surfers; lots of dropping in

DIRECTIONS From Byron, follow Lawson Street toward the lighthouse. At Palm Valley, a left turn takes you to a parking lot beside The Pass.

3 Broken Head

This lovely secluded beach community nestles at the southern end of a long beach running north through Suffolk Park to Cape Byron. Some protection from south winds is offered by the "Cocked Hat" rocks. A sand bottom funnels powerful right-handers along an outside bank, then past the rocks and into the beach. The beach breaks to the north can also push up some excellent waves.

WAVE TYPE Right

WAVE HEIGHT 2–8 ft (0.6–2.4 m)

BREAK TYPE Beach and point

BEST SWELL E–SE

BEST WIND SW–W

BEST TIDE Low–mid

BEST TIME December–June

HAZARDS Rocks, powerful shore break

DIRECTIONS Traveling south from Byron Bay toward Lennox Head on Broken Head Rd, turn left 1 km past the Suffolk Park Hotel and follow the signs to Broken Head Nature Reserve.

4 Lennox Head

This town has featured in surf movies and surfari itineraries since the 1960s. The headland towers over a long, boulder-lined point, where powerful, peeling waves reel over a sandy ribbon. Closer to town are reefs and beach breaks, best at high tide. South toward Ballina, quality breaks can be found at Boulders and Flat Rock. The North Wall at the Ballina river mouth is a swell magnet.

WAVE TYPE Right

WAVE HEIGHT 3–15 ft (0.9–4.6 m)

BREAK TYPE Point

BEST SWELL E–SE

BEST WIND SW–W

BEST TIDE All

BEST TIME January–May

HAZARDS Difficult entry and exit over slippery boulders; timing on sets needs to be spot on!

DIRECTIONS From Ballina, take the Coast Rd north. From Byron Bay, head south on Broken Head Rd then the Coast Rd. The road runs by the Bluff.

Gold Coast, Queensland

"Concrete Jungle," "Tinsel Town," "God's waiting room" — it seems everyone has an opinion about "The Goldy." One thing is certain, however: the Gold Coast is a magnet for pit pilots from around the world. Surfers have been riding the waves here since the 1920s, and every year the area continues to crank out drainpipe barrels in warm water.

While the Gold Coast is renowned for having some of the best sand-bottomed, right-hand, point-break waves on the planet, including Burleigh Heads, Currumbin Alley, Kirra (in its heyday), and the superhyped and supercrowded Superbank (also known as Stupor Bank) at Snapper Rocks, it can also provide quality beach breaks. The best chance of the point breaks

firing is during the cyclone season from December to April, but beach breaks can be found all year round. The most consistent break on the Gold Coast is the south-facing Duranbah — less than 1 mile (1.6 km) south of Snapper Rocks — and it can offer something when everywhere else is near flat.

The average summer maximum air temperature is 83°F (28°C), and the average winter maximum temperature is 72°F (22°C), while the average maximum water temperature ranges from 68°F (20°C) to 77°F (25°C). The closest international airport is Brisbane, which is around 47 miles (76 km) to the north; there is also a domestic air terminal, the Gold Coast Airport, situated at Bilinga, near Coolangatta.

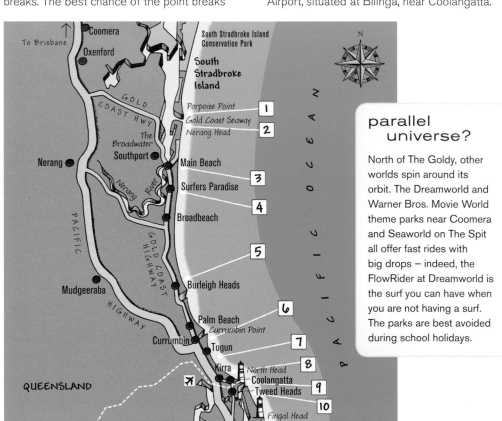

parallel universe?

North of The Goldy, other worlds spin around its orbit. The Dreamworld and Warner Bros. Movie World theme parks near Coomera and Seaworld on The Spit all offer fast rides with big drops — indeed, the FlowRider at Dreamworld is the surf you can have when you are not having a surf. The parks are best avoided during school holidays.

1 South Stradbroke Island

One of the most celebrated waves on the Gold Coast, South Straddie (also known as TOS – The Other Side) is the result of a regular influx of sand from the Gold Coast Sand Bypassing System. Together with offshore sandbars, these break up incoming swells into a myriad of peaky configurations. You'll get more tube time here than at most places in the world.

WAVE TYPE Left and right

WAVE HEIGHT 1–6 ft (0.3–1.8 m)

BREAK TYPE Sand

BEST SWELL NE–SE

BEST WIND W–NW

BEST TIDE Mid

BEST TIME March–September

HAZARDS Crowds, sharks, boats, sharp barnacles

DIRECTIONS Head north from Surfers Paradise on the Gold Coast Hwy, then take Waterways Dr. Turn left at the roundabout and follow Seaworld Dr until the road ends. To get to the island, either paddle across the seaway, or hail a water taxi.

2 The Spit

At the northern end of the Gold Coast, The Broadwater empties into the Pacific Ocean through the Gold Coast Seaway. Located on the southern side of the seaway, The Spit is one of only a few locations that offer protection from northerly winds. Good waves can be found either side of the jetty that pumps sand over to South Stradbroke Island.

WAVE TYPE Left and right

WAVE HEIGHT 1–5 ft (0.3–1.5 m)

BREAK TYPE Sand

BEST SWELL NE–SE

BEST WIND W–N

BEST TIDE Mid

BEST TIME October–January

HAZARDS Crowds, sharks

DIRECTIONS Head north from Surfers Paradise on the Gold Coast Hwy, then take Waterways Dr. Turn left at the roundabout and follow Seaworld Dr until the road ends. Walkways run from the parking lot to the beach.

3 Narrowneck

An artificial reef was built at Narrowneck in 1999 in order to create a buffer zone for the fragile beach separating the Pacific Ocean from the Nerang River. Although improving surf quality wasn't the main goal, the reef created a peaky wave that can, depending on sand movements, offer good rides during clean easterly groundswells.

WAVE TYPE Left and right

WAVE HEIGHT 1–6 ft (0.3–1.8 m)

BREAK TYPE Sand

BEST SWELL NE–SE

BEST WIND SW–NW

BEST TIDE Mid

BEST TIME January–October

HAZARDS Crowds

DIRECTIONS From central Surfers Paradise, follow Main Beach Pde north. Narrowneck is well signposted, but you'll have to park on the side of the road.

4 Surfers Paradise

Although the true surfer's paradise lies farther south at Snapper Rocks, there are almost 11 miles (18 km) of beach breaks between Burleigh Heads and the mouth of the Nerang River. Surfers Paradise lies in the heart of it all, and you'll have no trouble finding a good wave to surf here – just stroll up the beach and choose an empty peak.

WAVE TYPE Left and right

WAVE HEIGHT 1–6 ft (0.3–1.8 m)

BREAK TYPE Sand

BEST SWELL NE–SE

BEST WIND SW–NW

BEST TIDE Mid

BEST TIME January–October

HAZARDS Crowds

DIRECTIONS Drive along the Gold Coast Hwy from central Surfers Paradise and turn into one of the many side streets and parking lots adjacent to the beach.

5 Burleigh Heads

Burleigh Heads is a classic sand-on-rock point break, delivering memorable barrels on a thumping southeast groundswell. The wave quality can be a little dependent on sand buildup, but Burleigh picks up plenty of swell and even onshore days can be a lot of fun. The boulders lining the point are slippery, so you may prefer to paddle out from the cove – but watch out for exposed rocks at low tide.

WAVE TYPE Right

WAVE HEIGHT 1–10 ft (0.3–3.1 m)

BREAK TYPE Sand on rock

BEST SWELL SE

BEST WIND SW

BEST TIDE Mid

BEST TIME January–June

HAZARDS Crowds, rocks

DIRECTIONS In Burleigh Heads, turn off the Gold Coast Hwy onto Goodwin Tce, where you'll find plenty of street parking.

6 Currumbin Alley

The Alley used to be a longboarders' haunt. But the creation in 1994 of the Tweed River Entrance Sand Bypassing Project, a sand-dredging operation to the south, resulted in a longer wave that breaks through to the southern corner of Palm Beach. As a result, Currumbin is now more oriented toward high-performance surfing. Quality beach breaks are found north to Elephant Rock; an offshore bar is tackled by tow-surfers in large swells.

WAVE TYPE Right

WAVE HEIGHT 1–8 ft (0.3–2.4 m)

BREAK TYPE Sand

BEST SWELL E–SE

BEST WIND SW

BEST TIDE Mid

BEST TIME January–June

HAZARDS Crowds, rips

DIRECTIONS In Currumbin, turn east off the Gold Coast Hwy onto Duringan St and drive to the parking lot opposite Wallace Nicoll Park.

7 Flat Rock

A lesser-known wave, Flat Rock isn't as consistent or reliable as surrounding breaks, but offers good alternatives under peaky east and northeasterly swells. In particular, it is a worthy option when the wind is straight out of the south, though it doesn't work well when the surf is big. A good option for intermediate surfers looking to get away from the crowds.

WAVE TYPE Left and right

WAVE HEIGHT 1–5 ft (0.3–1.5 m)

BREAK TYPE Sand

BEST SWELL NE–E

BEST WIND S–W

BEST TIDE Mid

BEST TIME January–June

HAZARDS Rips

DIRECTIONS In Tugun, turn off the Gold Coast Hwy onto Wagawn St, and park on Pacific Pde. There is also parking at Kropp Park on Teemangum St.

8 Kirra

Formerly revered for its seemingly endless tubes, Kirra is currently a shadow of its former self, following the creation of the Tweed River Entrance Sand Bypassing Project in 1994, which flooded it with sand. Plans are afoot to rectify the damage done, but only time will tell if Kirra will return to its former glory.

WAVE TYPE Right

WAVE HEIGHT 2–6 ft (0.6–1.8 m)

BREAK TYPE Sand

BEST SWELL E

BEST WIND SE–SW

BEST TIDE Low

BEST TIME January–June

HAZARDS Crowds, rips, currents

DIRECTIONS Kirra is visible from Marine Pde when driving south from Coolangatta. Convenient street parking is available near Kirra and Coolangatta surf lifesaving clubs.

9 Snapper Rocks

Once an average point break, Snapper Rocks is now the jewel in the Gold Coast crown. Following the development of sand-pumping in the area, it has one of the longest and most perfect (and most crowded) sand-bottom point breaks in the world, affectionately known as The Superbank. It hosts the first stop on the World Championship Tour (WCT) each March.

WAVE TYPE Right

WAVE HEIGHT 1–6 ft (0.3–1.8 m)

BREAK TYPE Sand

BEST SWELL E or SE

BEST WIND SE–SW

BEST TIDE Mid

BEST TIME January–June

HAZARDS Crowds, crowds, crowds!

DIRECTIONS Marine Pde runs from Kirra to Snapper Rocks. There is street parking, but the large parking lot at Coolangatta Beach is a better option, as that is where you'll invariably come out of the water after a Superbank ride.

10 Duranbah

Duranbah (or D'Bah) is located in New South Wales, but Queensland surfers have claimed it as their own. Outer banks break up swell lines into peaky A-frames that unload onto the beach. The outer banks themselves sometimes offer good waves during large swells. The most reliable waves are a right-hander off the training wall, and a split peak in the middle.

WAVE TYPE Left and right

WAVE HEIGHT 1–6 ft (0.3–1.8 m)

BREAK TYPE Sand, with a rock groyne at the southern end

BEST SWELL E–SE

BEST WIND SW

BEST TIDE Low

BEST TIME January–June

HAZARDS Crowds

DIRECTIONS From Coolangatta, follow Boundary St or Marine Pde to the top parking lot, or continue down Hill St, turn left into Eden St and park on the side of Flagstaff Hill Rd.

High-rises line the golden sands at Surfers Paradise. In the distance is South Stradbroke Island.

Sunshine Coast, Queensland

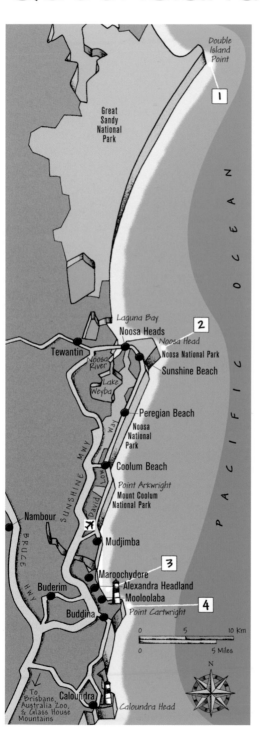

The Sunshine Coast extends from Noosa in the north to Caloundra in the south. Year-round warmth in and out of the water ensures a steady flow of visitors. The winter months can provide blue skies for weeks on end, while the summer's humidity can be uncomfortable. Summer's average maximum air temperature is 82°F (28°C) and the winter average temperature is 72°F (22°C). The average maximum water temperature ranges from 66°F (19°C) in winter to 77°F (25°C) in summer.

While images of warm, peeling waves and a rain-forest backdrop have drawn many surfers here since the early 1960s, the unfortunate reality is that the Sunshine Coast surf is often disappointingly inconsistent. The period from January to May provides the most hope. The stretch from Sunshine Beach through to Coolum often seems to attract the most swell, but, like other stretches along the Sunshine Coast, it is reliant on winds with some west in them for the surf to be clean and smooth.

The closest international airport is Brisbane, which is around 60 miles (97 km) south of Caloundra, and there is a domestic air terminal 3 miles (5 km) north of Maroochydore.

if there's no swell ...

Just 20 minutes drive south of Caloundra is Australia Zoo, which was set up by the late Steve Irwin of *Crocodile Hunter* fame. In the nearby Glass House Mountains, the half-mile (800-m) trek, beginning 2½ miles (4 km) south of the town of Coolum, to the top of 682-foot (208-m) Mount Coolum is rewarded by breathtaking 360-degree views from the summit.

1 Double Island Point

Situated in Great Sandy National Park, north of Noosa, Double Island Point offers beach breaks protected from the northerly wind. The best peaks are often found close to the northern end of the beach. On the northern side of the headland lies a long right-hand point that is often a great ride on a longboard, and can also offer exceptionally long rides for shortboards.

WAVE TYPE Right and left

WAVE HEIGHT 2–12 ft (0.6–3.7 m)

BREAK TYPE Beach and point

BEST SWELL E–SE

BEST WIND E–SE

BEST TIDE Low

BEST TIME February–May

HAZARDS Rocks, sharks

DIRECTIONS From Noosa Heads, drive to the Tewantin ferry, cross the Noosa River and drive north for an hour along the beach. You'll need an off-road vehicle and a mid to low tide to drive the beach. Check tide times before you depart.

2 Noosa National Park

The park contains five point breaks: Granite Bay, Tea Tree, Nationals, Little Cove, and First Point. They require a larger swell to break, so they can be fickle. However, when a cyclone in the Coral Sea sends strong groundswells southward, these bays offer perfect point surf with some extremely long rides – up to 1 mile (1.6 km) long. Koalas can be seen along the walking track.

WAVE TYPE Right

WAVE HEIGHT 3–12 ft (0.9–3.7 m)

BREAK TYPE Point

BEST SWELL NE–SE

BEST WIND SE

BEST TIDE Low

BEST TIME February–April

HAZARDS Crowds, rock jumps

DIRECTIONS In Noosa Heads, turn right into Hastings St. Follow the road to the National Park Entrance. The outer points can only be reached on foot.

3 Alexandra Headland

Also known as "The Bluff" or "Alex," this is a fun and easy wave that almost always provides something ridable. It has both a point break and an adjoining beach break. With quality beach breaks also on offer to the north at Maroochydore and south at Mooloolaba, this area is a hotspot of surfing activity.

WAVE TYPE Mostly right

WAVE HEIGHT 1–12 ft (0.3–3.7 m)

BREAK TYPE Point and beach

BEST SWELL E–SE

BEST WIND SE–S

BEST TIDE Low

BEST TIME February–May

HAZARDS Rocks

DIRECTIONS The point sits right next to Alexandra Pde, the main seafront road in Alexandra Headland. You can't miss it. Paddle out from the beach or from the rock shelf.

4 Point Cartwright

Standing on top of Alexandra Headland, you'll see whether or not Point Cartwright is breaking by looking to the prominent headland and tower to the southeast. This can be a challenging wave, particularly on the outside ledge called Platforms. Not for the fainthearted.

WAVE TYPE Right

WAVE HEIGHT 4–15 ft (1.2–4.6 m)

BREAK TYPE Point

BEST SWELL E–SE

BEST WIND SE–S

BEST TIDE Low

BEST TIME February–May

HAZARDS Rocks, shallow ledge on takeoff

DIRECTIONS From Nicklin Way in Buddina, take Point Cartwright Dr, then turn left onto Pacific Blvd. From the end of the road, it's a short walk over the headland to the point.

Introduction

the great winds

A typhoon is essentially the same as a hurricane or cyclone — a large, revolving, low-pressure weather system that generates powerful winds over a relatively small area. For a typhoon to develop, sea water must become very warm, usually more than 80°F (26.5°C). The name typhoon comes from the Cantonese word *taifung*, meaning "great wind." The area between Guam, the Philippines, and Japan is often called "Typhoon Alley."

Surfers at East Side Beach, Bali, Indonesia. Bali is the main hub for surf touring in Indonesia.

Eastern Asia has been a major surfing destination only for the past 30 years, although globe-trotting explorers such as Australian Peter Troy made forays into the region well before that time. By the mid-1970s, surf films such as *Sea of Joy*, *The Forgotten Island of Santosha*, and *Morning of the Earth* had created an image of the region as an exotic and affordable surfing destination, where waves were big and always on and crowds were small and rarely found.

Surfing destinations in Eastern Asia stretch from Japan south through the Philippines to Indonesia, and face both the Pacific and Indian oceans. The most reliable swells are those that spin across the Indian Ocean from South Africa, eventually crashing ashore on the western and southern coasts of the Indonesian archipelago. Partly for this reason, but also because it is affordable and relatively stable politically, Indonesia remains the most popular surfing destination in Eastern Asia. April to October is the best time for swell here. Islands such as Lombok, Sumba, Sumbawa, Timor, Sulawesi, and Roti all have world-class waves, but there are few places that can provide the kinds of comforts and distractions that Bali can offer. Indonesia was badly affected by the December 2004 tsunami, which left approximately 168,000 Indonesians dead, but is steadily recovering. The reefs of Nias and the Mentawai Islands have moved as a result, but all still continue to offer excellent waves.

Riding the Storms

On the northwestern shore of the Pacific, the surf is reliant on swells fueled by seasonal typhoons. The season runs from June to December, when warm water that pools in the western Pacific near Guam and the Philippines creates ideal conditions for typhoon incubation. In the Philippines, the typhoons usually come in from the east of Mindanao and head in a northwesterly direction before hitting the islands east of Luzon.

Japan lives in fear of typhoons, or tai fu, as they are called locally, which are renowned for the death and destruction they wreak. When the storms rev up and spin out, people everywhere, from the hi-tech cities to sleepy fishing towns, stop and brace themselves for the hellish onslaught that has been compared to being thrown into a giant blender. Surfers, on the other hand, start rubbing their hands together and pouring over weather charts. Surfing has become tremendously popular in Japan in recent years and the country is a safe and easy place to visit, though it can be costly.

Other parts of Eastern Asia offer limited opportunities, mainly on beach breaks. China's coastline remains largely unexplored by surfers, and its geography suggests it would rely more on windswell than groundswell. Hainan, an island in the South China Sea, was surfed by Australian Peter Drouyn in 1986 and has since developed a small local scene.

Vietnam does not get much surf but can produce overhead waves on its central coast during the peak of the typhoon season and it has some great beaches framed by points and reefs, which can generate perfect peelers when conditions are ideal. But being there on such occasions will be as much a matter of good fortune as good planning.

Similarly, Thailand lacks exceptional waves. The island of Phuket off the southwest mainland gets some waves during the country's April-to-September monsoon, but they are not of the quality that warrants a dedicated surfing expedition and closeouts are common.

Though Malaysia, too, lacks major waves, it does have the Sunway Lagoon indoor wave machine, which is capable of churning out waves of up to 6 feet (1.8 m). Situated about 45 minutes drive from Kuala Lumpur, it is the country's busiest tourist attraction.

Nias and Mentawai Islands, Indonesia

Perhaps no place on earth in the past 10 years has graced the covers of surfing magazines more than the Mentawais, a 200-mile (320-km) chain of coral-laden islands some 85 nautical miles (157 km) off the west coast of Sumatra in Indonesia. Its four main islands in the chain are Siberut, Sipura, North Pagai, and South Pagai. Generally, the waves here range from perfect to more perfect to perfectly perfect.

There are more than 80 surf spots in the region, but with three dozen boats each carrying an average of around 10 surfers each day during the April to October dry season, you are in for a rude shock if you think you will be here on your lonesome. Everybody who can afford it wants some of what's on offer here.

However, change is afoot. Tourism authorities have determined that the number of boats and surfers allowed to visit the islands will henceforth be controled. Land-based development will also be subject to sustainable planning, and mooring buoys will be installed to eliminate anchor damage to reefs.

North of the Mentawais lies the region's best-known wave, the mechanically perfect right-hander off Lagundri Bay on Nias Island, about 80 miles (128 km) off the Sumatran coast. The 2004 Boxing Day tsunami, which killed 1,000 people in the area, and the March 2005 earthquake altered much of Nias's coastline, in places moving it over 50 yards (45 m) inland and lifting the land as much as 8 feet (2.4 m). As a result, the "Lagundri Express" has become even more cylindrical.

Accommodation in many areas, notably Nias, consists of basic beach huts, known as losmen, though resorts are springing up. Cerebral malaria is present in populated areas, and should be taken seriously. Do your research on an appropriate preventative before you depart.

1 Asu, Nias

A classic Indonesian left, Asu is the northernmost island in the Hinako group, and the wave is located off the northwestern tip. Long lines of swell wrap around the coral reef, and the seasonal southeast trade winds blow straight offshore. The recent Nias earthquake raised the seafloor in the area as much as 6 ft (1.8 m), giving the wave new characteristics.

WAVE TYPE Left

WAVE HEIGHT 3–12 ft (0.9–3.7 m)

BREAK TYPE Reef point

BEST SWELL S–SW

BEST WIND SE

BEST TIDE Mid–high

BEST TIME April–November

HAZARDS Shallow reef, rocks, sea urchins, malaria

DIRECTIONS Fly to Nias Island, and take local transportation to Lagundri Bay, the main surfing center. Boat trips depart regularly from here.

2 Bawa, Nias

The southernmost island in the Hinako group, Bawa has a big and hollow right at its southeastern tip that has been compared favorably with Sunset Beach in Hawaii. Exposed to all seasonal groundswell, it generates some of the biggest waves in Indonesia. Here, too, the 2005 earthquake raised the seafloor by as much as 6 ft (1.8 m).

WAVE TYPE Right

WAVE HEIGHT 3–15 ft (0.9–4.6 m)

BREAK Type Reef point

BEST Swell S–SW

BEST Wind NW

BEST Tide Mid–high

BEST Time April–November

HAZARDS Shallow reef, rocks, sea urchins, malaria

DIRECTIONS Fly to Nias Island and take local transportation to Lagundri Bay. Boat trips depart regularly from here.

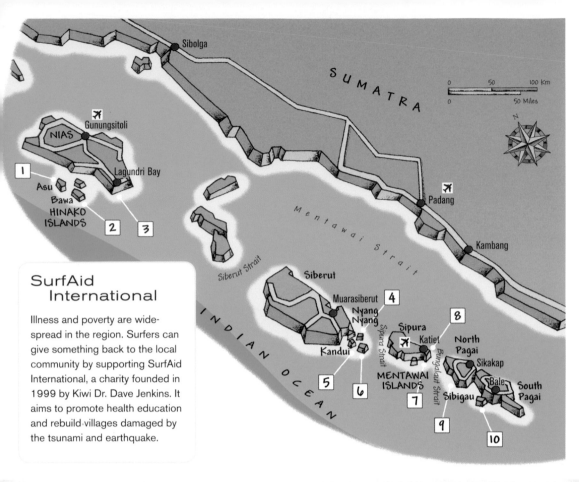

SUMATRA

Sibolga

0   50   100 Km
0   50 Miles

N

Gunungsitoli ✈

NIAS

Lagundri Bay

1

Asu

Bawa

HINAKO ISLANDS

2   3

Padang ✈

Kambang

Mentawai Strait
Siberut Strait

Siberut

SurfAid International

Illness and poverty are wide-spread in the region. Surfers can give something back to the local community by supporting SurfAid International, a charity founded in 1999 by Kiwi Dr. Dave Jenkins. It aims to promote health education and rebuild villages damaged by the tsunami and earthquake.

INDIAN OCEAN

Muarasiberut   4

Nyang Nyang

Kandui

Sipura   Sipura Strait

Katiet ✈

North Pagai

8

Sikakap

MENTAWAI ISLANDS   Bungalaut Strait

5

6

7

Sibigau

Bale

South Pagai

9

10

3 Lagundri Bay, Nias

A legendary wave, the inside reef at Lagundri Bay has been a surfer's nirvana for more than 30 years. A short but flawless right barrel, it has changed since the recent Nias earthquake and is said by many to have been improved by the rise in the seafloor.

WAVE TYPE Right

WAVE HEIGHT 3–10 ft (0.9–3.1 m)

BREAK TYPE Reef point

BEST SWELL S–SW

BEST WIND NW

BEST TIDE Mid–high

BEST TIME April–November

HAZARDS Shallow reef, rocks, sea urchins, malaria

DIRECTIONS Fly to Nias Island and take local transportation to Lagundri Bay.

4 Bankvaults, Nyang Nyang

A thick and hollow peak over a shallow reef at the eastern tip of Nyang Nyang Island, Bankvaults picks up all swells and delivers deep barrels and broken boards in equal measure. Its reliability during smaller swells makes it a favorite destination in the Mentawai Islands for charter boats.

WAVE TYPE Right

WAVE HEIGHT 3–12 ft (0.9–3.7 m)

BREAK TYPE Reef point

BEST SWELL S–SW

BEST WIND SE

BEST TIDE Mid–high

BEST TIME April–November

HAZARDS Shallow reef, powerful waves, crowds

DIRECTIONS Fly to Padang on Sumatra. More than 60 surf charter boats serve the Mentawai Islands from this port town, and there are several new land-based resorts on islands in the area.

5 Nokandui, Kandui

A long and screaming hollow left-hand barrel, Nokandui is located off the northwest corner of Kandui (Karangmajat) Island, in the Playgrounds area. It's enticing, yet not for the faint of heart: less-than-capable surfers can find themselves in the terrifying situation of straightening out onto near-dry reef, as the wave passes them by.

WAVE TYPE Left

WAVE HEIGHT 3–12 ft (0.9–3.7 m)

BREAK TYPE Reef point

BEST SWELL S–SW

BEST WIND SE

BEST TIDE Mid–high

BEST TIME April–November

HAZARDS Shallow reef, powerful waves, crowds

DIRECTIONS Fly to Padang on the coast of Sumatra island. More than 60 surf charter boats serve the Mentawai Islands from this port town, and there are several new land-based resorts on islands in the area.

6 Rifles, Kandui

A very long right tube, Rifles works only on the biggest of southerly-angled swells and northwest winds. Such is the quality of the wave, located off the southeast corner of Kandui (Karangmajat) Island, that boat captains will pull the anchor at the first sign of a favorable swell and wind forecast and head for Rifles on the chance it will be breaking.

WAVE TYPE Right

WAVE HEIGHT 3–12 ft (0.9–3.7 m)

BREAK TYPE Reef point

BEST SWELL S–SW

BEST WIND NW

BEST TIDE Mid–high

BEST TIME April–November

HAZARDS Shallow reef, powerful waves, crowds

DIRECTIONS Fly to Padang on the coast of Sumatra, then take a charter boat. There are several resorts in the area.

A big left-hander, Thunders on South Pagai Island is renowned for its consistency, particularly in summer.

7 Lance's Right, Sipura

Named after the Australian surfer Lance Knight, who discovered it in the mid-1980s, this is one of the world's best waves, a photogenic right-hander in front of Katiet village on the southern tip of Sipura Island. Often perfect, it's the number-one spot on every charter itinerary, and the "Keyhole" anchorage in front of the lineup can host as many as 15 boats on a good swell, with additional land-based surfers in the water.

WAVE TYPE Right

WAVE HEIGHT 3–12 ft (0.9–3.7 m)

BREAK TYPE Reef point

BEST SWELL S–SW

BEST WIND NW

BEST TIDE Mid–high

BEST TIME April–November

HAZARDS Shallow reef, powerful waves, crowds

DIRECTIONS Fly to Padang, then take a charter boat or charter flight to Sipura Island. There are several new resorts in Katiet village, by the wave.

8 Lance's Left, Sipura

Situated on the opposite side of Sipura Island from Lance's Right and linked by a trail through the forest from Katiet village is Lance's Left. It's at its best on westerly-angled swells and takes a southeast wind. Another popular spot for surf charter boats, it may host as many as ten boats when the swell and wind conditions are favorable.

WAVE TYPE Left

WAVE HEIGHT 3–12 ft (0.9–3.7 m)

BREAK TYPE Reef point

BEST SWELL S–SW

BEST WIND SE

BEST TIDE Mid–high

BEST TIME April–November

HAZARDS Shallow reef, powerful waves, crowds

DIRECTIONS Fly to Padang, then take a charter boat or charter flight to Sipura Island. There are several new resorts in Katiet village, by the wave.

9 Macaroni's, North Pagai

Voted the world's "funnest" wave by many top professional surfers, Macaroni's on North Pagai Island is a short but perfectly shaped left-hander, breaking over a reef shelf into a deep bay. There's a barrel section on the takeoff followed by several juicy maneuver sections as the wave bends into the bay. It's surfable on all tides, and most winds and swells.

WAVE TYPE Left

WAVE HEIGHT 3–8 ft (0.9–2.4 m)

BREAK TYPE Reef point

BEST SWELL S–SW

BEST WIND NE (rare)

BEST TIDE Mid–high

BEST TIME April–November

HAZARDS Shallow reef, powerful waves, crowds

DIRECTIONS Fly to Padang on the coast of Sumatra, then take a charter boat or the ferry to Sikakap on North Pagai. There's a new land-based luxury resort at Macaroni's, which has speedboats that can take you to other breaks.

10 Thunders, South Pagai

A top destination for every Mentawai surf charter, Thunders is a big left-hander off the northwest side of South Pagai Island. The main drawcard is extreme consistency, as Thunders is exposed to all swells from the southern Indian Ocean, and can produce quality waves from waist-high to triple overhead.

WAVE TYPE Left

WAVE HEIGHT 3–15 ft (0.9–4.6 m)

BREAK TYPE Reef point

BEST SWELL S–SW

BEST WIND SE

BEST TIDE Mid–high

BEST TIME April–November

HAZARDS Shallow reef, powerful waves, crowds

DIRECTIONS Fly to Padang on the coast of Sumatra, then take a charter boat. There are several new land-based resorts on South Pagai Island, some offering speedboats to access other breaks.

1 One Palm Point, Java

Located off Panaitan Island, off the west coast of Java, this is one of the world's best but most dangerous waves. Ridiculously shallow, it produces some of the longest and most perfect tubes found anywhere. The swell really needs to be well overhead in order to break in slightly deeper water.

WAVE TYPE Left

WAVE HEIGHT 5–18 ft (1.5–5.5 m)

BREAK TYPE Reef

BEST SWELL SW

BEST WIND E–SE

BEST TIDE Mid–high

BEST TIME April–October

HAZARDS Shallow water and sharp coral reef, isolated location

DIRECTIONS It's best to travel with a reputable charter-boat operator.

2 Grajagan, Java

Arguably the world's best left, Grajagan (G-Land) is a consistently good but demanding wave, inspiring both fear and elation. It has four sections: Kong's, Money Trees, Launching Pad, and Speedies; they rarely link up, but there's enough length of ride on each section, with the wave getting hollower and faster as it goes.

WAVE TYPE Left

WAVE HEIGHT 4–25 ft (1.2–7.6 m)

BREAK TYPE Reef

BEST SWELL SW

BEST WIND E–SE

BEST TIDE Mid–high

BEST TIME April–October

HAZARDS Sharp coral reef, sea snakes in the lagoon, Speedies' shallow end section, isolation

DIRECTIONS As G-Land is in a remote national park in eastern Java, it is best to visit on a tour with one of the surf camps at G-Land. Book before you leave or in Bali.

Java, Bali, and Lombok, Indonesia

Although almost certainly ridden in the 1960s, Bali has provided a rite-of-passage for surfers, particularly Australians, since its first widely publicized ride, made by 15-year-old Sydneysider Steven Cooney, at Uluwatu in 1971. Cooney rode on a 5-ft 9-in (1.8-m) single fin without a leash, and his ride was captured by the lens of Alby Falzon for the seminal surfing flick *Morning of the Earth*. Today, Bali remains the starting or ending point for most surf expeditions through Indonesia.

Waves are to be found in Bali most of the year, with the May-to-October dry season firing in swells fanned by reliable offshore winds. From Medewi on the southwest coast down to Green Ball Bay tucked around the corner from Uluwatu, there are some world-class left-handers to be found. During the wet season from December to March, the winds are

offshore on the southeast surf breaks, which are mostly right-handers. Tides are critical.

Lombok, 31 miles (50 km) east of Bali, is around 50 miles (80 km) from top to bottom and about 43 miles (70 km) across. Some say it's like Bali used to be, but the crowds, especially at the sometimes-perfect, but

3 Legian Beach, Bali

Legian's beach breaks are perfect for learners when small (shoulder high) but become thumping and dangerous when the swell is large (double overhead). High tide helps the waves to peel better into the rips and channels. Low tide is surfable but tends to close out more. A bonus is that Legian's is usually less crowded than Uluwatu, Padang, or Bingin.

WAVE TYPE Left and right

WAVE HEIGHT 2–18 ft (0.6–5.5 m)

BREAK TYPE Beach

BEST SWELL SW

BEST WIND E

BEST TIDE Mid–high

BEST TIME March–October

HAZARDS Rips

DIRECTIONS Legian Beach adjoins Kuta Beach to the north. It can be accessed from numerous points along the coast. There are many hotels and restaurants on the beachfront.

4 Kuta and Airport Reefs, Bali

Kuta Reef is a perfect ride, up to 100 yards (100 m) or so, that's a little easier than places like Uluwatu. For this reason, plus the fact it's close to Kuta, it gets crowded. Low tide is too shallow. To the south are Airport Lefts and Airport Rights. The lefts are a little bigger but less mechanical than Kuta Reef; the right is sucky and can handle serious size.

WAVE TYPE Lefts and a right

WAVE HEIGHT 4–15 ft (1.2–4.6 m)

BREAK TYPE Reef

BEST SWELL SW

BEST WIND E

BEST TIDE Mid–high

BEST TIME April–October

HAZARDS Sharp coral reef

DIRECTIONS From Kuta, travel south to the village of Tuban. Hire a boat from the beach here and you can check out all three waves in one trip if you wish.

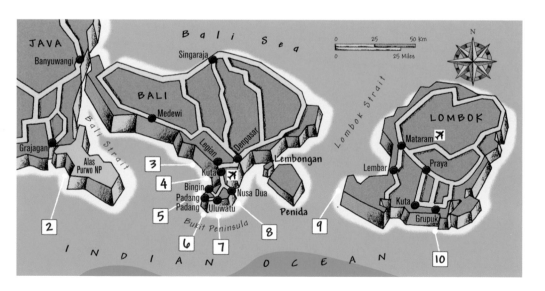

often-fickle Desert Point, can be as big as those at Uluwatu. Stretching west from Bali, Java has 746 miles (1,200 km) of Indian Ocean coastline. The jewel in the Javanese crown is Grajagan or G-Land, which became a commercial surf camp in the late 1970s. The best time to surf Java and Lombok is between April and September.

tread warily

Sharp reefs at many of these destinations mean that good insurance is essential. Sell your soul, lose your passport, gamble away your money, but don't part with your reef booties.

A surfer launches himself into the barrel of a wave off the coast of Java, Indonesia.

5 Bingin, Bali

Bingin is a short but extremely mechanical barrel. The takeoff zone is tight and usually crowded; the end section is perilously shallow. To the south of the reef is Impossibles, a long, wally left that offers some enjoyable sections; it's a place to escape the crowds. Nearby is Dreamland, a fun right that's the softest and safest wave on the Bukit Peninsula.

WAVE TYPE Left

WAVE HEIGHT 5–12 ft (1.5–3.7 m)

BREAK TYPE Reef

BEST SWELL SW

BEST WIND E

BEST TIDE Mid

BEST TIME April–October

HAZARDS Sharp coral reef

DIRECTIONS Travel south from Kuta, turn right into Pecatu village, and follow the signs to Bingin. The journey takes about 35 to 40 minutes.

6 Padang Padang, Bali

Padang Padang is a world-class barrel that only breaks once Uluwatu gets really big. The sharp reef has holes and canyons, making it particularly dangerous, the crowds can be tough, and the wave doesn't break well under head high. But when it all comes together, mind-blowing pits are on offer to anyone with the ability and ticker. At least the paddle out is safe and easy!

WAVE TYPE Left

WAVE HEIGHT 6–15 ft (1.8–4.6 m)

BREAK TYPE Reef

BEST SWELL SW

BEST WIND E

BEST TIDE Mid–high

BEST TIME April–October

HAZARDS Sharp coral reef, canyons in reef, pitching lip

DIRECTIONS Drive south from Kuta for about 40 minutes. Turn right off the main road when you see the Padang Padang signs.

7 Uluwatu, Bali

Even if you don't surf this wave, the views from the adjacent warungs (small restaurants) are spectacular. The approach to the break is through the famous Ulu cave and it can be intimidating when the swell is up; the cave is also your only exit point, so your timing has to be right at high tide. Uluwatu is never flat, always crowded, and offers plenty of juice.

WAVE TYPE Left

WAVE HEIGHT 4–30 ft (1.2–9.1 m)

BREAK TYPE Reef

BEST SWELL SW

BEST WIND E–SE

BEST TIDE Low tide

BEST TIME April–October

HAZARDS Sharp coral reef, shallow end section, powerful wave, missing the cave when trying to come back in

DIRECTIONS Drive 45 minutes south of Kuta along the main road of the Bukit Peninsula. The turnoff is clearly signposted.

8 Nusa Dua, Bali

When the swell is small, this long right reef break with varying sections is an easy ride. However, on a booming double-overhead swell, it has plenty of power. Between April and October, you'll need to surf it early in the morning. Come December, however, with the arrival of the trade winds, the many breaks along this coast are offshore all day long.

WAVE TYPE Right

WAVE HEIGHT 4–25 ft (1.2–7.6 m)

BREAK TYPE Reef

BEST SWELL S

BEST WIND W

BEST TIDE All

BEST TIME December–March

HAZARDS Reef

DIRECTIONS This is the main beach at the town of Nusa Dua. Hire a boat to take you out to the lineup.

9 Desert Point, Lombok

Desert Point is one of the best waves on the planet, offering barrel rides of up to 20 seconds. It is super-fast with a growing end section that can devour even the most experienced shack-master. It needs a huge swell to fire up and even with that can be fickle, with tides and strong currents wreaking havoc. Worth the wait, though.

WAVE TYPE Left

WAVE HEIGHT 6–15 ft (1.8–4.6 m)

BREAK TYPE Reef

BEST SWELL SW

BEST WIND E

BEST TIDE Mid–high

BEST TIME April–October

HAZARDS Sharp coral reef, killer end section

DIRECTIONS Catch a ferry from Bali to the port of Lembar (on the island of Lombok), and hire a driver to take you to this isolated outpost.

10 Grupuk, Lombok

Grupuk is a large bay and village on the south coast of Lombok. The outside right picks up plenty of swell and can be ridden even on huge days. Inside the bay is a much smaller right that offers a short but enjoyable ride over reef that is not too gnarly. On the eastern side is a left that can also be quite good.

WAVE TYPE Left and right

WAVE HEIGHT 5–18 feet (1.5–5.5 m)

BREAK TYPE Reef

BEST SWELL SW

BEST WIND NW–NE

BEST TIDE Mid–high

BEST TIME April–November

HAZARDS Coral reef

DIRECTIONS Drive about 30 minutes east along the main road from Kuta (in Lombok, not Bali!) to the small fishing village of Grupuk. You will need to hire a boat with a driver to access these waves.

Philippines

With more than 7,100 islands, the Philippines has a multitude of breaks, but many are difficult to access and are dependent on inconsistent swell periods. There are three main surf areas. The large island of Luzon in the north has the most surf and the most surfers, on its northeast coast. In the northeast, Catanduanes is the site of Majestics, a world-class wave, though very fickle. The island of Siargao in the east has Cloud 9 — some call it "Crowd Line" — which is probably the country's best-known wave.

The Philippine climate is tropical, with a dry season from April to June and a rainy season from June to October. The hottest months are April and May. Surf here relies on easterly swells generated by typhoons, most of them heading toward Japan, during the July-to-November tropical storm season. The Habagat is the southwest monsoon, characterized by a southwest wind that buffets the northern half of the country through the wet season. The Amihan monsoon, driven by a northeast wind, blows across the northern Philippines during the dry season. In all, around 15 to 20 typhoons each provide a few days of head-high or double-overhead waves with offshore winds. Make no mistake, the place can crank, but timing is critical!

On domestic flights, some smaller planes may not take surfboards, so it pays to check ahead; overland and ferry travel might be a better option at times. Road conditions vary, however: the highways to the well-known surf destinations are okay, but once you leave the main roads you'll be better off with a vehicle that has stronger than standard suspension, ideally a four-wheel-drive.

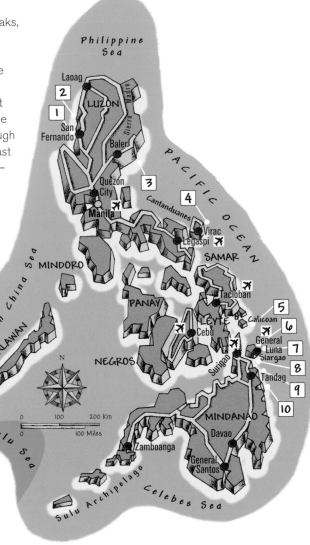

tread warily

Razor sharp coral breaks are a hazard on many Philippine beaches, and they are not the only danger surf travelers might have to contend with. As well as active volcanoes and the occasional earthquake or typhoon, the Philippines are afflicted by terrorism and high levels of crime. Check your government's travel advisories before you set off.

1 Urbiztondo Beach, Luzon

An open beach break facing the South China Sea, Urbiztondo takes all swells. It is popular with beginners and as a surf contest venue and can be crowded on weekends and holidays, but the peaks are often empty during the week.

WAVE TYPE Left and right

WAVE HEIGHT 3–5 ft (0.9–1.5 m)

BREAK TYPE Sandbar

BEST SWELL NW–N

BEST WIND NE–E

BEST TIDE All

BEST TIME November–February

HAZARDS Weekend crowds, beginners, heavy traffic, petty thieves

DIRECTIONS Drive or take a bus north from Manila along the highway for six to eight hours, depending on traffic, to San Fernando, capital of La Union Province. Urbiztondo is just north of town in the municipality of San Juan, barangay Urbiztondo.

2 Monaliza Point, Luzon

The Philippines' most popular surf spot and a national competition venue, Monaliza is accessible by car from Metro Manila, and can be packed on weekends. Long rights break over a reef shelf, and there are several takeoff spots depending on tide and swell direction.

WAVE TYPE Right

WAVE HEIGHT 3–8 ft (0.9–2.4 m)

BREAK TYPE Reef shelf, some rocks

BEST SWELL NW–N

BEST WIND NE–E

BEST TIDE All

BEST TIME November–February

HAZARDS Weekend crowds, beginners, heavy traffic, petty thieves

DIRECTIONS Drive or take a bus north from Manila along the highway (six to eight hours, depending on traffic) to San Fernando, capital of La Union Province. The point is north of town in the municipality of San Juan, barangay Urbiztondo, by the Monaliza guesthouse.

3 Cemento, Luzon

This reef break offers thick, hollow rights, regular barrels, and a cutback section as the wave backs off into deeper water. Positioning is critical and the takeoff zone tight – and dangerous, as it runs over a shallow live coral reef. The "Baler Boys" ride it well, and are friendly toward visitors who show respect.

WAVE TYPE Right

WAVE HEIGHT 3–6 ft (0.9–1.8 m)

BREAK TYPE Live coral reef

BEST SWELL N–NE

BEST WIND S–SW

BEST TIDE High

BEST TIME July–November

HAZARDS Weekend crowds; coral reef; powerful, hollow waves; typhoons making landfall

DIRECTIONS From Manila, drive or take a bus north over the Sierra Madre mountains to Baler in Aurora Province. The journey can take up to 12 hours. Cemento is a short walk from the main beach at Sabang in Baler.

4 Puraran Bay, Catanduanes

This high-quality, hollow right reef break is fueled by inconsistent seasonal typhoon swells. The waves can be fun up to head high, and become a huge open barrel on bigger swells. Takeoff is over a shallow, seaweed-covered reef and the wave ends in a deep channel, quite far from shore. Local surfers are friendly, but resident foreigners regularly intimidate visitors.

WAVE TYPE Right

WAVE HEIGHT 3–10 ft (0.9–3.1 m)

BREAK TYPE Coral reef

BEST SWELL N–E typhoon

BEST WIND S–SW

BEST TIDE High, or low tide on small swells

BEST TIME July–November

HAZARDS Hostile expats, coral reef, powerful waves, typhoons making landfall; communist rebels active in area, but rarely bother visitors

DIRECTIONS Fly from Manila to Virac on Catanduanes, then take a tricycle or minivan to the beach accommodation at Puraran Bay.

5 ABCD, Calicoan

Situated on scenic Calicoan Island, these right and left breaks are on an easily accessible sand beach right in front of The Surf Camp, a deluxe resort with luxury cottages and a swimming pool. The surf breaks into a channel in the barrier reef, producing fun waves up to 6 ft (1.8 m) high.

WAVE TYPE Left and right

WAVE HEIGHT 3–6 ft (0.9–1.8 m)

BREAK TYPE Coral reef

BEST SWELL N–E

BEST WIND S–SW

BEST TIDE All

BEST TIME July–November

HAZARDS Shallow coral reef, rocks

DIRECTIONS Fly from Manila to Tacloban city in Leyte, then hire a minivan taxi for the three-hour drive over the San Juanico Bridge to Calicoan via Guiuan in southern Samar.

6 Cloud 9, Siargao

This right reef break at Tuason Point on Siargao Island, in Surigao del Norte Province, is by far the best known in the Philippines. It has a thick peak takeoff, as the wave focuses on the shallow reef, then a clean open barrel leading into a narrow channel. It can be very hollow and dangerous, and the takeoff is critical.

WAVE TYPE Right with some lefts

WAVE HEIGHT 3–8 ft (0.9–2.4 m)

BREAK TYPE Coral reef

BEST SWELL N–E typhoon

BEST WIND S–SW

BEST TIDE High (very shallow at low tide)

BEST TIME July–November

HAZARDS Shallow coral reef, crowds, rocks, strong current in narrow channel

DIRECTIONS Fly from Manila to Cebu city, then to Siargao; or take a ferry to Surigao city in Mindanao followed by a boat to Dapa in Siargao. Then take a jeepney to the town of General Luna or accommodation at Tuason Point.

7 Tuesday Rock, Siargao

Located at the base of a small island 2½ miles (4 km) offshore from Cloud 9, this right reef-shelf break is accessible only by boat. Large swells wrap around the base of the island, and break into a deep channel. The wave is long and workable, with barrel sections.

WAVE HEIGHT 3–12 ft (0.9–3.7 m)

BREAK TYPE Coral reef

BEST SWELL N–E

BEST WIND S–SW

BEST TIDE High (very shallow at low tide)

BEST TIME July–November

HAZARDS Shallow coral reef, rocks

DIRECTIONS Fly from Manila to Cebu city, then to Siargao; or take a ferry to Surigao city in Mindanao followed by a boat to Dapa in Siargao. Then take a jeepney to General Luna or accommodation in the Tuason Point area.

8 Pansukian Reef, Siargao

A right reef break with clean hollow barrels, Pansukian lies some 3 miles (4.8 km) offshore (boat access only) from Pansukian Tropical Resort and General Luna. Sheltered, it requires a big typhoon swell to break and the waves will be about half the size of more exposed waves like Cloud 9. It's usually uncrowded.

WAVE TYPE Right

WAVE HEIGHT 3–6 ft (0.9–1.8 m)

BREAK TYPE Coral reef

BEST SWELL N–E

BEST WIND S–SW

BEST TIDE High (very shallow at low tide)

BEST TIME July–November

HAZARDS Shallow coral reef, rocks, strong current in channel

DIRECTIONS Fly from Manila to Cebu city, then to Siargao; or take a ferry to Surigao city in Mindanao followed by a boat to Dapa in Siargao. Then take a jeepney to Pansukian Tropical Resort, General Luna, or Tuason Point.

Within reach of Manila, Urbiztondo Beach in La Union Province is the Philippines' most popular surf area.

9 Lanuza River Mouth, Mindanao

A tide-sensitive river-mouth sandbar break that can go from easy and fun on a high tide with a small swell, to long, grinding barrels on a low tide and big swell, Lanuza is difficult to catch. But when it breaks on a big swell and low tide, it's one of the best waves in the Philippines.

WAVE TYPE Right

WAVE HEIGHT 3–12 ft (0.9–3.7 m)

BREAK TYPE Gravel sandbar at river mouth

BEST SWELL N–E

BEST WIND S–SW

BEST TIDE Low

BEST TIME July–November

HAZARDS River-borne rubbish, sharks, bandits

DIRECTIONS Fly from Manila to Cebu city, then to Surigao city, or take the ferry to Surigao city. Catch a local bus to Lanuza town (unfortunately, the highway is notorious for bandits and rebel New People's Army holdups). Stay in nearby Tandag, as there is no formal accommodation in Lanuza.

10 Jelly's Point, Mindanao

Located on the far end of Lanuza Bay, Jelly's can only be reached by boat. It's a long and hollow right reef point, and usually twice as big as the more protected waves inside the bay. There is a fishing village on the beach. Never crowded, and rarely surfed.

WAVE TYPE Right

WAVE HEIGHT 3–12 ft (0.9–3.7 m)

BREAK TYPE Reef point

BEST SWELL N–E

BEST WIND S–SW

BEST TIDE Mid–high

BEST TIME July–November

HAZARDS Shallow reef, rocks, sea urchins

DIRECTIONS Fly from Manila to Cebu city, then to Surigao city; or take the ferry to Surigao city. Catch a local bus to Tandag town (unfortunately, the highway is notorious for bandits and rebel New People's Army holdups). Accommodation is available in Tandag; hire a boat locally to get to Jelly's Point.

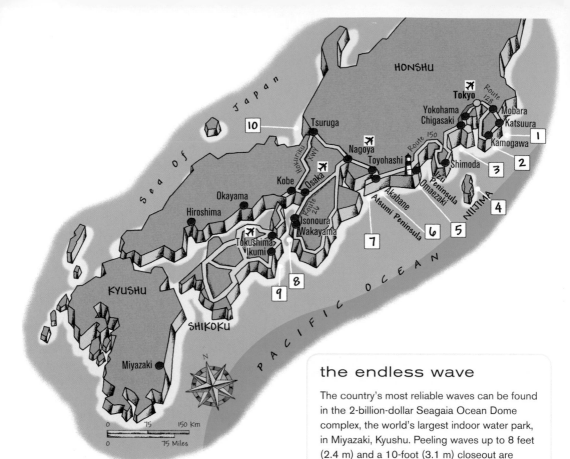

the endless wave

The country's most reliable waves can be found in the 2-billion-dollar Seagaia Ocean Dome complex, the world's largest indoor water park, in Miyazaki, Kyushu. Peeling waves up to 8 feet (2.4 m) and a 10-foot (3.1 m) closeout are possible on its "Great Bank." You can't take your own board, but must hire one on site.

Japan

The Japanese islands of Honshu, Hokkaido, Shikoku, and Kyushu, as well as thousands of smaller islands, are rarely visited by wave-seeking foreigners. However, they are home to more than 750,000 surfers, and can offer some superb wave action. Most of it takes place on the eastern, Pacific-facing coasts, which catch the deep ocean swells and typhoons. The coast facing the Sea of Japan gets swells from local storms but also long periods of onshore winds.

Summer offers the best waves and weather, while spring and fall provide the calmest conditions, fewer crowds, usually clear and sunny weather, and comfortable water temperatures. Most waves come from small lows off the coast, or prolonged periods of onshore wind. Spring seems to get more swell than fall. Winter is for the brave. In most places, it is near freezing and you'll need a full suit, gloves, hood, and boots. However, there will be no crowds and the weather is often clear, with crisp offshore winds. Winters aside, it's wise to avoid weekends and public holidays — you won't believe the lineup for the lineup!

Swell direction is a big factor in Japan, and on any given swell it is almost impossible to know for sure what will be working without heading down to the coast and looking at the water movement. Somewhere that was huge and out of control on the last typhoon can be flat on the next, and then perfect on the one after. At the height of the typhoon season, August and September, when the storms pump through with a regularity of almost one a week, there is a lot of searching to do!

Transport, accommodation, and other services are all first-rate, though the language can be a challenge for many visitors. Coastal pollution is a problem in a few areas, especially near cities and after rain near river mouths.

1 Malibu

Malibu is a right reef break located in the town of Katsuura. When it's on, Malibu is always crowded and it's probably one of Japan's most famous surfing spots, thanks partly to the Quiksilver Pro being held here in 2005. It offers a bowling section to carve up or pull into, a long fun wall to go to town on, and some hollower sections inside.

WAVE TYPE Left and right

WAVE HEIGHT 2–6 ft (0.6–1.8 m)

BREAK TYPE Reef

BEST SWELL E–S

BEST WIND N

BEST TIDE All

BEST TIME June–October

HAZARDS Rocks, beginners, rips during large swells, typhoons making landfall

DIRECTIONS From Mobara, take Route 128 through Ohara to Katsuura. The road goes right past Malibu and there is plenty of parking.

2 Maruki

A beach break in the town of Kamogawa, Maruki is one of the most consistent spots in the Chiba region, and is popular with surfers from Tokyo and Yokohama. It is best in an 11-foot (3.4-m) northeast swell and northerly winds, when big fat lefts roll in and suck up on the inside. A long rock platform on the eastern side provides access to the lineup when it's too hard to paddle out.

WAVE TYPE Left and right

WAVE HEIGHT 2–11 ft (0.6–3.4 m)

BREAK TYPE Beach

BEST SWELL NE or S

BEST WIND N

BEST TIDE All

BEST TIME March, July–October

HAZARDS Crowds, rips during large swells, typhoons making landfall

DIRECTIONS Follow Route 128 from Tokyo; it passes the beach as you come out of the tunnel south of Amatsu. There is parking by the beach.

3 Chigasaki

At the center of the Shonan resort region and close to Tokyo, Chigasaki gets crowded beyond belief in summer. It is prone to long flat spells and the waves are usually small, but it comes alive during the late summer and early fall typhoon season. Waves get up to 7 ft (2.1 m) during typhoons, but anything over that height generally closes out.

WAVE TYPE Left and right

WAVE HEIGHT 2–7 ft (0.6–2.1 m)

BREAK TYPE Beach

BEST SWELL SE

BEST WIND NW

BEST TIDE Low–mid

BEST TIME July–October

HAZARDS Crowds, beginners, typhoons making landfall

DIRECTIONS In Tokyo, jump on the JR Tokaido Line and get off at Chigasaki Station. From the south exit, walk down any of the main roads, which all lead to the beach.

4 Habushiura Beach

Situated on Niijima Island, this long, beautiful beach, with clean, clear blue water, has good-quality beach breaks generated by outside sandbanks. The sands provide a range of options and it is seldom crowded. It can be dangerous for swimmers at high tide, however, as the sand drops out near the shore.

WAVE TYPE Left and right

WAVE HEIGHT 2–8 ft (0.6–2.4 m)

BREAK TYPE Beach

BEST SWELL NE

BEST WIND W

BEST TIDE Low

BEST TIME March–December

HAZARDS Rips, typhoons making landfall

DIRECTIONS Catch the ferry from Tokyo or from Shimoda at the tip of the Izu Peninsula. Either take your car on the ferry or (much better) hire a bicycle on the island.

5 Omaezaki

Omaezaki is a famous fishing town with a lighthouse and a great surf beach. The beach collects most swell from the west but with enough swell from the east–southeast it produces long left-breaking waves. It's a favorite among experienced surfers for its consistent wave shape. It will close out over 7 ft (2.1 m).

WAVE TYPE Left and right

WAVE HEIGHT 1–8 ft (0.3–2.4 m)

BREAK TYPE Beach with some reef

BEST SWELL E

BEST WIND NE

BEST TIDE All

BEST TIME March–Dec

HAZARDS Rocks, currents, typhoons making landfall, nuclear power plant!

DIRECTIONS From Hamamatsu, take Route 150 along the beautiful Enshu Coast and follow the signs to Omaezaki. The beach road starts from under the lighthouse and runs west. You can surf anywhere along there.

6 Long Beach

This popular beach in Akabane Cho in Tahara city attracts all levels of surfers and is often crowded at weekends. However, it is an attractive beach with some nice (occasionally really nice) left-handers off the point. The beach to the west also gets good waves. Long Beach is the venue for the annual Tahara Pro WQS contest.

WAVE TYPE Left and right

WAVE HEIGHT 1–6 ft (0.3–1.8 m)

BREAK TYPE Point and beach

BEST SWELL SE

BEST WIND NW

BEST TIDE All

BEST TIME March–December

HAZARDS Rocks, beginners, rips during large swells, typhoons making landfall

DIRECTIONS From Toyohashi city, head to Route 42, following the coast to Irago. Turn off Route 42 at Akabane. The beach is well signposted.

7 Sentan

When the swell is massive from a typhoon or low-pressure system, Sentan often becomes the only remaining option as other spots begin to close out. A long point break with left-breaking waves, it is typically slow and full, but in the right conditions experienced surfers can find a few workable sections and even a barrel.

WAVE TYPE Left

WAVE HEIGHT 2–8 ft (0.6–2.4 m)

BREAK TYPE Long point

BEST SWELL S

BEST WIND NE–E

BEST TIDE Low–mid

BEST TIME July–October

HAZARDS Strong currents, concrete breakwaters, rocks, crowds, beginners, typhoons making landfall

DIRECTIONS Sentan is at the tip of the Atsumi Peninsula. From Toyohashi, take Route 259 and follow the road signs to Irago; the beach is right next to the Irago ferry terminal.

8 Isonoura

Isonoura is the closest surf spot to the city of Osaka. Most of the year it is small and flat; however, when the summer typhoon season arrives and pushes up a good southerly swell, it comes alive with clean lines in the 2–5 ft (0.6–1.5 m) range, occasionally bringing hollow barrels. When it is 3 ft (0.9 m) or less, it gets unbelievably crowded!

WAVE TYPE Left and right

WAVE HEIGHT 1–5 ft (0.9–1.5 m)

BREAK TYPE Beach

BEST SWELL S–SW

BEST WIND NW–N

BEST TIDE All

BEST TIME August–November

HAZARDS Crowds, typhoons making landfall

DIRECTIONS Head south from Osaka on Route 26 to Isonoura. A maze of streets leads to the beach — best to ask for directions! Alternatively, take the train to Isonoura, on the Nankai Kada line; the beach is just west of the station.

When all else fails, the Seagaia Ocean Dome at Miyazaki offers constant, dependable surf.

9 Ikumi

Located on Shikoku, Ikumi catches a lot of swell and usually has the biggest surf in the area. Conditions are best when the swell is small to medium as it tends to close out when over 8 ft (2.4 m). The facilities, which include parking, toilets, showers, and accommodation, are excellent, but it can get crowded.

WAVE TYPE Left and right

WAVE HEIGHT 2–8 ft (0.6–2.4 m)

BREAK TYPE Beach break

BEST SWELL E–SE

BEST WIND SW–W

BEST TIDE All

BEST TIME July–November

HAZARDS Crowds on weekends, typhoons making landfall

DIRECTIONS Drive across the bridge from Kobe to Tokushima or take the ferry from Wakayama to Tokushima. Then follow Route 55 south to Ikumi.

10 Tsuruga

This beautiful area offers a number of different beach breaks. Conditions are often forgiving and the waves slow-breaking, making it ideal for beginners – in summer especially, small, easy waves can be enjoyed here. But there is also a good range of other waves for more experienced surfers. It's at its best in the fall months, when you will need a wetsuit.

WAVE TYPE Left and right

WAVE HEIGHT 1–4 ft (0.3–1.2 m)

BREAK TYPE Beach

BEST SWELL NW–NE

BEST WIND SE–SW

BEST TIDE All

BEST TIME September–December

HAZARDS Concrete breakwater, occasional strong currents, typhoons making landfall

DIRECTIONS Take the Hokuriku Expressway from Osaka and turn off at the Tsuruga exit. Then follow Route 8 to the coast.

CHAPTER 8

The Indian Ocean

Introduction

Madagascar

Réunion and Mauritius

Maldives

Sri Lanka

Introduction

The Indian Ocean has more than 41,000 miles (almost 66,000 km) of coastline exposed to long fetches of storm swell, as well as a great diversity of coastal environments, so it's not surprising that there are thousands of surf breaks on its shores that remain unknown. To find them, you'll need time, money, patience, a taste for exotic cultures, and a subdued aversion to risk. New frontiers aplenty await the adventurous. Are you ready?

Covering an area of 42,599 million sq miles (68,556 million sq km), the Indian Ocean is the third largest of the world's five oceans (behind the Pacific and Atlantic oceans, but ahead of the Southern and Arctic oceans). It has some of the longest traveling swells in the world, most notably along the 6,200-mile (almost 10,000-km) corridor between the southern tips of Africa and Australia.

The climate north of the equator is affected by a monsoon season from October until April, during which strong northeast winds blow; from May until October, south and west winds prevail. In the Arabian Sea, the monsoon brings rain to the Indian subcontinent; in the Southern Hemisphere, the winds generally are milder, but summer storms near Mauritius can be severe.

Indian Ocean surf areas are generally far-flung and hard to get to. Reaching the Maldives from Los Angeles, for example, requires around 30 hours of travel. Several flights may be required to reach some destinations and tourist infrastructure can be little developed. Tropical diseases and occasional political instability can also be hazards, so make sure you check travel advisories and obtain the appropriate inoculations and preventative medicines before you head off. The rewards, however, include fascinating traditional cultures, pristine beaches, and uncrowded but world-class waves.

New Frontiers

In addition to the better-known, or at least developing, surf areas featured on the following

Local fishermen at work in sight of one of Madagascar's most consistent waves, Jelly Babies, near Anakao.

The Indian Ocean's top surf spots are concentrated on several of its large islands.

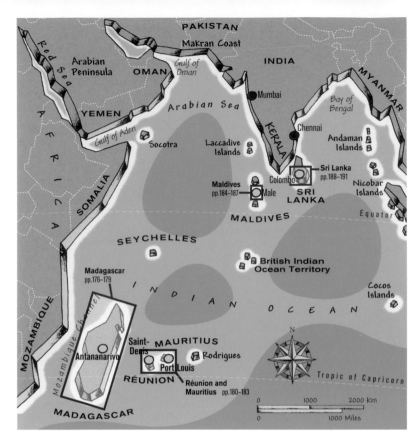

pages — Madagascar, Réunion and Mauritius, the Maldives, and Sri Lanka — several other Indian Ocean destinations are beginning to feature on the surf explorer's radar and can offer thrills aplenty for those willing to put in the hard yards.

All of the Arabian Sea's south-facing shores, in Pakistan, Oman, Yemen, India, and Somalia, have waves going unridden. When it edges Somalia and the Arabian Peninsula, the ferocity of the southwest monsoon can ignite some of the strongest tropical winds on the planet, creating exciting surfing conditions. While it is yet to be embraced by any but the most adventurous of surfers, Yemen is developing a reputation as a reliable wave magnet with opportunities galore along its 118-mile (190-km) coastline, including head-high beach and reef breaks.

To the south, the Seychelles Banks, in the Seychelles Islands, provide a barrier to most of the available swell moving into the country's main island of Mahe. The outer islands also have many large and unpublicized breaks.

Pakistan remains a frontier that few have dared to visit with the intention of riding waves, yet it has more than 600 miles (965 km) of coastline. The Makran Coast, in particular, offers much potential, even though it tends to attract more windswells than groundswells. Surfing's contemporary Marco Polo, Englishman Stuart Butler, has surfed Pakistan, Oman, and Yemen and found better-than-average waves in all locations, with some nearing perfection in both Yemen and Pakistan.

India's southwest coast has some quality waves, including a point break near Mumbai (formerly Bombay) and some reasonable, if inconsistent, waves in the southwestern state of Kerala. On the eastern side of India, good waves can be found around Chennai (formerly Madras). Right around the Bay of Bengal, there are waves worth traveling for, even in Myanmar (formerly Burma), though here the controling military junta will not allow surfers to wander the coast without supervision.

guaranteed surf

The Indian Ocean provides some of the longest fetch swells on the planet. These are particularly reliable during the Southern Hemisphere fall and winter (March to August). Indeed, a visit of a couple of weeks to this part of the world in this period is about as close as you can get to a guarantee of good waves.

Madagascar

Formerly a French colony, the island nation of Madagascar lies in the Indian Ocean, about 240 miles (386 km) southeast of Mozambique on the African mainland. The population, approaching 20 million, is mainly of African and Indonesian origin, mixed with some Indian, Chinese, and French. The main language is Malagasy, though French is also spoken. English is rare.

Madagascar suffers from significant social problems, including the sad but omnipresent colonial triple legacy of poverty, homegrown despots, and endemic corruption. Eighty per cent of the island has been deforested and soil erosion is a major problem. Add to this low life expectancy, poor health care, periodic famine, and shark-infested waters, and it's not difficult to see why it hasn't featured in many surf itineraries. But that is changing due to a combination of a push from local tourism authorities and a desire among adventurous surfers to seek out new frontiers.

The fourth largest island in the world, with approximately 3,000 miles (4,828 km) of coastline, Madagascar offers abundant opportunities for surfing on coasts where the weather and water are mild to tropical year-round. From May to September, the southwest and southern coasts are positioned to pick up the same Roaring Forties swells that pump the breaks of South Africa and Indonesia. December to March sees cyclone swells batter the east-facing spots and the dominant northeast wind provide a good setup for offshore conditions.

International flights arrive at the capital Antananarivo. The island is so large that it is best to fly from there to regional centers on the national carrier (known locally as "Air Mad"), then hire a car. Alternatively, you can grab a zebu cart outside the cities or a *pousse-pousse* (rickshaw) in flatter areas. But the most popular and cheapest way to get around is by *taxi-brousse* (bush taxi). Often overcrowded, slow and susceptible to mechanical failure, these taxis also offer travellers with plenty of time a heady combination of risk and fun.

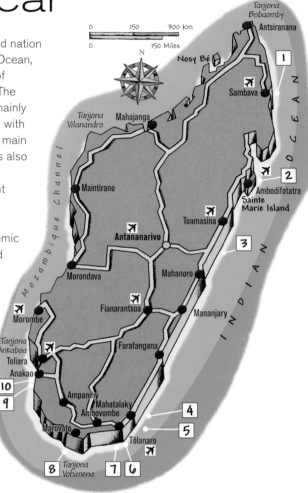

paddle power

Because many Madagascan breaks are on reefs up to a mile offshore, you'll need to be a super fit *vazaha* (Malagasy for foreigner) able to *vezo* (paddle) to reach these waves, or have access to a motorboat or *pirogue* (local sailing boat). But the rewards are well worth the extra hassles.

1 Sambava

This fast-breaking hollow wave wraps around the point. It needs a bit of size to come alive, and the best time can be the rainy cyclone season when there are east–northeast swells. Another good point lies a few kilometres southeast along the coast – ask for directions.

WAVE TYPE Right

WAVE HEIGHT 3–8 ft (0.9–2.4 m)

BREAK TYPE Reef point

BEST SWELL E

BEST WIND SW–W

BEST TIDE Low–mid

BEST TIME May–August, December–February

HAZARDS Malaria, pollution, sharks, rocks

DIRECTIONS Fly or drive to Sambava. The spot is in the town, just south of the river mouth.

2 Sainte Marie Island

Punchy waves ledge up here and offer fast, enjoyable rides. It's best to arrive with a surfing companion, otherwise you'll be surfing solo in supposed shark territory. If it's flat, try the east coast of the island farther south, which receives more swell and offers rich potential, especially on the outer reefs in the south.

WAVE TYPE Left and right

WAVE HEIGHT 3–10 ft (0.9–3.1 m)

BREAK TYPE Reef

BEST SWELL E–SE

BEST WIND W

BEST TIDE All

BEST TIME March–September

HAZARDS Malaria, sharks, coral

DIRECTIONS From the airport south of Ambodifotatra, drive north for approximately 28 miles (45 km) to Ambodiatafana village on the northeastern tip of the island. The wave is a short walk north of the village.

3 Ambila Lamaitso

The white-sand shoreline beside this village is straight and peaks can be found anywhere, depending on the sandbanks and tide. One of the best is a left sandbar that can become hollow and powerful, offering long rides when it's on. Ask a local to point it out.

WAVE TYPE Left and right

WAVE HEIGHT 3–10 ft (0.9–3.1 m)

BREAK TYPE Beach

BEST SWELL E–SE

BEST WIND W–NW

BEST TIDE All

BEST TIME March–October

HAZARDS Malaria, sharks, rips

DIRECTIONS From Antananarivo, head east to the coast via Moramanga township and Brickaville, from where it's another 6 miles (10 km) to Ambila Lamaitso. Good waves lie north and south of the village. Check conditions by driving south along the dirt road on the isthmus between the coast and the river.

4 Manafiafy

This scenic headland is made up of rocky reefs and small white-sand beaches. Exposed reefs here provide consistent quality left and right breaks. If the reefs aren't working, check the beach break just south of the headland, in Mananivo Bay.

WAVE TYPE Left and right

WAVE HEIGHT 3–15 ft (0.9–4.6 m)

BREAK TYPE Reef

BEST SWELL SW

BEST WIND W–NW

BEST TIDE Low–mid

BEST TIME March–October

HAZARDS Malaria, sharks, rocks

DIRECTIONS Driving north from Tôlanaro, turn east toward the coast approximately 6 miles (10 km) after the village of Mahatalaky. The wave is situated at Manafiafy village, off a scenic rocky headland at the northern end of Mananivo Bay.

5 Lokaro Island

Groundswells hit the exposed reef of this small island, creating dredging lefts and rights. Because of the difficult access, crowds are minimal to nonexistent. The wave becomes very powerful as it gets bigger, so bring extra boards and leashes.

WAVE TYPE Left and right

WAVE HEIGHT 3–15 ft (0.9–4.6 m)

BREAK TYPE Reef

BEST SWELL S

BEST WIND NW

BEST TIDE All

BEST TIME March–October

HAZARDS Malaria, sharks, rocks, tricky access

DIRECTIONS The island is 12 miles (20 km) north of Tôlanaro. Hire a boat in the town to take you there.

6 Libanona Beach

The mixture of reef and beach breaks here serves up fun rides. Look out for waves breaking off the small rocky outcrop in the far north of the bay, where swells are constantly shifting the sand around. Due to its easy access and consistency, this is one of the most popular options in the Tôlanaro area, and one of the few places in Madagascar where you might expect to share the water with other surfers.

WAVE TYPE Left and right

WAVE HEIGHT 3–12 ft (0.9–3.7 m)

BREAK TYPE Reef and beach

BEST SWELL S–SW

BEST WIND N–NE

BEST TIDE All

BEST TIME March–October

HAZARDS Malaria, sharks, rocks

DIRECTIONS The beach is right in the town of Tôlanaro, on the southern side of the headland.

7 Baie Des Singes

This long stretch of beach is a mixture of reef and sand. If you get the right combination of tide and swell, you can ride good-size waves with long walls, which are ideal for top-to-bottom carving. Get there early in the morning to enjoy the surf before the trade winds blow it out.

WAVE TYPE Left and right

WAVE HEIGHT 3–12 ft (0.9–3.7 m)

BREAK TYPE Reef and beach

BEST SWELL SE–S

BEST WIND W–NW

BEST TIDE Mid–high

BEST TIME March–October

HAZARDS Malaria, sharks, rips, rocks

DIRECTIONS From Tôlanaro, walk south along the beach for about a couple of miles (2–3 km) and look for the peaks.

8 Lavanono

The main wave here is a fun left-hand point break suitable for all levels and all boards when small. At over 6 ft (1.8 m), however, the wave comes alive, gaining intensity with long workable walls. There are also several potential reef setups just a short walk east along the coast.

WAVE TYPE Left

WAVE HEIGHT 3–16 ft (0.9–4.9 m)

BREAK TYPE Point and reef

BEST SWELL S–SW

BEST WIND NE

BEST TIDE Low–mid

BEST TIME March–October

HAZARDS Malaria, sharks, coral

DIRECTIONS Lavanono is at the southern tip of Madagascar. Heading southwest from Tôlanaro, the road for Lavanono is about 25 miles (40 km) past the turnoff for Cape Sainte Marie. A four-wheel-drive vehicle is required.

9 Jelly Babies

This mechanical peak, which has an easy takeoff, offers long rides both ways. It also generates some barrels, as well as fun sections with plenty of lip to smack. Jelly Babies is a high-performance wave, ideal for warming up before attempting the more serious options in the area.

WAVE TYPE Left and right

WAVE HEIGHT 3–12 ft (0.9–3.7 m)

BREAK TYPE Reef

BEST SWELL S

BEST WIND Light E

BEST TIDE Mid–high

BEST TIME March–October

HAZARDS Malaria, sharks, coral

DIRECTIONS Jelly Babies is on an outer reef southeast of Anakao. To get there, hire a dugout (with skipper) in Anakao or book a surf charter boat.

10 Flame Bowls

A long left-hand point off Anakao, Flame Bowls breaks down an offshore reef and terminates off the end of an atoll. Along the way, it becomes hollow, heavy, and solid. One of the premier waves in the Vezo reef area, it's for experts only.

WAVE TYPE Left

WAVE HEIGHT 3–15 ft (0.9–4.6 m)

BREAK TYPE Point break over coral

BEST SWELL S

BEST WIND SE

BEST TIDE Mid–high

BEST TIME March–October

HAZARDS Malaria, sharks, coral

DIRECTIONS Hire a dugout (with skipper) in Anakao or book a surf charter boat.

Riding to the top of the peak at Flame Bowls, one of Madagascar's most challenging waves.

Réunion and Mauritius

Réunion is a French-governed territory located about 420 miles (676 km) east of Madagascar. Home to fewer than 800,000 people, it is almost elliptical in shape, measuring only 30 miles (48 km) across at its widest point, and has just 128 miles (207 km) of coastline. Yet it offers some of the most consistently good surf in the Indian Ocean, especially on its west coast between May and September.

About 110 miles (180 km) northeast of Réunion is the star of the 1974 hippy surf-travel film *The Forgotten Island of Santosha*, Mauritius, or, more specifically, Tamarin Bay. Tamarin often makes lists of the best waves on Earth, but it only rarely breaks above 6 ft (1.8 m) and, when it does, local surfers can be fiercely territorial. However, if you are fortunate enough to be there on one of the couple of dozen days a year when the place is firing from Roaring Forties swells, you can expect to be racing down a left-hander for almost 300 yards (300 m).

There are also several other excellent waves along the 109 miles (177 km) of Mauritius's coastline. The island enjoys a tropical climate modified by southeast trade winds, with a warm, mostly dry winter (May to November) and a hot, wet, humid summer (November to May). The

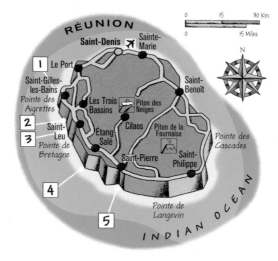

southwest corner attracts the most consistent surf, at its best April to September.

Getting to these islands can be expensive, with most direct flights originating in Europe and Africa. Hire cars and buses are available locally, and tourist facilities are good but not cheap. On Réunion, buses called cars jaunes (yellow coaches) ply the main routes and taxis can be hired, even for a whole day. The bus services on Mauritius are adequate, but tend to be slow. The two islands are linked by flights and a ferry that runs a few times a month.

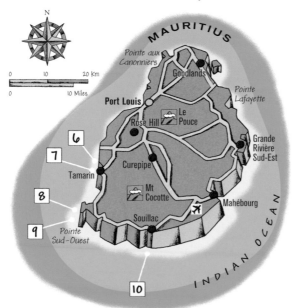

small but deadly

Réunion has a well-deserved reputation as a shark zone. These fearsome fish are most abundant off the west coast of the island, especially during the summer cyclone season (November to April). At the time of writing, Réunion's marine observatory had recorded 24 shark attacks off the island's shores since 1980, 13 of which were fatal.

1 L'Hermitage, Réunion

This wave is situated on a reef pass and has both a left and right break. The left is more commonly surfed, and is a short and hollow wave best at head high and in light winds. The reef is very shallow, and known for its big sharks.

WAVE TYPE Right and Left

WAVE HEIGHT 3–6 ft (0.9–1.8 m)

BREAK TYPE Coral reef

BEST SWELL S–SW

BEST WIND N

BEST TIDE Mid–high

BEST TIME April–November

HAZARDS Powerful waves, sharp reef, strong currents, sharks

DIRECTIONS Take a taxi or rental car from the airport near St.-Denis to St.-Gilles-les-Bains. The wave is on the outer reef. Ask the locals for advice on the currents.

2 Les Trois Bassins, Réunion

A popular beach area for locals and international visitors, Trois Bassins has several reef breaks that work on various tides and winds, with The Peak being the most popular. All are located just a short paddle from shore in shallow waters over sharp coral reefs.

WAVE TYPE Left and right

WAVE HEIGHT 3–6 ft (0.9–1.8 m)

BREAK TYPE Reef

BEST SWELL S–SW Indian Ocean groundswell

BEST WIND SE

BEST TIDE Mid–high (low tide can be dangerous)

BEST TIME April–November

HAZARDS Sharp coral reef, sharks, localism, sea urchins

DIRECTIONS Take a taxi or rental car from the airport near St.-Denis to St.-Gilles-les-Bains. The Trois Bassins area is in front of the main sand beach.

3 St.-Leu, Réunion

This classic left-hand wave is world-famous as a competition venue and one of the best and most consistent surfing waves in the Indian Ocean. Starting from the top of a long and shallow coral reef, the wave increases in size as it wraps and bowls 90 degrees around the reef, ending in a deep channel well known for its big sharks.

WAVE TYPE Left

WAVE HEIGHT 3–12 ft (0.9–3.7 m)

BREAK TYPE Reef

BEST SWELL S–SW Indian Ocean groundswell

BEST WIND SE

BEST TIDE Mid–high

BEST TIME April–November

HAZARDS Sharp coral reef, powerful waves, sharks, localism

DIRECTIONS Take a taxi or rental car from the airport near St.-Denis to St.-Leu on the west coast. The wave is behind the small harbor.

4 Étang-Salé, Réunion

One of the few beach breaks on Réunion, Étang-Salé is a good spot for smaller days and popular with local surfers and bodyboarders. It's a thumping hollow shore break on a black-sand beach. The takeoff zone and breaking patterns change with the sandbanks.

WAVE TYPE Left and right

WAVE HEIGHT 3–6 ft (0.9–1.8 m)

BREAK TYPE Sandbar

BEST SWELL S–SW

BEST WIND N

BEST TIDE All

BEST TIME April–November

HAZARDS Powerful shorebreak, hot sand, strong currents, sharks

DIRECTIONS Take a taxi or rental car from the airport near St.-Denis to the west coast, and follow the signs to Étang-Salé. Turn off before the first bridge, then park and walk.

5 St.-Pierre, Réunion

This powerful reef-break right-hander lies in front of the small harbor at St.-Pierre. There is easy access via the rock jetty and strong current, but this spot is shallow and powerful. Falling in the wrong place means an almost certain encounter with the sharp reef, and, like every spot in Réunion, St.-Pierre has a reputation for big sharks. The peak takeoff is followed by a barrel section that gets crazy with size – once over 6 ft (1.8 m), it's dangerous.

WAVE TYPE Right (though can go left when small)

WAVE HEIGHT 3–10 ft (0.9–3.1 m)

BREAK TYPE Coral reef

BEST SWELL S–SW Indian Ocean groundswell

BEST WIND E–SE

BEST TIDE Mid–high (low tide can be dangerous)

BEST TIME April–November

HAZARDS Sharp coral reef, strong currents, sharks

DIRECTIONS Take a taxi or rental car from the airport near St.-Denis to St.-Pierre on the southwest coast, a drive of several hours.

6 Black Rocks, Mauritius

Across Tamarin Bay from the shallow reef of the classic left-hander is an easier right, at a cluster of black rocks on the shoreline, hence the name. The wave will break consistently in the winter season, and is a popular weekend surfing area for locals.

WAVE TYPE Right

WAVE HEIGHT 3–6 ft (0.9–1.8 m)

BREAK TYPE Sand and rocks

BEST SWELL S–SW Indian Ocean groundswell

BEST WIND N–NE

BEST TIDE Low–mid

BEST TIME April–November

HAZARDS Rocks

DIRECTIONS Take a taxi or rental car from the airport near Mahébourg on the east coast to Tamarin on the west coast. Black Rocks is a short walk north of Tamarin Public Beach.

Early-morning waves roll in at St.-Leu, the most renowned surf spot on the island of Réunion.

7 Tamarin Bay, Mauritius

This legendary wave is a long and hollow left-hander, offshore on the seasonal southeast trade winds. The reef is sharp and shallow. Tamarin needs the biggest of Southern Hemisphere winter swells to work, which happens only several times in a season.

WAVE TYPE Left

WAVE HEIGHT 3–12 ft (0.9–3.7 m)

BREAK TYPE Reef point

BEST SWELL S–SW Indian Ocean groundswell

BEST WIND SE

BEST TIDE Mid–high (low tide can be dangerous)

BEST TIME April–November

HAZARDS Shallow reef, localism, sea urchins, petty thieves

DIRECTIONS Take a taxi or rental car from the airport near Mahébourg on the east coast to Tamarin on the west coast. The wave is clearly visible from Tamarin Public Beach in the middle of town, behind the fishing boats.

8 Passe de L'Ambulante, Mauritius

South of Tamarin is the large rock of Le Morne Brabant. The lagoon in front of it is breached by several passes, the largest of which, L'Ambulante, has the island's most consistent wave. It is both a left and a right, which break into the deeper water of the pass. Getting there requires a long paddle or short boat ride.

WAVE TYPE Left and right

WAVE HEIGHT 3–8 ft (0.9–2.4 m)

BREAK TYPE Reef pass

BEST SWELL S–SW Indian Ocean groundswell

BEST WIND SE

BEST TIDE Mid–high (low tide can be dangerous)

BEST TIME April–November

HAZARDS Shallow reef, sea urchins, strong current on outgoing tide, kitesurfers and windsurfers

DIRECTIONS Take a taxi or rental car from the airport at Mahébourg to the Le Morne area in the southwest of the island. Access the beach next to the entrance to the Berjaya Hotel and turn right. The wave is well offshore.

9 One Eye's, Mauritius

Farther south on the same barrier reef as L'Ambulante is One Eye's, another reef pass with a good left. It's quite consistent in winter, but can be dangerous on a ferocious outbound current and a dropping tide.

WAVE TYPE Left

WAVE HEIGHT 3–6 ft (0.9–1.8 m)

BREAK TYPE Reef pass

BEST SWELL S–SW Indian Ocean groundswell

BEST WIND SE

BEST TIDE Mid–high (low tide can be dangerous)

BEST TIME April–November

HAZARDS Shallow reef, sea urchins, long paddle from shore, strong current on outgoing tide

DIRECTIONS Take a taxi or rental car from the airport at Mahébourg to the Le Morne area in the southwest. Access the beach next to the entrance to the Berjaya Hotel and turn left. The wave is well offshore — paddle out or hire a boat.

10 Souillac, Mauritius

A coral-reef left-hander in front of the town of Souillac, this is an excellent wave that nearly always has swell in the winter months of April to October. Unfortunately, it is also affected by the winter southeast trade winds, when it is usually onshore and unridable. Early mornings are best for less wind.

WAVE TYPE Left

WAVE HEIGHT 3–8 ft (0.9–2.4 m)

BREAK TYPE Reef pass

BEST SWELL S–SW

BEST WIND N or NE

BEST TIDE Mid–high

BEST TIME April–November

HAZARDS Shallow reef, long paddle from shore, sharks at river mouth

DIRECTIONS Take a taxi or rental car from the airport at Mahébourg to accommodation in the Le Morne area on the west coast. Souillac (which has few tourist facilities) is about an hour away by car.

Maldives

Located about 435 miles (700 km) southwest of Sri Lanka, the Maldives consists of about 1,190 islands spread over 26 low-lying atolls along a 475-mile (764-km) strip. According to the *Guinness Book of Records*, it is the world's flattest country, with no natural land higher than 7.9 ft (2.4 m) above sea level. It also has the smallest population of any Asian country at around 300,000 people.

After being shipwrecked near the capital Male in 1973, two Aussie surfers, Tony Hinde and Mark Scanlon, recognized that the swells from the Roaring Forties created ideal surfing conditions. Hinde returned in 1974 to explore the islands, stayed, and became a Maldivian citizen. In 1990, he founded a surf resort in Tari. Still the islands remained relatively unsurfed, until about 1993, when surf magazines did what surf magazines do.

International flights arrive at Male International Airport, on Hulhule Island. Ferries and taxi boats provide transport between the airport, the capital, and other islands. Air taxis also operate between islands but aren't for those on a tight budget. English is widely spoken.

The government has heavily regulated the tourism industry to ensure surf slums don't spring up. You can't just arrive in the country and do your own thing; instead you need to have prebooked your accommodation with a land- or boat-based agency. If you choose to stay on land, be mindful that you will be reliant on your resort's surf taxis, known locally as *dhonis*.

The southwest monsoon, from April till October, provides the best conditions, with April to June having the lion's share of offshore days.

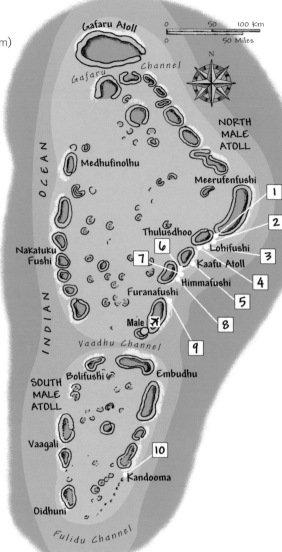

if there's no swell ...

Scuba divers from around the world rave about the high visibility in the turquoise waters that surround the Maldives. If you haven't taken the plunge as yet, the country offers an ideal environment in which to develop a different kind of interest in the ocean.

The Indian Ocean

Maldives

1 Chickens

The northernmost wave in North Male Atoll, Chickens can produce a long and incredibly fast ride over a reasonably deep and flat reef bottom. It's a high-performance wave that can also offer quality barrels on bigger swells. Only surf here if you can at least set your first turn quickly and maintain a high-speed line.

WAVE TYPE Left

WAVE HEIGHT 3–15 ft (0.9–4.6 m)

BREAK TYPE Reef

BEST SWELL ESE–SE

BEST WIND NW

BEST TIDE Low

BEST TIME April–October

HAZARDS Strong currents, shallow end section

DIRECTIONS This is the break on the northern side of the channel at Thulusdhoo. Boat access only.

2 Cokes

The island of Thulusdhoo is known as Cokes (or Colas) because of the local Coca-Cola plant. The wave of the same name is the most challenging wave and also the best barrel on North Male Atoll. The takeoff is steeper than most Maldivian waves and is better suited to shortboards. The ride is fast with numerous barrel opportunities, and the end section throws a chunky barrel that can't always be completed.

WAVE TYPE Right

WAVE HEIGHT 3–15 ft (0.9–4.6 m)

BREAK TYPE Reef

BEST SWELL SE–S

BEST WIND SW–W

BEST TIDE All

BEST TIME April–October

HAZARDS Shallow and powerful end section, stonefish

DIRECTIONS Breaks directly in front of the island of Thulusdhoo. Boat access only.

3 Lohifushi

The island of Lohifushi has recently been upgraded to become a four-star resort called Huduran Fushi. A quality, fast wave breaks a stone's throw from the beach and, although the resort claims exclusivity, according to the local government anyone is free to surf it. It's a good wave but can get crowded, with over 100 surfers sometimes staying at the resort at once.

WAVE TYPE Left

WAVE HEIGHT 3–15 ft (0.9–4.6 m)

BREAK TYPE Reef

BEST SWELL ESE–SE

BEST WIND NW

BEST TIDE All

BEST TIME April–October

HAZARDS Strong currents, fast end section

DIRECTIONS Paddle out from the sunset bar in front of the break.

4 Ninjas

Under normal conditions, Ninjas offers a slower, fatter ride compared with its neighbors, which particularly suits longboarders and less-experienced surfers. The takeoff is soft and there are multiple cutback sections. However, the end section closes out and it is easy to get caught inside here.

WAVE TYPE Right

WAVE HEIGHT 3–15 ft (0.9–4.6 m)

BREAK TYPE Reef

BEST SWELL SE–S

BEST WIND SW–W

BEST TIDE Mid

BEST TIME April–October

HAZARDS Stonefish, sharp rocks on inside reef

DIRECTIONS Just across the channel from Lohifushi. Boat access is best, but you can also rock-hop or paddle out from the Club Med island of Kanifinolhu.

Internationally renowned Brazilian surfer Adriano de Souza takes to the air at Kakuni in the Maldives.

5 Pasta Point

Pasta Point, on Kaafu Atoll, is reserved for the exclusive use of guests at the Dhonveli Resort, run by Tony Hussein Hinde, one of the Australians shipwrecked here in the 1970s. The wave is fast and high quality, though it works best when there is some north in the wind (as with all the lefts here). Together with Sultans, Honkys, and Jails to the south this forms one of the world's greatest setups.

WAVE TYPE Left

WAVE HEIGHT 3–15 ft (0.9–4.6 m)

BREAK TYPE Reef

BEST SWELL SE–S

BEST WIND NW

BEST TIDE Low

BEST TIME April–October

HAZARDS Strong currents

DIRECTIONS Paddle out from the Dhonveli Resort.

6 Sultans

Named with the Maldives' monarchist history in mind, Sultans is one of the most enjoyable waves you could find anywhere. There's an easy takeoff, which may be followed by a long wall, barrel, cutback, or a string of high-performance maneuvers. The ride ends with a racy, hollow end section.

WAVE TYPE Right

WAVE HEIGHT 3–15 ft (0.9–4.6 m)

BREAK TYPE Reef

BEST SWELL SE–S

BEST WIND SW–W

BEST TIDE Low

BEST TIME April–October

HAZARDS Crowds, fast and shallow end section; unexploded bombs left from days when island was used as a bombing range

DIRECTIONS Breaks directly in front of the local island of Thanburdhoo. Boat access only.

7 Honkys

This is arguably the Maldives' best wave, though it needs a northerly wind, which is rare during the swell season. A straightforward drop is followed by a long, fast section, allowing competent shortboarders to perform some of the best turns of their life. As the wave passes over "Fred's Ledge," it bends back on itself, creating a powerful barrel and end section.

WAVE TYPE Left

WAVE HEIGHT 3–15 ft (0.9–4.6 m)

BREAK TYPE Reef

BEST SWELL SE–S

BEST WIND NW–N

BEST TIDE Low

BEST TIME April–October

HAZARDS Strong currents, Fred's Ledge

DIRECTIONS Located on the southern side of Sultans. Boat access only.

8 Jails (aka Jailbreak)

Named for the local jail, this wave was off-limits to surfers until the correctional center was downgraded to a drug rehabilitation center in the 1990s. One of the best in the Maldives, it's a perfect, down-the-line wave that can have different sections and may barrel at any point. As at Chickens, you'll need to set your first turn early in order to make the section. Do that on a big swell and you may score the ride of your life.

WAVE TYPE Right

WAVE HEIGHT 3–15 ft (0.9–4.6 m)

BREAK TYPE Reef

BEST SWELL SE–S

BEST WIND SW–W

BEST TIDE Low

BEST TIME April–October

HAZARDS Fast and shallow end section, strong currents

DIRECTIONS Breaks directly in front of the island of Himmafushi. Boat access only.

9 Tombstones

Tombstones will break only in a big swell or when the swell is from the southeast. It never gets big and offers a soft, rolling longboard wave in its first section. However, the second section turns into a fast and hollow linkup, breaking in just a couple of feet of water, which can be dangerous – hence the name. It's often flat though, so don't bother with it unless Sultans is well overhead.

WAVE TYPE Right

WAVE HEIGHT 3–8 ft (0.9–2.4 m)

BREAK TYPE Reef

BEST SWELL Large SE

BEST WIND S–SW

BEST TIDE All

BEST TIME April–October

HAZARDS End section, strong currents

DIRECTIONS Breaks off the northern corner of the island of Furanafushi. Boat access is best.

10 Riptides

Due to a major swell block to the south, the surf at this South Male Atoll is normally smaller than in the north. The wave breaks in the middle of a channel and requires light winds only. It's a shifting right peak that can be difficult to line up, but once you connect, it offers fun drops, occasional tubes, and plenty of cutback practice. It becomes more challenging with size, but is rarely big.

WAVE TYPE Right

WAVE HEIGHT 3–8 ft (0.9–2.4 m)

BREAK TYPE Reef

BEST SWELL SE

BEST WIND Light W

BEST TIDE All

BEST TIME April–October

HAZARDS Strong currents (keep a support boat with you at all times)

DIRECTIONS Riptides is in the first channel south of Kandooma. Boat access only.

Sri Lanka

Just 20 miles (32 km) across the Palk Strait from the southern tip of India lies the teardrop-shaped island of Sri Lanka. Formerly a British colony known as Ceylon, it has a population of around 20 million people and 832 miles (1,340 km) of coastline.

International flights arrive at Colombo. For long journeys, the best way to travel is to hire a minivan and driver. Tuk-tuks are the cheapest option for shorter journeys. Buses are slow and driving is not recommended.

From May to October, the southwest monsoon produces offshore winds on the east coast. The focus of surfing here is Arugam Bay, 195 miles (314 km) southeast of Colombo. It was hippy central in the late 1970s and early 1980s, and is still often very crowded. From October to March, the northeast monsoon creates offshore conditions on the west coast. Hikkaduwa, 60 miles (100 km) south of

Colombo, is the hub here. Crowds can be a problem at Hikkaduwa, too, along with pollution and aggressive locals, but, on the other hand, there is nearly always something to surf here.

A great alternative to these centers is the south coast between Galle and Dondra. The roads are rough, but the region is inexpensive, the food sensational, the people hospitable, and the waves little ridden. A fascinating 17th-century port, Galle bore the brunt of the 2004 tsunami, which claimed 35,000 lives and displaced half a million people in Sri Lanka.

1 Beruwala

A generally weak beach break, Beruwala is far enough south to pick up fairly regular swell. Good sandbanks can form at the southern end of the beach, close to the mouth of the Bentota River. The area has plenty of accommodation.

WAVE TYPE Left and right

WAVE HEIGHT 2–6 ft (0.6–1.8 m)

BREAK TYPE Beach

BEST SWELL S–SW

BEST WIND E

BEST TIDE All

BEST TIME November–April

HAZARDS Poor water quality

DIRECTIONS From Colombo, drive south on Highway 2 (Galle Rd) for 34 miles (55 km) to Beruwala. There are footpaths to the beach between the big hotels.

2 Hikkaduwa

Hikkaduwa has a range of good breaks, and everything else a surfer needs. Main Reef is an A-frame peak providing good but invariably crowded rides in both directions. A short distance to the north is Benny's, an offshore reef which offers powerful, hollow lefts in a big swell. To the south, Inside Reef is another good left.

WAVE TYPE Left and right

WAVE HEIGHT 2–8 ft (0.6–2.4 m)

BREAK TYPE Reef

BEST SWELL S–SW

BEST WIND E

BEST TIDE All

BEST TIME November–April

HAZARDS Crowds, territorial locals, sharp coral

DIRECTIONS From Galle, drive west on Highway 2 for 10½ miles (17 km) to Hikkaduwa. Main Reef is in the middle of the Wewala area.

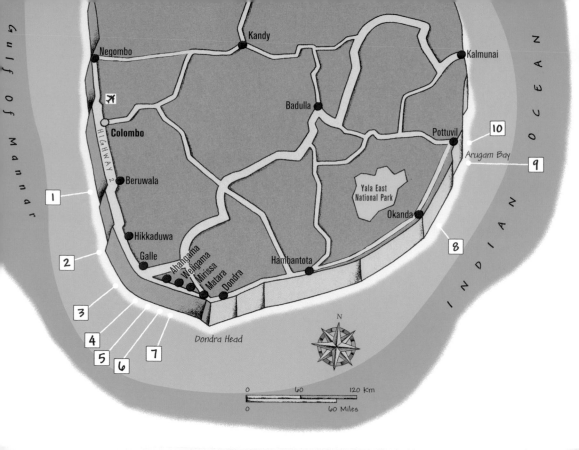

3 Galle

On a large swell, a good, hollow left breaks off the jetty at the eastern end of Galle Bay. And even when the swell isn't big enough to get the jetty firing, you will still find small peaks in the middle of the bay, which are perfect for beginners.

WAVE TYPE Left

WAVE HEIGHT 2–6 ft (0.6–1.8 m)

BREAK TYPE Reef

BEST SWELL S–SW

BEST WIND N

BEST TIDE All

BEST TIME November–April

HAZARDS Pollution, fishing boats

DIRECTIONS From the fort in Galle, drive east along the coast road for just over a mile (2 km) to reach the jetty.

4 The Rock

The Rock is one of the best waves on the south coast. As the name suggests, a large boulder on the shore makes it easy to find. It offers both a left and a right. The left is the longer wave and can give rides of over 100 yards (100 m); the right is shorter but more powerful. An incoming tide is best.

WAVE TYPE Left and right

WAVE HEIGHT 3–8 ft (0.9–2.4 m)

BREAK TYPE Reef

BEST SWELL S–SW

BEST WIND N

BEST TIDE All

BEST TIME November–April

HAZARDS Sharp coral, territorial locals

DIRECTIONS From Galle, drive east on Highway 2 for 6 miles (10 km) to Ahangama village. The Rock is opposite the Kabalana Hotel.

5 Midigama

The main break at Midigama, a left, is a cruisy, fun wave that can offer the occasional tube when offshore. You get to it by paddling out from the Hiltens Beach Resort. Farther down the beach, a short, punchy right breaks over a shallow reef in front of Ram's guesthouse.

WAVE TYPE Left and right

WAVE HEIGHT 2–6 ft (0.6–1.8 m)

BREAK TYPE Reef

BEST SWELL S–SW

BEST WIND N

BEST TIDE Low–mid

BEST TIME November–April

HAZARDS Shallow reef at Ram's

DIRECTIONS From Galle, drive east on Highway 2 for 7½ miles (12 km). Look for the signs for Hiltens Beach Resort and Ram's guesthouse.

6 Weligama

This beautiful curved bay is home to a series of fun beach breaks, which are gentle enough for novices without being gutless. The sheltered location makes Weligama a mellow alternative to the nearby reefs and can offer more protection in a big swell.

WAVE TYPE Left and right

WAVE HEIGHT 2–6 ft (0.6–1.8 m)

BREAK TYPE Beach

BEST SWELL S–SW

BEST WIND N

BEST TIDE All

BEST TIME November–April

HAZARDS Crowds

DIRECTIONS From Galle, drive east on Highway 2 for just over 15 miles (25 km). The best waves are in the middle of the beach.

From its origins as a fishing village, Hikkaduwa evolved through the 1970s and 1980s into a major resort.

7 Mirissa

Mirissa, a beautiful, quiet spot, is home to a well-protected right-hand reef break tucked in behind the headland. It's a short but punchy wave, reached by a tricky paddle. There is also a left at the eastern end of the beach, which works in a big swell.

WAVE TYPE Right

WAVE HEIGHT 3–6 ft (0.9–1.8 m)

BREAK TYPE Reef

BEST SWELL SW

BEST WIND N

BEST TIDE Low

BEST TIME November–April

HAZARDS Difficult entry, sea urchins

DIRECTIONS From Galle, drive east on Highway 2 for approximately 19 miles (30 km). Mirissa can also be reached by means of a ten-minute tuk-tuk ride from Weligama.

8 Okanda

Just inside Yala East National Park is Okanda Point, a sand-bottomed, right-hand point break. This is a performance wave with a hollow inside section. It picks up plenty of swell and can provide rides of up to 500 yards (500 m) or so. Difficult access means it is rarely crowded.

WAVE TYPE Right

WAVE HEIGHT 3–6 ft (0.9–1.8 m)

BREAK TYPE Point

BEST SWELL E–S

BEST WIND W–NW

BEST TIDE Mid

BEST TIME April–September

HAZARDS Rocks

DIRECTIONS From Arugam Bay, drive south along the coast road for just over 12 miles (20 km). You will need a four-wheel-drive vehicle.

9 Arugam Bay

The right-hand point break here is Sri Lanka's most famous wave and justifiably so: extending up to 500 yards (500 m), it offers great rides with a mixture of tubing sections and workable walls. It picks up more swell than neighboring spots, and the length of the wave means it can handle a crowd.

WAVE TYPE Right

WAVE HEIGHT 2–8 ft (0.6–2.4 m)

BREAK TYPE Point

BEST SWELL E–S

BEST WIND W–NW

BEST TIDE All

BEST TIME April–September

HAZARDS Sharp coral, crowds in peak season

DIRECTIONS From Pottuvil town, drive 1½ miles (2.5 km) south to Arugam Bay. The point is a ten-minute walk from the southern end of the beach.

10 Pottuvil Point

Set in a stunning location, and usually smaller and less crowded than Arugam Bay, this right-hand, sand-bottomed point break can produce extremely long rides of up to 800 yards (800 m). More often, the wave breaks in sections, but it can be fun to try to link these together. It needs a big swell to work, however.

WAVE TYPE Right

WAVE HEIGHT 3–6 ft (0.9–1.8 m)

BREAK TYPE Point

BEST SWELL E–S

BEST WIND W–NW

BEST TIDE Low–mid

BEST TIME April–September

HAZARDS Boulders, remote location

DIRECTIONS It's a 30-minute tuk-tuk ride from Arugam Bay, then a ten-minute walk.

CHAPTER 9

Western Europe

Introduction

Where the often stormy Atlantic meets Europe's rugged and rain-stained coastline, surfers can enjoy an outstanding variety of cool-water waves, ranging from pulverizing reefs and long, hollow points to gentle beach breaks. The surf is rarely flat and averages 1–3 ft (0.3–0.9 m) in summer, with 59–68°F (15–20°C) sea temperatures, and 4–10 ft (1.2–3.1 m) during the mild fall, winter, and spring in 41–50°F (5–10°C) waters. During the chilly winters, waves like Mundaka in northern Spain excel, but quick-changing conditions make weather forecasting an essential part of the European surfer's knowledge. Wetsuited warriors edge deeper every year into inhospitable but sometimes epic surf frontiers such as northern Scotland, Norway, and Iceland. The most recent discovery has been the tow-in spot Alieens, on the west coast of Ireland, where huge waves break close to the dramatic Cliffs of Moher.

Generalizations are almost impossible in Europe, its politics and economy being as diverse as its landscape, which ranges from rocky coastlines to rich farmland and snow-capped peaks. While snow falls in the Alps, the arid south can have months of scorching sun, and the lush north months of yeasty rain. Europe is a melting pot of different languages and traditions, where efforts to speak the local lingo are always appreciated. Politically stable with little in the way of threatening sea life, Europe is a safe and popular surfing destination. Pollution, once widespread, has been reduced, in part thanks to the efforts of environmental groups such as Surfers Against Sewage and Surfrider Foundation Europe.

The downside to visiting Europe is the relatively high cost of living, making camping the only cheap travel option. However, road and train networks are superb, and air travel is affordable and convenient.

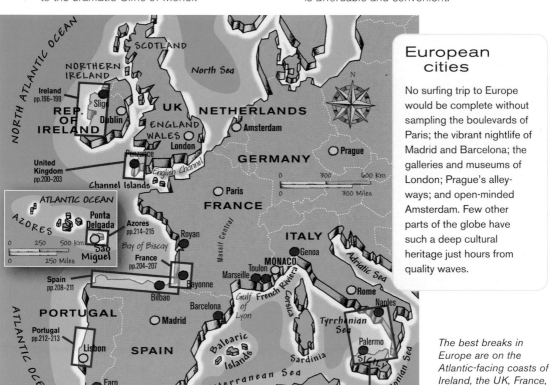

European cities

No surfing trip to Europe would be complete without sampling the boulevards of Paris; the vibrant nightlife of Madrid and Barcelona; the galleries and museums of London; Prague's alley-ways; and open-minded Amsterdam. Few other parts of the globe have such a deep cultural heritage just hours from quality waves.

The best breaks in Europe are on the Atlantic-facing coasts of Ireland, the UK, France, Spain, and Portugal, and in the Azores.

Mundaka, in the Basque Country of Spain, is one of the finest surf spots in the whole of Europe.

The Climate

European waters should be much colder than they are, considering their 40–60° north latitude. Thankfully, the Gulf Stream helps coastal Europe to escape extremes of weather with a constant flow of mild mid-Atlantic water. Low-pressure systems follow the Gulf Stream's course, sending swell as they deepen, tracking northeast. Between October and May in fall, winter, and spring, these strong, wet, windy weather systems hit the UK and Ireland. In the process they send big, often clean surf to points, reefs, and beaches in France, Spain, Portugal, Madeira, the Canary Islands, and the Azores. In ideal conditions, the low pressures spin in the North Atlantic, while a high pressure system over mainland Europe creates clear weather and offshore winds. This pattern is more common between June and August in summer, when surf is smaller, because the lows are less frequent, travel farther north, and dissipate earlier.

The European summer can be a balmy 68–86°F (20–30°C), making possible boardshorts sessions in 68°F (20°C) water at places like the world-famous stretch of powerful beach breaks in Hossegor, France. September to November is the prime time for all European surfing, with frequent long-fetch groundswells from the southwest and fairly warm weather and water. This is when Europe hosts ASP world tour contests and most surfers travel the coast, regularly enjoying perfect conditions.

The tidal range in Europe is large, averaging 10–20 ft (3.1–6.1 m). A tide chart is essential as breaks work best at certain tides. The sheltered Mediterranean is the exception. Surprisingly, the Med can enjoy short-lived windswells from a number of different directions, which send waves to parts of southern France and western Italy. In the North Sea, deep depressions entering from the North Atlantic can send swell to the east coast of the UK, Norway, Germany, and the Netherlands.

Europe's connection with surfing goes back to Captain James Cook, who captained the first group of Westerners to witness surfing in Hawaii in 1778. Cook grew up in a place where some of the hollowest left-handers in the UK break, at Staithes, Yorkshire. Here Cook felt the lure of the sea before he embarked on his Pacific voyages.

Almost two centuries later, in the 1950s and 1960s, traveling South African, Australian, and Californian surfers brought the sport to Biarritz in France, and Jersey (Channel Islands) and Cornwall in the UK. Today, the hundreds of thousands of surfers all over Europe are a welcome addition to the continent's cosmopolitan, sophisticated, and always evolving culture and economy.

1 Rossnowlagh Beach

Rossnowlagh is a small but popular family-oriented seaside resort in South Donegal. Its magnificent 2-mile (3.2-km) stretch of beach offers gentle waves suitable for beginners; it's also a fun spot for longboarders. The beach is home to one of Ireland's largest and oldest surf clubs, and the town has a surf shop and plenty of accommodation.

WAVE TYPE Left and right

WAVE HEIGHT 1–6 ft (0.3–1.8 m)

BREAK TYPE Beach

BEST SWELL W

BEST WIND E

BEST TIDE Mid–high

BEST TIME Year-round

HAZARDS Weaver fish concealed under the sand (the sting can be very painful). Beware of soft sand areas if you take your car onto the beach.

DIRECTIONS From Sligo city, take the N15 to Ballyshannon, then the R231 to Rossnowlagh.

2 The Peak

The Peak is located at Bundoran in South Donegal. Its high-quality reef produces long, hollow lefts and shorter but quality rights. Both the European Surfing Championships and the Quiksilver World Masters Championships have been held here. The town of Bundoran has three surf schools and two surf shops.

WAVE TYPE Left and right

WAVE HEIGHT 2–10 ft (0.6–3.1 m)

BREAK TYPE Reef

BEST SWELL W

BEST WIND E

BEST TIDE Low–mid

BEST TIME September–April

HAZARDS Rocks, crowds, sewage

DIRECTIONS From Sligo city, take the N15 to Bundoran. As you approach the center of town, you'll see The Peak to your left.

Ireland

Tucked away in Ireland's convoluted coastline are some of the finest waves in the whole of Europe. Below moss-covered hills and towering cliffs are spitting 6–10-ft (1.8–3.1-m) peaks and rolling 4-ft (1.2-m) points. Rights and lefts spin for hundreds of yards — cold, greasy, and green over kelp beds — until they are finally exhausted on sharp rocky shores. Ireland has recently gained widespread recognition for its wealth of waves, and few areas remain uncharted. North Atlantic swell strikes hard at crowded hotspots such as Easky, Bundoran, and Lahinch. Long, rolling rides accessed via memorable countryside make Ireland magic, and visitors are quickly won over by the unique culture — and the stout beers.

In the mild, damp winters, water temperature is 46°F (8°C), demanding a 5/3 mm wetsuit, boots, gloves, and hood. There is continuous swell from the southwest, west, and north. In the strong prevailing southwest wind, the excellent north-facing reef and point breaks around Easky and Bundoran (The Peak) are the best places to be, with waves for both the intermediate and advanced surfer. When the wind turns southeast, County Clare has a wide choice of beautiful easier-to-ride long points and a few hollow reefs that are suitable for the expert. Either side of summer, in April to May and September to November, is the best time to surf in Ireland, when you can shed some neoprene and enjoy calmer weather and the powerful 6-ft (1.8-m) clean swells.

A rental car is essential from arrival at international airports in Dublin, Knock, Shannon, and Belfast, or the regional airports closer to the best waves at Galway or Sligo. But be patient during long drives searching for the offshore winds, and savor the slow pace of life and the rolling countryside of the Emerald Isle.

3 Strandhill Beach

The beach is located in the seaside town of Strandhill, not far from Sligo City. It offers good-quality peaks suitable for experienced or advanced surfers. There are two surf schools and a surf shop, and the County Sligo Surf Club has its clubhouse in the Maritime Centre at the seafront.

WAVE TYPE Left and right

WAVE HEIGHT 1–6 ft (0.3–1.8 m)

BREAK TYPE Beach

BEST SWELL W–NW

BEST WIND NE–E

BEST TIDE Mid–high

BEST TIME Year-round

HAZARDS Rocks, strong rips, tricky entry and exit on spring high tide

DIRECTIONS Take the R292 from Sligo city for about 6 miles (10 km) to Strandhill.

4 Easky Left

This left-hander breaks into the mouth of the Easky River in the shadow of thirteenth-century Roslea Castle at Easky, an attractive coastal village in West Sligo. The Irish Surfing Association has its headquarters here. This wave is well known and can get crowded.

WAVE TYPE Left

WAVE HEIGHT 2–8 ft (0.6–2.4 m)

BREAK TYPE Point

BEST SWELL W

BEST WIND S

BEST TIDE Mid–high

BEST TIME September–April

HAZARDS Dangerous currents, rocks, crowds

DIRECTIONS Take the N59 (Sligo–Ballina Rd), then turn off at Dromore West for Easky. As you approach the village, turn left immediately before the school and then left into the parking lot overlooking Easky Left at the end of the road.

a glass of Guinness

The pub is the heart of every Irish community. Après surf, it is the ultimate place to enjoy food, music, and Guinness. Although Guinness is now a global brand, available in many places worldwide, there's nothing like sampling the brew on its home soil. The creamy texture and rich barley flavor perfectly complement a long, cold surf session.

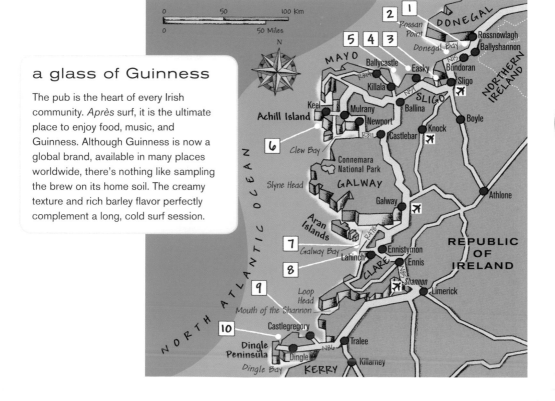

5 Kilcummin

This powerful left-hander is located behind the harbor wall at Kilcummin, peeling down the point toward the harbor when it breaks. This location, north of Ballina, may appear isolated, but when few other nearby waves are surfable, it gets busy. Kilcummin is one of the few spots on the west coast that's offshore in a westerly.

WAVE TYPE Left

WAVE HEIGHT 2–10 ft (0.6–3.1 m)

BREAK TYPE Reef

BEST SWELL NW–N

BEST WIND W

BEST TIDE Low

BEST TIME November–March

HAZARDS Strong currents

DIRECTIONS Take the R314 from Ballina toward Ballycastle, and turn right after Killala for Kilcummin Harbour.

6 Keel

Keel Beach is scenically located in the village of Keel on Achill Island just off the west coast of County Mayo. The beach offers good-quality peaks in the right conditions. Achill is a popular tourist destination, particularly in the summer when the beach gets busy with surfers and other water users.

WAVE TYPE Left and right

WAVE HEIGHT 2–6 ft (0.6–1.8 m)

BREAK TYPE Beach

BEST SWELL SW

BEST WIND NE

BEST TIDE Breaks through the tide

BEST TIME Year-round

HAZARDS Crowds in summer, weaver fish hiding under the sand (the sting can be very painful)

DIRECTIONS From Castlebar, follow the R311 to Newport, then the N59 to Mulrany. From here, take the R319 across the bridge to Achill Island and follow the signs to Keel.

Swooping up high at The Peak, near Bundoran on the west coast of Ireland

7 Crab Island

This quality right-hander breaks on the back of Crab Island, a tiny island off Doolin Harbour. The swell coming out of deep water forms long, hollow right-handers when it hits the island. Keep in mind that the wave size viewed from shore is always deceptive, appearing smaller than it actually is.

WAVE TYPE Right

WAVE HEIGHT 2–10 ft (0.6–3.1 m)

BREAK TYPE Reef

BEST SWELL W

BEST WIND E

BEST TIDE Low–mid

BEST TIME September–April

HAZARDS Strong currents, shallow reef, long paddle out

DIRECTIONS From Lahinch, take the R478 to Doolin. Check Crab Island from the harbor.

8 Lahinch Beach

This popular beach offers good-quality peaks for the more experienced surfer. Immediately south of the beach lies a series of top-quality lefts that peel back toward the beach. The town of Lahinch offers plenty of accommodation and is home to the West Coast Surf Club and several surf shops and schools.

WAVE TYPE Left and right

WAVE HEIGHT 2–6 ft (0.6–1.8 m)

BREAK TYPE Beach

BEST SWELL W

BEST WIND E

BEST TIDE Low–mid

BEST TIME Year-round

HAZARDS Crowds, dangerous on spring high tide, tricky exit

DIRECTIONS From Ennis, take the N85 through Ennistymon to Lahinch.

9 Brandon Bay

This large, horseshoe-shaped bay, located on the north side of the Dingle Peninsula in County Kerry, offers a variety of breaks. The beach faces northwest, and picks up west-to-northwest swell. It's popular with surfers and windsurfers throughout the year.

WAVE TYPE Left and right

WAVE HEIGHT 2–6 ft (0.6–1.8 m)

BREAK TYPE Beach, reef

BEST SWELL W–NW

BEST WIND E

BEST TIDE All

BEST TIME Year-round

HAZARDS Strong currents in places

DIRECTIONS Take the N86 from Tralee to Castlegregory. There are several places to access the beach from there.

10 Ballydavid

This quality right-hand point break can be seen from the harbor at Ballydavid, a small village on the Dingle Peninsula in County Kerry. It needs a really big swell before it starts to work. It's heavy, particularly on the takeoff, and offers a hollow ride.

WAVE TYPE Right

WAVE HEIGHT 6–10 ft (1.8–3.1 m)

BREAK TYPE Point

BEST SWELL Big W–NW

BEST WIND S

BEST TIDE All

BEST TIME November–March

HAZARDS Heavy takeoff

DIRECTIONS Take the N86 from Tralee to Dingle, and from there follow the R559 to Ballydavid. Check the wave from the harbor.

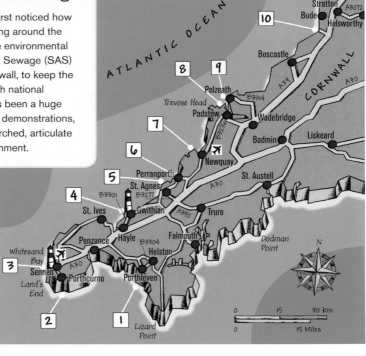

Surfers Against Sewage

It was Britain's surfers who first noticed how much raw sewage was floating around the British coastline. In 1990 the environmental action group Surfers Against Sewage (SAS) was born in St. Agnes, Cornwall, to keep the ocean clean by engaging with national politics. Since then, SAS has been a huge success, staging flamboyant demonstrations, as well as making well-researched, articulate representations to the government.

United Kingdom

The UK's 7,723-mile (12,429-km) coastline encompasses some of the most stunning beaches in Europe and an estimated 500,000 surfers. The long reach of the continental shelf takes the sting out of swell, so surfing here is generally less demanding than in France, Spain, and Portugal. The weather is mild, wet, and changeable, but surf conditions are easy to predict and best between September and November. In the north, intimidating 6-ft (1.8-m) reefs and bitter 41°F (5°C) winters demand total wetsuit cover. The largest surf scenes are in the warmer southwest, which enjoy year-round 2–8-ft (0.6–2.4-m) waves. Summer 3/2 mm wetsuits are perfect for the 61°F (16°C) water temperatures.

Cornwall is the focus of surf culture. The Cornish landscape is a mixture of wild moorland, Neolithic remains, and a post-industrial landscape of abandoned tin mines. A granite bedrock defines the peninsula. Waves come from all directions, breaking on brilliant white quartz sand and into coves tucked under steep cliffs. In contrast to the heather and gorse of the moors, the tourist surf towns of St. Ives, Padstow, and Bude offer a Mediterranean feel and culinary sophistication. Unfortunately, the granite does not erode to form reef breaks, making beaches the only option, with fickle conditions dependent upon the huge tidal changes and ever-shifting sandbars. The exception to this is the outstanding hollow right reef break at Porthleven on the south Cornish coast.

Surf City UK is Newquay on the north Cornish coast, where nine golden beaches are concentrated. Once a fishing port, today it houses most of the thriving British surf industry and in August stages an ASP surf contest, during which the normal wintertime population of 22,000 swells to 250,000. Newquay has a regional airport and is about 260 miles (418 km) from London. Be prepared for the shift from the multicultural buzz of London to slower paced Cornwall, where, in places, time seems to have stood still.

1 Porthleven

Porthleven offers a collection of rock-bottom breaks of varying quality, the focal point being The Reef, a triangular outcrop just to the north of the town's harbor that can throw up powerful, barreling A-frames. Requiring a rare combination of north or northeast winds and a clean southwest swell to work, Porthleven comes alive only a handful of times a year.

WAVE TYPE Left and right

WAVE HEIGHT 2–12 ft (0.6–3.7 m)

BREAK TYPE Reef

BEST SWELL SW or big W–NW

BEST WIND N–NE

BEST TIDE Low or high

BEST TIME September–March

HAZARDS Uneven, barnacle-encrusted reef; crowds

DIRECTIONS From Helston, follow the signs for Porthleven (B3304), and then take the small coast road up the hill just to the north of the harbor.

2 Porthcurno

Porthcurno is a stunningly beautiful cove offering punchy waves well suited to bodyboarding. Its sheltered aspect renders it worth checking on the back end of Atlantic storms as the winds go from southwest to northwest. Porthcurno is famous for its clifftop Minack Theatre, and for being Britain's first link to the USA via telegraph.

WAVE TYPE Left and right

WAVE HEIGHT 2–6 ft (0.6–1.8 m)

BREAK TYPE Beach

BEST SWELL SW or big W–NW

BEST WIND N

BEST TIDE Low

BEST TIME December–March

HAZARDS Getting cut off at the eastern end at high tide

DIRECTIONS From Penzance, follow the A30 west for 5 miles (8 km) and then turn onto the B3283 (and hope you don't get stuck behind a tractor!).

3 Sennen/Gwenver

Located just to the north of Land's End (the most westerly point in the British Isles) is Whitesand Bay, comprising two beach breaks separated by a rocky outcrop. Sennen, at the southern end, is an average, somewhat closey wave offering shelter in unruly conditions. Gwenver, meanwhile, is Cornwall's biggest swell magnet, although its sandbars are notoriously fickle.

WAVE TYPE Left and right

WAVE HEIGHT 2–10 ft (0.6–3.1 m)

BREAK TYPE Beach

BEST SWELL All

BEST WIND SE–S

BEST TIDE Mid

BEST TIME All

HAZARDS Strong rips at Gwenver

DIRECTIONS From Penzance, take the A30 west for about 10 miles (16 km) and then turn right to signposted Sennen Cove.

4 Gwithian

Rumor has it that, at low tide many years ago, a barrel was seen here… Favored by longboarders and beginners due to its gently shelving contour, Gwithian is a reliable, well-patrolled beach break with good facilities nearby. Godrevy Lighthouse, inspiration for Virginia Woolf's *To the Lighthouse*, sits majestically just offshore.

WAVE TYPE Left and right

WAVE HEIGHT 2–10 ft (0.6–3.1 m)

BREAK TYPE Beach

BEST SWELL NW

BEST WIND SE

BEST TIDE All

BEST TIME August–April

HAZARDS Hoards of novice surfers in peak season

DIRECTIONS From Hayle, take the B3301 coast road north for about 2 miles (3.2 km), past Gwithian, and then take a left turn to Godrevy National Trust Park.

5 Trevaunance Cove

During big swells this quaint, sheltered cove can deliver great punchy waves (mainly right-handers) and even the odd barrel. Its major drawback is a lack of space; there's not much room for maneuver here – either in the water or at the parking lot – which sometimes results in a tetchy atmosphere.

WAVE TYPE Right and occasional left

WAVE HEIGHT 2–8 ft (0.6–2.4 m)

BREAK TYPE Beach

BEST SWELL W–NW

BEST WIND S

BEST TIDE Mid

BEST TIME October–March

HAZARDS Often looks smaller than it is from the parking lot; aggressive locals

DIRECTIONS From Truro, take the A390 to Chiverton Cross roundabout and then the B3277 to St. Agnes.

6 Perran Sands

A vast expanse of exposed beach backed by an even bigger area of dunes, Perran Sands offers some welcome space (neighboring beaches can be overcrowded). Owing to wedges caused by the headlands, the waves tend to break better at either end, with the north end (Penhayle Corner) picking up the most swell.

WAVE TYPE Left and right

WAVE HEIGHT 2–10 ft (0.6–3.1 m)

BREAK TYPE Beach

BEST SWELL W

BEST WIND SE

BEST TIDE Mid–low

BEST TIME August–April

HAZARDS Long walk for access

DIRECTIONS From the A30, take either the B3284 or the B3285 to Perranporth, then head for Droskyn Point for a great panorama. If it's too small or crowded here, make for the holiday park and/or take a walk.

7 Fistral Beach

The best of Newquay's several beach breaks, Fistral is the venue for the annual Rip Curl Boardmasters event, held in August. An offshore reef (bombora) known as The Cribber – now becoming popular with tow-in surfers – will break a couple of times a year when swells of more than 10 ft (3.1 m) combine with southeast winds. More sheltered options lie just around the corner to the north.

WAVE TYPE Left and right

WAVE HEIGHT Beach: 2–8 ft (0.6–2.4 m); The Cribber: 10–15 ft (3.1–4.6 m)

BREAK TYPE Beach, reef

BEST SWELL W–NW

BEST WIND SE

BEST TIDE Low

BEST TIME August–April

HAZARDS Crowds

DIRECTIONS The beach is about 2 miles (3.2 km) from the center of Newquay. Follow the signs.

8 Harlyn Bay

Tucked away behind Trevose Head, and therefore lying dormant for most of the summer months, Harlyn Bay comes into its own when big winter swells close out the west-facing beaches, such as nearby Constantine and Booby's. The waves here aren't fantastic (lacking in power and tending to close out), but interesting rights will peel off the rocks at the eastern end at high tide.

WAVE TYPE Left and right

WAVE HEIGHT 2–8 ft (0.6–2.4 m)

BREAK TYPE Beach

BEST SWELL NW

BEST WIND S

BEST TIDE Mid

BEST TIME November–March

HAZARDS None

DIRECTIONS Follow the B3276 north from Newquay or west and then south from Padstow. Take the turnoff (easy to miss) to Harlyn Bay.

The waves of Fistral Beach, near Newquay, challenge the world's top professionals every August.

9 Polzeath

Polzeath offers a gently shelving, average-quality beach break, which is ideal for learning the basics. The adjacent coastline, near the busy beach resort of Polzeath, also boasts ample parking, a large surf shop, good campsites, and great walking on the South West Coast Path.

WAVE TYPE Left and right

WAVE HEIGHT 2–8 ft (0.6–2.4 m)

BREAK TYPE Beach

BEST SWELL W–NW

BEST WIND SE

BEST TIDE Low–mid

BEST TIME August–April

HAZARDS Rip at southern end of beach

DIRECTIONS From Wadebridge, take the B3314 north for about 3 miles (5 km), then follow the signs to Polzeath.

10 Widemouth Bay

Probably the best beach break in an area lacking good ones, Widemouth Bay is a fun wave that tends to break better at around three-quarter tide. Due to the uneven topography, what is a vast expanse at low tide will morph into a small cove as the tide comes in, magnifying the crowd. Rocky outcrops just to the south can yield great waves to those in the know.

WAVE TYPE Left and right

WAVE HEIGHT 2–8 ft (0.6–2.4 m)

BREAK TYPE Beach

BEST SWELL W–NW

BEST WIND SE

BEST TIDE Mid–high

BEST TIME August–April

HAZARDS Rocks at high tide

DIRECTIONS From Holsworthy, follow the A3072 west to Stratton, then take the A39 south for 1 mile (1.6 km), and turn right for the parking lot.

France

Southwest France is the birthplace and hub of European surfing. Visitors from all over the globe come here to sample hollow beach breaks, classy culture, magnificent food, and great beers and wines.

The Silver Coast, as it's known, extends from Royan in the north to Biarritz in the south. The 160-mile (260-km) long stretch of coastline is backed by pine forest and lakes, while the deep Bay of Biscay unloads swell right onto the steeply shelving sand with full force. There's a powerful and sometimes dangerous north-to-south current flow, and good sandbars come and go with tide and swell. Unfortunately, the breaks tend to close out at size, until you reach the jagged coastline south of the city of Biarritz, where both big-wave and beginner breaks sit in close proximity.

In the short, cold winters, the 8-ft (2.4-m) surf is dangerous and powerful, while in the long, warm summers, when the sea temperature climbs to 70°F (21°C), the surf is consistently 3 ft (0.9 m). Most surfers drive the *péage* (toll) roads from Paris or Biarritz airport to join summer crowds and nightlife at Hossegor. Fall brings the best waves and the beach breaks can be super hollow, but crowds create tension. Farther south, at Biarritz on the Basque Coast – where European surfing began in the late 1950s – the waves are excellent, with a stunning architectural backdrop.

Other parts of the Atlantic coast have good surf, too. The 800-mile (1,290-km) rugged coastline of Brittany has climate and surf conditions similar to those of Cornwall in England. Along the Mediterranean, the French Riviera enjoys short-lived swells when northwest or east winds send waves to beach breaks around Marseille and Toulon. The Riviera is one of the most glamorous resort areas in the world, with Monaco, Nice, and Cannes attracting a moneyed, glitzy set.

French lifeguards

Don't mess with French lifeguards! These highly qualified beach patrollers, with their blue and red uniforms, have the right to confiscate your surfboard if you ride a wave into the blue-flagged swimming area. Respect the signs or you might get arrested and fined. Keep out of trouble by surfing peaks a good distance from the swimming area.

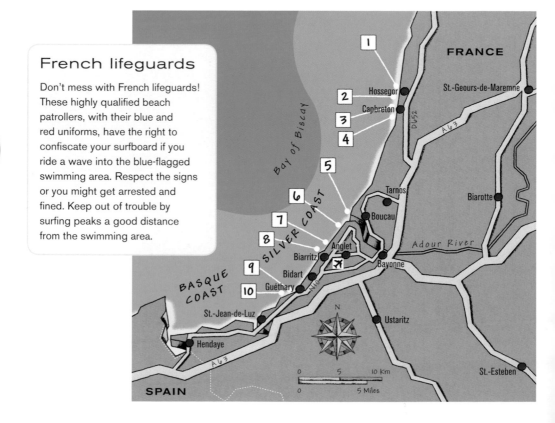

1 Les Culs Nuls

A thumping beach break that throws up epic barrels in the right conditions, Les Culs Nuls ("The Naked Asses") is a nude beach that can serve up waves similar to those farther south, only with less of a crowd. Watch the changing tide as peaks will pop up and disappear all over the place.

WAVE TYPE Left and right

WAVE HEIGHT 1–6 ft (0.3–1.8 m)

BREAK TYPE Beach

BEST SWELL W–NW

BEST WIND E–SE

BEST TIDE Varies depending on the sandbanks

BEST TIME March–May, September–November

HAZARDS Rips

DIRECTIONS From Hossegor's principal beach of La Centrale, follow the main beach road north for about 1¼ miles (2 km) to Les Culs Nuls.

2 La Gravière

Mainly a right, La Gravière is a fast, hollow wave that can claim a lot of boards in the right (or wrong!) conditions. This renowned wave attracts crowds, but the deep, long barrels make up for this.

WAVE TYPE Right and occasional left

WAVE HEIGHT 3–12 ft (0.9–3.7 m)

BREAK TYPE Beach

BEST SWELL W–NW

BEST WIND E–SE

BEST TIDE High

BEST TIME March–May, September–November

HAZARDS Breaking boards, rips, crowds

DIRECTIONS La Gravière is about 500 yards (500 m) north of Hossegor's La Centrale beach.

3 La Centrale

La Centrale, the main beach in Hossegor, can attract big crowds, both on the sand and in the water. Soft when it's small, this wave can hold a number of different peaks along the length of the beach. La Nord, the famous outside bank of La Centrale, has seen some of Europe's biggest tow-in sessions go down.

WAVE TYPE Left and right

WAVE HEIGHT 2–6 ft (0.6–1.8 m)

BREAK TYPE Beach

BEST SWELL W–NW

BEST WIND E–SE

BEST TIDE Low

BEST TIME March–May, September–November

HAZARDS Inexperienced surfers, rips, crowds

DIRECTIONS La Centrale is a short distance west of the center of Hossegor. Just follow the signs.

4 La Piste

La Piste is a beach break that can produce clean tubes and fun, fast waves. Tom Curren had a few legendary sessions here in the mid-1990s that generated a lot of video footage. It's also the home of the annual Quiksilver King of the Groms contest, attracting the world's best junior surfers.

WAVE TYPE Right

WAVE HEIGHT 2–6 ft (0.6–1.8 m)

BREAK TYPE Beach

BEST SWELL W–NW

BEST WIND SE–S

BEST TIDE All

BEST TIME Year-round

HAZARDS Localism

DIRECTIONS From Hossegor, take the D652 south a short distance over the river to the town of Capbreton. Walk south along the beach to La Piste, which breaks in front of some old concrete army bunkers.

La Gravière, near Hossegor, is a beach break that can hold huge swells and serve up big, meaty barrels.

5 Boucau

Head past the industrial eyesores of the local port and you'll find good beach breaks at Boucau. Located just north of the Adour River, it can produce lefts breaking off the groyne, then peaks along the beach. Remember to lock your car – thieves are a problem.

WAVE TYPE Left and right

WAVE HEIGHT 2–6 ft (0.6–1.8 m)

BREAK TYPE Beach

BEST SWELL W–NW

BEST WIND SE–S

BEST TIDE All

BEST TIME Year-round

HAZARDS Thieves

DIRECTIONS From Capbreton, take the D652 then the A63 south (direction: Boucau), turn off onto the D85, and follow the signs to Boucau. The beach is immediately north of the Adour River. Make your way through the industrial area to the beach parking lot.

6 Les Cavaliers

One of the swell magnets for the region, Les Cavaliers is a series of thumping beach breaks that can hold a lot of swell. At the northern end of the beach is a big breakwall. You can use the rip running inside it to get out the back, from where you can drift down the beach till you find a wave to your liking.

WAVE TYPE Right (off the breakwall); left and right (rest of the beach)

WAVE HEIGHT 2–10 ft (0.6–3.1 m)

BREAK TYPE Beach

BEST SWELL W–NW

BEST WIND SE–S

BEST TIDE Mid–low

BEST TIME Year-round

HAZARDS Rips, thumping shore break

DIRECTIONS Head north on the coast road from Biarritz through the western edge of Anglet till you get to Les Cavaliers parking lot.

7 Anglet

Anglet is a series of beach breaks near the town of the same name. From north to south, they are Chambre d'Amour (apparently named in honor of a couple who drowned), Sables d'Or, and Marinella. These are relatively tame waves compared to others in the area. The breaks can get very crowded and, occasionally, very good.

WAVE TYPE Left and right

WAVE HEIGHT 2–6 ft (0.6–1.8 m)

BREAK TYPE Beach

BEST SWELL W–NW

BEST WIND SE–S

BEST TIDE All

BEST TIME Year-round

HAZARDS Crowds

DIRECTIONS Follow the coast road north from Biarritz to the western edge of Anglet. Park along the beachfront.

8 Grande Plage

Biarritz is a grand old town with a big casino looking over the ocean and a lighthouse perched high on the rocks. Bars and clubs bustle after dark, and glamor is imperative on the beaches. As well as surfing, try swimming out to and climbing the smaller islands for a spot of cliff-jumping into the ocean. Biarritz isn't cheap, but it's fun.

WAVE TYPE Left and right

WAVE HEIGHT 2–6 ft (0.6–1.8 m)

BREAK TYPE Beach

BEST SWELL W–NW

BEST WIND SE–S

BEST TIDE All

BEST TIME Year-round

HAZARDS Crowds, pollution

DIRECTIONS The Grande Plage is a short distance west of the center of Biarritz.

9 Avalanche

Avalanche is a famous wave found outside another break, Alcyons, near the town of Guéthary. When a big swell is hitting, head here with your biggest gun and have a go at some of the biggest waves you'll ever encounter in Europe.

WAVE TYPE Left

WAVE HEIGHT 6–15 ft (1.8–4.6 m)

BREAK TYPE Reef

BEST SWELL NW–N

BEST WIND SE–S

BEST TIDE Low–mid

BEST TIME Year-round

HAZARDS Big waves, rocky bottom, rips, crowds

DIRECTIONS From Biarritz, follow the N10 south, via Bidart, to Guéthary. Avalanche is on the south side of Guéthary's harbor.

10 Lafitenia

Possibly the best right-hand point break in the Basque Country, Lafitenia is a long wave that can barrel on the inside section in the right conditions and holds a lot of swell. There is plenty of accommodation nearby, including campgrounds. The wave can get very crowded.

WAVE TYPE Right

WAVE HEIGHT 4–10 ft (1.2–3.1 m)

BREAK TYPE Reef

BEST SWELL NW–N

BEST WIND SE

BEST TIDE Mid–low

BEST TIME Year-round

HAZARDS Big waves, crowds, rocky bottom

DIRECTIONS Lafitenia is about ⅔ mile (1 km) south of Avalanche. Head south from Guéthary on the coast road, or north from St.-Jean-de-Luz on the N10. Park high on the hillside and walk.

Spain

With its high-quality river mouths and top-class locals, Spain is a thrilling and challenging place for a surfer. The waves, mainly confined to wintertime, are often dangerous and powerful. Summer waves are fickle, but this time of year offers a great opportunity to explore the mountainous terrain of the Picos de Europa and Cordillera Cantábrica in between surfing 2-ft (0.6-m) beach breaks. There are cultural delights, too. From mid-July to September towns come alive with weekend parties, including the running of the bulls in Pamplona.

The Atlantic coast of Andalusia, in southern Spain, has shelving beach breaks that unload with power. But it is the north, "Green Spain," that has the finest waves. The climate is far removed from the dry continental, desertlike inland plateau. In the cold, windy winter, when sea temperatures are 54°F (12°C), world-famous breaks such as Mundaka and, to its

time off in San Sebastián

The city of Donostia-San Sebastián (better known simply as San Sebastián) has some of Europe's most vibrant nightlife. After surfing the city's beach break at Zurriola, a stroll around the bay and harbor will calm the spirit before some Rioja and tapas tasting, and dancing in the old town. On weekends the streets bustle with Basque flair.

west, Menakoz, come alive with 10-ft (3.1-m) bone-crushers. The indented coast maximizes the frequent swells, with numerous river-mouth and beach breaks along the Basque Country, Cantabria, and Asturias — all of them accessible

1 Pantin

Pantin is the biggest swell-puller in the region, and as a result gets crowded at the height of summer on small swell conditions when it's the best bet for a wave in northern Galicia. It's been home to a summer European pro contest for a number of years. Pantin will also hold a bit of winter juice and can have hollow, barreling peaks. Big parking lots, free camping.

WAVE TYPE Left and right

WAVE HEIGHT 2–8 ft (0.6–2.4 m)

BREAK TYPE Beach

BEST SWELL W–NW

BEST WIND S

BEST TIDE Low

BEST TIME September–November

HAZARDS Strong rips

DIRECTIONS From Ferrol, follow the AC556 north past Valdoviño, then take the Pantin turnoff.

2 Tapia

This consistent beach break not far from the Galician border in western Asturias is usually a good bet for a wave in minimal conditions. It usually has a decent-shaped left, as well as various peaks. A relative swell-puller, Tapia, like Pantin, is home to a long-standing European pro contest, and is popular year-round, particularly in summer.

WAVE TYPE Left and right

WAVE HEIGHT 2–8 ft (0.6–2.4 m)

BREAK TYPE Beach

BEST SWELL W–NW

BEST WIND S

BEST TIDE Low–mid

BEST TIME September–November

HAZARDS None

DIRECTIONS Follow the N634 east from Ribadeo, then take the Tapia de Casariego turnoff.

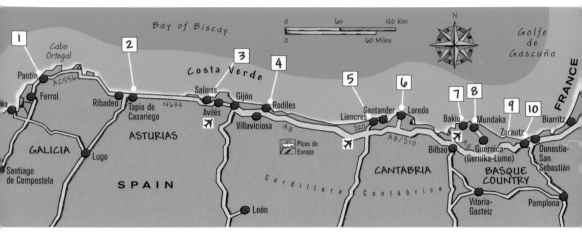

by road from international airports at Madrid, Bilbao, and Santander. The farther west you travel, the more uncrowded the waves.

It's essential that you try some Spanish to get by and gain the respect of the locals.

Without some understanding of the language, Spain can feel intimidating and conservative. But if you have the right attitude, the Spanish people will welcome you warmly into a wonderful and ancient lifestyle.

3 Salinas

Salinas is a consistent beach break, with waves getting bigger the farther east you go along the beach. It works on all tides. Often crowded, Salinas can also be fairly dirty. With a backdrop that's not exactly scenic (a lot of concrete), this is nevertheless one of the most popular beach breaks in the state.

WAVE TYPE Left and right

WAVE HEIGHT 2–8 ft (0.6–2.4 m)

BREAK TYPE Beach

BEST SWELL W–NW

BEST WIND SE

BEST TIDE All

BEST TIME September–November

HAZARDS Pollution, crowds

DIRECTIONS Follow the A8 from Gijón, turn on to the A181 to Avilés, and take the N632A to Salinas.

4 Rodiles

A sand-bottomed river-mouth left in a beautiful setting, Rodiles is often referred to as "Mundaka's little sister." Though it's usually not as long or hollow, it's pretty damn good nevertheless. It needs a decent-sized swell. Although famous as a left, Rodiles can occasionally have rights, too. It's set in a nature reserve, and you park among eucalyptus trees overlooking the break.

WAVE TYPE Left and occasional right

WAVE HEIGHT 4–8 ft (1.2–2.4 m)

BREAK TYPE River mouth

BEST SWELL NW

BEST WIND S–SW

BEST TIDE Low–mid

BEST TIME December–February

HAZARDS Car crime

DIRECTIONS From Gijón, drive east on the A8, take the Villaviciosa turnoff, then follow signs to Rodiles.

5 Liencres

This is a good-quality beachie, with powerful peaks up and down a long beach, depending on the banks. Being the closest consistent beach break west of Santander, Liencres is the hub of that city's surf scene and, as a result, is usually crowded on the better peaks. There's a big parking lot.

WAVE TYPE Left and right

WAVE HEIGHT 2–8 ft (0.6–2.4 m)

BREAK TYPE Beach

BEST SWELL W–NW

BEST WIND SE

BEST TIDE Low

BEST TIME September–November

HAZARDS Crowds, some localism

DIRECTIONS Follow the S20 west from Santander, then take the Liencres turnoff shortly after Santa Cruz de Bezana.

6 Santa Marina

Santa Marina is a gnarly, big-wave spot off the island that gives the break its name. The wave has a big, steep wall with heavy tube sections, requiring a big swell to work with east winds, which usually happens during winter and at only a handful of other times per year.

WAVE TYPE Right

WAVE HEIGHT 4–15 ft (1.2–4.6 m)

BREAK TYPE Reef

BEST SWELL W–NW

BEST WIND E

BEST TIDE Mid

BEST TIME December–February

HAZARDS Rocks, cleanup sets

DIRECTIONS From Santander, follow the A8/S10 east, then the CA145 north toward Marina de Cudeyo, through Somo then toward Loredo. The wave breaks off the island of Santa Marina, just off Loredo.

7 Bakio

Bakio is a consistent beach break within a scenic 20-minute drive of Mundaka. It has waves on small days when Mundaka is flat, and as a result, some rounds of the Billabong Pro Mundaka WCT in October are usually held here. The peaks are of average quality; Bakio gets good when sandbars allow. It's often crowded, particularly in summer.

WAVE TYPE Left and right

WAVE HEIGHT 2–8 ft (0.6–2.4 m)

BREAK TYPE Beach

BEST SWELL NW

BEST WIND S

BEST TIDE Mid

BEST TIME September–November

HAZARDS Some car crime in summer

DIRECTIONS From Mundaka, take the BI2235 to Bermeo, then follow the BI3101 through the forest toward Bakio.

8 Mundaka

Mundaka is far and away one of Europe's best surf spots, and on its day can rival any left anywhere. It's always crowded, and getting waves on the peak is unlikely when it's firing. But with several hundred yards of hollow wall reeling off, visitors can still have their moments by spreading out.

WAVE TYPE Left

WAVE HEIGHT 3–12 ft (0.9–3.7 m)

BREAK TYPE River mouth

BEST SWELL N

BEST WIND S

BEST TIDE Low

BEST TIME September–February

HAZARDS Crowds

DIRECTIONS From San Sebastián, follow the A8 west toward Bilbao, take the Amorbieta–Etxano turnoff, and then the BI635 to Guernica (Gernika-Lumo). From there, follow the signs to Bermeo then Mundaka.

9 Roca Puta

Roca Puta is an intimidating spot just off the coast road with a difficult takeoff right on the rocks. Entry and exit from the water can be hairy, particularly on bigger days; the peak is usually pretty packed with a tight-knit crew. Just around the corner is Playa Gris, a spot that has provided multiple entries for big-wave surfers in the Billabong XXL awards.

WAVE TYPE Right

WAVE HEIGHT 6–15 ft (1.8–4.6 m)

BREAK TYPE Reef, point

BEST SWELL NW–N

BEST WIND S

BEST TIDE Mid

BEST TIME December–February

HAZARDS Rocks, tricky entry and exit

DIRECTIONS From Zarautz, head west along the N634 coast road. The break is visible from the road about 2 miles (3.2 km) before (east of) Zumaia.

10 Zarautz

This north-facing beach break stretches from in front of the town of Zarautz to the end of the bay to the east. It offers multiple peaks, the best often in front of the surf club (Surf Eskola). Zarautz is a hotbed of surfing talent and home to some of Spain's top pros and red-hot groms. Parking is often tricky.

WAVE TYPE Left and right

WAVE HEIGHT 1–6 ft (0.3–1.8 m)

BREAK TYPE Beach

BEST SWELL NW–N

BEST WIND S–SW

BEST TIDE Mid

BEST TIME September–November

HAZARDS Parking

DIRECTIONS From San Sebastián, follow the A8 west, and turn off to Zarautz town just before the Zarautz toll (*peaje*) station.

Mundaka is famed for its screaming barrels of up to four tube sections, depending on the sandbanks.

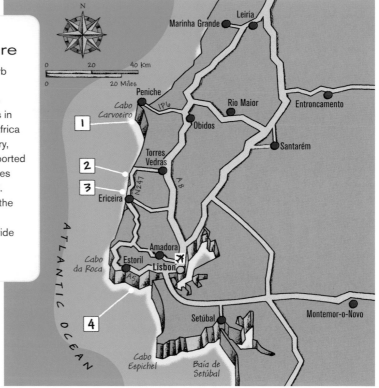

Portugal's coffee culture

Coffee in Portugal is superb and deeply woven into the nation's history. During the colonial period, plantations in São Tomé and Angola in Africa supplied the mother country, and coffee culture was exported to Brazil. Espresso machines are everywhere in Portugal. A rich *bica* espresso from the bakery will give you extra strength for the next tube ride and pick you up from the previous night's excesses.

Portugal

Portugal is a great seafaring nation, having played a crucial role during the Age of Discovery in the 1400s, when Prince Henry the Navigator helped open up trading routes around the Cape of Good Hope. Portugal has become a great surfing nation since the sport erupted here in the 1980s, and the country remains an inexpensive, wave-rich destination for traveling surfers. Its west-facing coastline consistently enjoys strong Atlantic swells that focus on heavy 8-ft (2.4-m) right-hand point breaks and powerful closeout beach breaks. The Portuguese locals surf with passion and commitment — this is what it takes to deal with the thundering barrels at Supertubos and the daunting sharp reef at Coxos.

The lack of a continental shelf accentuates the power of the Atlantic swell. The deep water and the cold Canaries Current keep the water temperature as cool as 64°F (18°C) in the summer, when the air can be 82°F (28°C).

But in winter, when the surf is at its best, the water stays a mild 61°F (16°C), making a 4/3 mm wetsuit perfect.

Lisbon has an international airport. Rental cars are inexpensive and the roads excellent. Lisbon waves offer a good mix of beaches and reefs, but they are crowded and polluted. Obvious hotspots are around the whitewashed stone town of Ericeira and the fishing heartland of Peniche. Both locations have a good variety of waves for intermediate and advanced surfers. The farther north you go, the wetter the climate and the worse the wave quality. Southward, into the arid Algarve, the temperatures are higher and point breaks numerous and long. Cheap flights are available to Faro from many European cities, and, although prices have risen recently, Portugal still offers better value than any other European surf destination. The locals really like it if you try a couple of Portuguese words, but the language is tough to master.

1 Supertubos

This powerful, hollow wave just south of Peniche has excellent, predominantly left barrels, and is considered one of Europe's finest beach breaks. Very popular with local bodyboarders, it's usually crowded. The water is consistently colder here than at other spots in Portugal. It's sometimes prone to closing out.

WAVE TYPE Left and right

WAVE HEIGHT 2–8 ft (0.6–2.4 m)

BREAK TYPE Beach

BEST SWELL SW

BEST WIND NE

BEST TIDE Low–mid

BEST TIME December–February

HAZARDS Car crime, crowds, aggressive bodyboarders, smell of fish from nearby fish-processing plant

DIRECTIONS From Lisbon, take the A8 north, then at Obidos follow the IP6 toward Peniche. The turnoff to the beach is about ⅔ mile (1 km) before the town.

2 Coxos

This right-hand point break is widely regarded as the best wave in Portugal. It comes out of deep water and breaks with power along a series of hollow sections in front of sharp rock ledges. Entry and exit is tricky on solid swells, so watch where and how the locals do it. Coxos is the home break of some of Portugal's (and Europe's) finest pro surfers.

WAVE TYPE Right

WAVE HEIGHT 3–12 ft (0.9–3.7 m)

BREAK TYPE Point

BEST SWELL NW

BEST WIND E

BEST TIDE Low–mid

BEST TIME December–February

HAZARDS Rocks, sea urchins, tricky entry and exit

DIRECTIONS Drive from Ericeira north along the N247 coast road, turn left at Ribamar, and follow dirt tracks for a couple of minutes.

3 Ribeira d'Ilhas

This series of right-breaking reefs is pretty consistent, and can have ridable surf under a range of swell and wind conditions when none of the other breaks in the Ericeira area are on. The 5-Star WQS contest is held here in September. An excellent surf camp overlooks the break.

WAVE TYPE Right

WAVE HEIGHT 2–10 ft (0.6–3.1 m)

BREAK TYPE Reef, point

BEST SWELL NW

BEST WIND E

BEST TIDE Mid

BEST TIME December–February

HAZARDS Crowds

DIRECTIONS Drive north from Ericeira for a few minutes along the N247 coast road, then turn into the parking area above the break to check it.

4 Carcavelos

Close to the city of Lisbon, this high-quality beach break suffers from crowds and pollution. Nevertheless, Carcavelos produces excellent, hollow, mainly left peaks, which break in view of the walls of a medieval fortress. A straight southwest swell usually provides the most favorable conditions.

WAVE TYPE Left and occasional right

WAVE HEIGHT 2–10 ft (0.6–3.1 m)

BREAK TYPE Beach

BEST SWELL SW

BEST WIND NE

BEST TIDE All

BEST TIME September–November

HAZARDS Crowds, pollution

DIRECTIONS From central Lisbon, take the A5 west (direction: Costa do Estoril), and turn off onto the N6-7 toward Carcavelos.

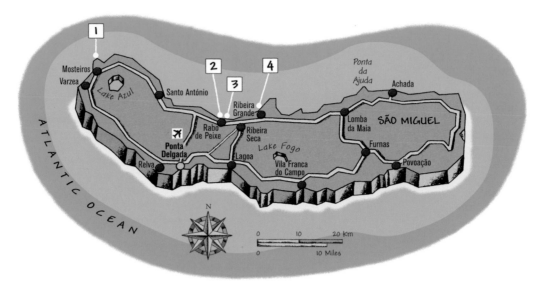

Azores

The surf-pounded Azores are nine dramatic volcanic islands in the middle of the Atlantic, about 800 miles (1,300 km) from Lisbon. Stormy seas are so ubiquitous here that Portuguese sailors often referred to the Azores as "the Disappearing Isles" because the islands' peaks often seemed swamped by the swells.

The islands form the highest peak of the Mid-Atlantic Ridge, which runs from Iceland to the Antarctic, and the volcanic rock has formed steep topography. São Miguel is the largest and most populated island and has north-facing beaches such as Ribeira Grande, which have black sand and fun surf with small tides.

Despite the remote setting, surf culture is strong and local surfers should be respected. Between September and May, Azorean surf is regularly bigger than 10 ft (3.1 m) and very powerful. Long drops and fast-breaking sections thunder over sharp lava volcanic reefs. The proximity to the source of the swell also means that conditions can change very quickly. This can prove extremely hazardous when a small, clean swell at one of the many remote breaks quickly transforms into a wild disorganized sea. Swell size, inaccessibility, and reef shape make surfing in the Azores not for the novice.

The azure water is teeming with sea life, including sharks, squid, and jellyfish. In spring and summer (April to September) it is warm with light northwest winds, 3-ft (0.9-m) waves, and 72°F (22°C) sea temperatures, making surfing in boardshorts a possibility. In fall and winter (October to March) the air is cool, but the sea averages 61°F (16°C), suiting a 3/2 mm wetsuit. The swells can peak at 15 ft (4.6 m) and come from all directions, with a dominant southwest airflow. Winds and rainfall quickly chase swell, which is short-lived and disorganized due to the island's proximity to the source of the storm. Spring and fall are the best surf periods for clean surf and calm and warm weather.

São Miguel's international airport is at Ponta Delgada in the southwest. You can rent cars from the airport. The tight-cornering cliff-edge roads rival the surf for thrills.

the Azores High

The Azores High is a mid-Atlantic high-pressure weather system that is invariably centered over the islands. The clockwise rotation of the Azores High has a crucial impact on European and African weather and surf. In an ideal situation, it can protect Europe with clear weather, keeping lows moving to the northeast, and sending perfect, clean waves to the shores of Western Europe.

1 Ponta dos Mosteiros

Situated in the extreme northwest corner of the island of São Miguel, this powerful open ocean spot needs a medium-sized swell to start to break, and can hold swells of up to around 16 ft (4.9 m). Like most spots on the island, it's best suited to experienced surfers.

WAVE TYPE Left and right

WAVE HEIGHT 4–15 ft (1.2–4.6 m)

BREAK TYPE Reef

BEST SWELL NW

BEST WIND SE

BEST TIDE Mid

BEST TIME November–February

HAZARDS Sharp rocks, big waves

DIRECTIONS From Ponta Delgada, take the coast road west in the direction of Relva, and continue all the way to the northwest tip of the island. About 1¼ miles (2 km) after Varzea, take a left turn to Mosteiros.

2 Rabo de Peixe

Considered by many to be the best surf spot on the island, this left is situated in the village of the same name. This wave used to be a right barrel, but the construction of a jetty has changed it into a hollow left. While it's still an excellent wave, many claim the pre-jetty right was even better.

WAVE TYPE Left

WAVE HEIGHT 4–10 ft (1.2–3.1 m)

BREAK TYPE Reef

BEST SWELL N–NE

BEST WIND S–SW

BEST TIDE Mid

BEST TIME November–February

HAZARDS Sea urchins, rocks, aggressive locals

DIRECTIONS From Ribeira Grande, head west on the coast highway through Ribeira Seca, and then continue for another 2½ miles (4 km) to Rabo de Peixe.

3 Areais

A relatively flat-bottomed point break, Areais is the most consistent wave on the north coast of São Miguel. Although not as dangerous as other spots on the island, it's still not suitable for novices. The wave breaks relatively short, left and right.

WAVE TYPE Left and right

WAVE HEIGHT 3–8 ft (0.9–2.4 m)

BREAK TYPE Point

BEST SWELL NW

BEST WIND S

BEST TIDE All

BEST TIME November–February

HAZARDS Sometimes dangerous rips

DIRECTIONS Head west from Ribeira Grande on the coast highway for about 3 miles (5 km), then take a right turn about 1¼ miles (2 km) before Rabo de Peixe to check this spot.

4 Ribeira Grande

This beach break with a sand-and-rock bottom is situated in front of the biggest town on the north coast of São Miguel, Ribeira Grande. The wave packs a punch and isn't suitable for total beginners, although it's less intimidating than most spots on the north coast.

WAVE TYPE Left

WAVE HEIGHT 4–8 ft (1.2–2.4 m)

BREAK TYPE Beach

BEST SWELL N

BEST WIND S

BEST TIDE Mid–high

BEST TIME November–February

HAZARDS Rips

DIRECTIONS From Ponta Delgada, first take the coast road east for about 1¼ miles (2 km) in the direction of Lagoa, then turn left following signs across the island to Ribeira Grande.

Italy

Surfing the coast of Italy is something to be savored. While the cultural experience of this ancient area is ever-present, the swells are short-lived with a small fetch and wave period. In winter the waves can be 3 ft (0.9 m) and clean with 55°F (13°C) water, and a 3/2 mm full wetsuit may be required. "It's not a place you're looking for, it's a wind condition," explains Nik Zanella, editor of Italy's stylish *SurfNews* magazine. "Where's the longest fetch going to strike? It can take a lot of traveling to be there when it happens. But the rewards are worth it. Italian surfers are excellent forecasters."

The Mediterranean's waters are the most heavily navigated on Earth, but in Italy surfing has only recently become popular, mainly around Tuscany, Genoa, and Rome. For the visitor, crime and pollution are hazards, but Italian surfers are welcoming to respectful travelers. Away from the major urban areas,

in Sicily and southern Italy, crowded lineups and territorial locals are unknown.

The quality of the surf ranges from clean, small beach breaks to fun, mushy point breaks and occasional sharp, limestone reefs. In summer, between July and August, when the water is 75°F (24°C), two-week flat spells are common. This is also possible in January and February due to cold continental high pressure. During other parts of the year the Mediterranean is notorious for sudden and violent short-lived storms from the mixing of Atlantic, African, and European weather systems. The associated winds can deliver swells to every coast, particularly between March and May. The usual source of swell is the consistent Mistral north wind, which supplies waves on the north- and west-facing coastlines.

Blink and you'll miss it. But it's worth taking a board to supplement the cultural buzz.

the Mistral

The Mistral is a strong katabatic wind that cools above the Massif Central mountain range of France and funnels down the Rhône Valley, speeding up before it reaches the Gulf of Lyon. It is the main source of swell in the Mediterranean, sending waves to the southeast to be savored by Italian surfers.

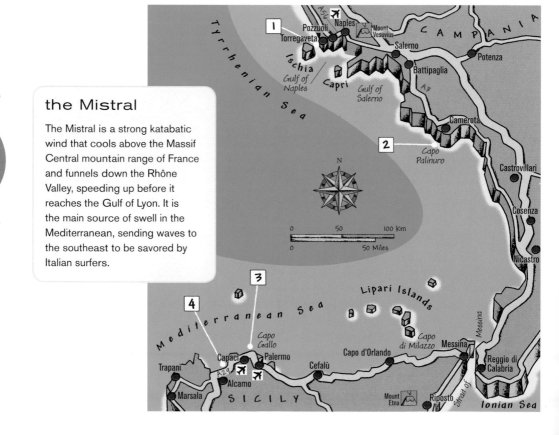

Tyrrhenian Sea

A56
Naples
Pozzuoli
Torregaveta
Mount Vesuvius
Salerno
C A M P A N I A
Potenza
Ischia
Gulf of Naples
Capri
Gulf of Salerno
Battipaglia
A3
Camerota

2
Capo Palinuro
Castrovillari

Cosenza

N

0   50   100 Km
0   50 Miles

Nicastro

3
Lipari Islands

4
Mediterranean Sea

Messina

Capo Gallo
Capo di Milazzo
Messina
Capo d'Orlando

Capaci
Palermo
Cefalù
Trapani
A29
Alcamo
Marsala
S I C I L Y
Mount Etna
Riposto
Reggio di Calabria

Strait of

Ionian Sea

1 Capolinea

Situated a short distance west of the city of Naples, Capolinea is a broad bay that picks up a range of Mediterranean swells from the northwest, southwest, and southeast. A series of left and right peaks works okay on messy swells and can handle the onshore wind, as well as a bit of size.

WAVE TYPE Left and right

WAVE HEIGHT 1–6 ft (0.3–1.8 m)

BREAK TYPE Reef

BEST SWELL SE–NW

BEST WIND N

BEST TIDE All

BEST TIME December–February

HAZARDS None

DIRECTIONS The town of Torregaveta lies at the southern end of the bay, about 18 miles (29 km) from Naples. Follow the A56 west in the direction of Pozzuoli, after which you navigate around Lago Averno, through Bacoli, to Torregaveta.

2 Le Dune

This beach break is located not far from the town of Camerota in the Campania region. Le Dune picks up all west and northwest swells, mainly rights, and still works reasonably well with medium-strength onshore winds. As a bonus, it's usually not crowded.

WAVE TYPE Right and occasional left

WAVE HEIGHT 1–6 ft (0.3–1.8 m)

BREAK TYPE Beach

BEST SWELL W–NW

BEST WIND NW

BEST TIDE All

BEST TIME December–February

HAZARDS None

DIRECTIONS From the town of Battipaglia, take the A3 south, then the SS517 west to Camerota.

3 Isola delle Femmine

This range of zippy, hollow peaks, located northwest of the city of Palermo, often provides the most consistent surf in the region. These peaks require a northwest swell but can't handle much onshore wind. Being close to Palermo and relatively consistent, this spot has a tendency to get crowded.

WAVE TYPE Left and right

WAVE HEIGHT 1–6 ft (0.3–1.8 m)

BREAK TYPE Beach

BEST SWELL NW

BEST WIND SE

BEST TIDE All

BEST TIME December–February

HAZARDS Crowds

DIRECTIONS Take the A29 west from Palermo, and follow the signs.

4 Ciammarita

Ciammarita picks up northwest swells, the most common swell direction on Sicily's north coast. Breaking in the bay are several sand-bottomed A-frame peaks that can handle the onshore wind as long as it's not howling. Ciammarita is usually less crowded than surf spots closer to Palermo.

WAVE TYPE Left and right

WAVE HEIGHT 2–6 ft (0.6–1.8 m)

BREAK TYPE Beach

BEST SWELL NW

BEST WIND SE

BEST TIDE All

BEST TIME December–February

HAZARDS None

DIRECTIONS From Palermo, take the A29 west in the direction of Trapani. After about 30 miles (48 km), turn onto the SS113 toward the village of Trappeto and, just before the village, turn off to Spiaggia di Ciammarita.

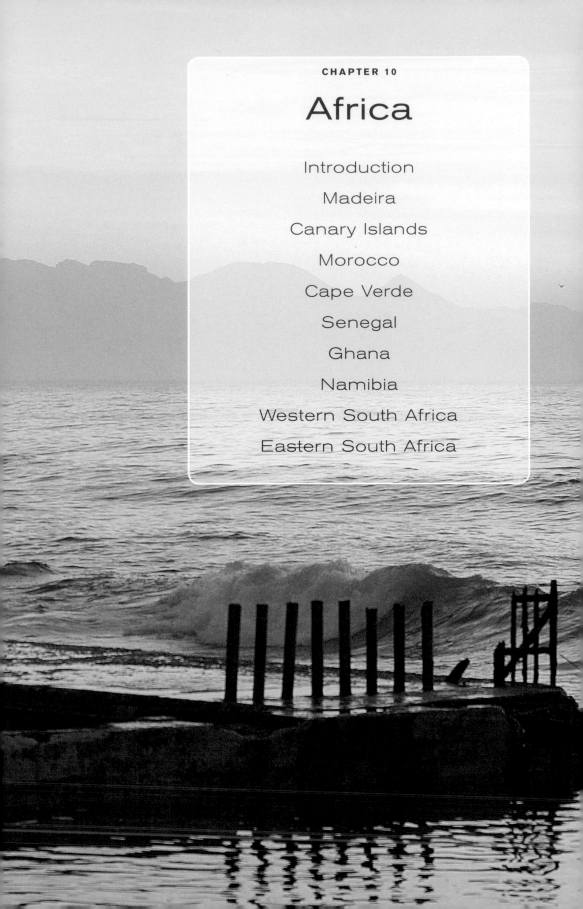

Introduction

Africa is the second-largest continent, covering a fifth of the world's land area. Surrounded predominantly by the Atlantic and Indian oceans, and with 22,920 miles (36,888 km) of coastline, Africa has more than 30 countries where surfing is possible, including those bordering the Mediterranean Sea.

The northwest coast from Morocco to Senegal, including the offshore archipelagoes of the Canaries, Madeira, and Cape Verde, is well positioned to receive North Atlantic swell, which is biggest between November and February. This area is typified by an abundance of powerful right reef breaks. The northeast trade winds create favorable offshore winds at many of these waves. The Canaries Current keeps the water cool, although it does warm up between June and October, which unfortunately aren't the ideal surfing months.

The west coast from Senegal to South Africa receives swell from intense low-pressure systems originating near Patagonia's Cape Horn. These systems cross the South Atlantic on their way past the bottom of Africa. This swell is at its biggest between about April and September, with the bulk of its power hitting the shores of South Africa and Namibia; at this time of year, Cape Town's peninsula waves are often large, raw, and stormy. The swell loses size from Angola northward, particularly in the countries bordering the Gulf of Guinea, as it travels longer distances over a shallow continental shelf before it arrives at the coast. The positive side of this is that although countries like Ghana, Liberia, and Gabon rarely get solid surf, what does arrive is usually clean and organized. The predominant southwest wind is onshore for much of the west coast; however, this wind becomes more variable as it hits the land. The Benguela Current affects the west coast, especially in the south, making for extremely frigid waters year-round.

South Africa's south- and southeast-facing coasts, as well as Mozambique's, also receive strong South Atlantic southwest swells between April and September. However, these same storms also send southeast swells as they track below the coast of Africa. From December to

Atlantic swells hit the the reef at The Dunes, South Africa, creating some challenging waves.

Morocco and South Africa are the undoubted stars of African surfing, but several other countries are known for quality waves; still others are uncharted surf territory.

March, occasional cyclones can also light up southeast-facing coasts with east swell. This entire coast has an enormous variety of waves as well as the highest density of right points on the planet, between Cape St. Francis and Durban. The weather here is more settled than the exposed Western Cape and the predominant southwest winds favor many of the spots. The water gets warmer farther east along the coast as the Atlantic mixes with the Indian Ocean and the warm Agulhas Current.

The Challenges of Travel

South Africa is the only country that's fairly easy to traverse in search of waves. Most of Africa's waves are remote, and a four-wheel-drive vehicle is the best way to find them. This comes with its own set of problems, however, like negotiating flooded roads, crossing borders, and avoiding land mines in former war zones. Sharks are a major concern, especially along the coasts of Mozambique and southeastern South Africa, where great white, tiger, and bull sharks have been responsible for many fatal attacks on surfers. Other hazards include crime, such as carjackings and robbery, especially in South Africa, and pollution near big coastal cities, particularly in Morocco.

Diseases such as malaria, AIDS, and cholera are also a concern. Seek medical advice about these before traveling. Once in Africa, it's best to drink bottled or boiled water. With common sense, however, most problems can be avoided, and the sense of adventure and quality of waves that a surf trip to this continent provides make the obstacles part of the magical surf experience that only wild Africa can provide.

the king who loves to surf

King Mohammed VI of Morocco, who claims descent from the Prophet Mohammed, wields absolute power in his country. He also has a great love for surfing and is the president of the lavish Oudayas Surf Club in Rabat, where he's been known to surf. This means that it's not a good idea to drop in on the locals of Rabat – one of them could just be the king.

Madeira

Known as the Rock Garden of the Atlantic because of its picturesque terraced settlements, Madeira is one of the peaks of an ocean mountain range reaching 6,104 ft (1,860 m) above sea level, 310 miles (500 km) from the coast of Africa. These peaks form the Madeira archipelago, an autonomous region of Portugal, of which Madeira is the largest member. The island's rugged coastline descends dramatically into the ocean, and this geography, combined with an exposed coast, make it a serious big-wave location. With the exception of Machico, the island's waves are suitable only for advanced surfers.

The biggest waves are seen from November to February, when northwest swells arrive from the North Atlantic. The predominant wind is northeast, which is favorable for the southwest-facing breaks such as Jardim do Mar and Paúl do Mar, although the island's steepness offers some natural protection from the wind. The north coast is often onshore, so dawn or evening sessions are worth considering.

Funchal, the capital, has an international airport. The climate is moderate with average temperatures rarely getting below 55°F (13°C) or above 79°F (26°C). While the southern side of the island is almost always bathed in sun, the north is often shrouded in a cool mist. Wear full wetsuits from November to June, when water temperatures average 61–66°F (16–19°C); a springsuit can be worn from July to October in temperatures around 70°F (21°C).

Jardim do Mar's seawall

Despite widespread protest and condemnation, in 2005 the the government built a seawall at the village of Jardim do Mar, home to the best wave on the island. Although the wave is still very good when the swells are big, the wall has made the wave worse on smaller days, as well as more dangerous because cement blocks placed in the water are close to the breaking waves. The wall has also marred the beauty of what was once a stunning village.

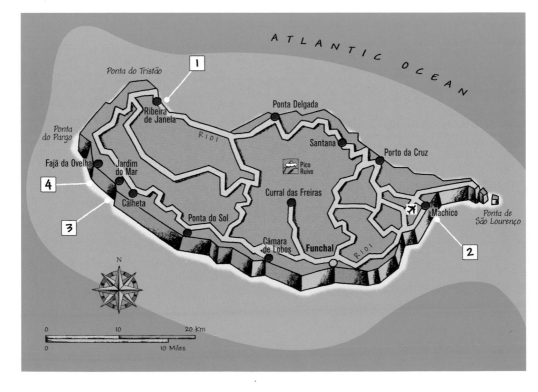

1 Contreira

This long, reeling left point picks up as much swell as anywhere on Madeira. However, to get Contreira at its best you need a calm, windless day and a medium-sized swell. Nearby Ribeira da Janela (to the west) is another top-quality left point break.

WAVE TYPE Left

WAVE HEIGHT 6–12 ft (1.8–3.7 m)

BREAK TYPE Point

BEST SWELL W–N

BEST WIND SW

BEST TIDE All

BEST TIME November–February

HAZARDS Rocks, currents

DIRECTIONS From Ribeira da Janela, drive east on the R101 for a short distance. The point is opposite a sign advertising a restaurant.

2 Machico

Madeira is not a place for the fainthearted, but if a more mellow scene is required it can be found at Machico. Localized southeast winds can generate onshore waves here when the rest of the island is flat, and the beach break is the tamest the island has to offer.

WAVE TYPE Left and right

WAVE HEIGHT 4–8 ft (1.2–2.4 m)

BREAK TYPE Beach

BEST SWELL SE

BEST WIND NW

BEST TIDE Low–mid

BEST TIME November–February

HAZARDS Rocks

DIRECTIONS From Funchal, drive east for 12½ miles (20 km) on the R101 to Machico.

3 Jardim do Mar

The spot that put the island on the map as a serious big-wave destination, Jardim do Mar is an extremely powerful wave that's suitable only for the very experienced surfer. The full impact of a seawall constructed a few years ago is as yet unclear, but this wave can still hold anything the Atlantic throws at it.

WAVE TYPE Right

WAVE HEIGHT 6–20+ ft (1.8–6.1+ m)

BREAK TYPE Point

BEST SWELL W–N

BEST WIND NE

BEST TIDE All

BEST TIME November–February

HAZARDS Boulders, currents, hazardous entry and exit

DIRECTIONS From Calheta, drive west on the R101, then turn left onto a minor road, which takes you to Jardim do Mar.

4 Paúl do Mar

Consistently bigger than nearby Ponta Pequena and Jardim do Mar, this wave is a fast, barreling right that breaks terrifyingly close to the concrete seawall built to protect the fishing village from the might of the Atlantic. Paúl do Mar is a very challenging wave.

WAVE TYPE Right

WAVE HEIGHT 6–20+ ft (1.8–6.1+ m)

BREAK TYPE Point

BEST SWELL W–N

BEST WIND NE

BEST TIDE All

BEST TIME November–February

HAZARDS Rocks, currents, difficult entry and exit

DIRECTIONS From Jardim do Mar, walk for 30 minutes along the cliff path to Ponta Pequena; Paúl do Mar is a 20-minute walk from there.

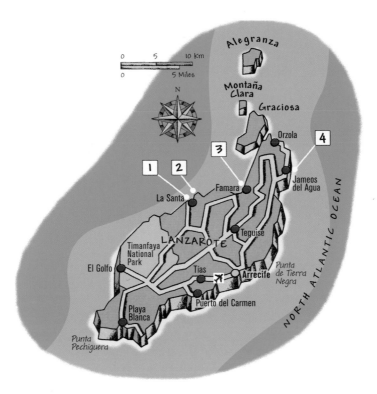

Canary Islands

The Canary Islands, a volcanic archipelago of seven islands and several islets, are less than 70 miles (113 km) off the African coast. They are an autonomous region of Spain. Lanzarote is the island with the most consistent surf. Its main town is Arrecife, where the international airport is located.

The island's contrasting waves range from the heavy slabs around La Santa to the long, stretching beach break of Playa de Famara. Beginners love Playa de Famara, and a couple of surf schools operate there. But novice surfers have few other options, as most of the island's waves break over lava reef where some experience is needed. Waves such as Morro Negro and San Juan (near Playa de Famara) have a consistency, power, and quality to keep most surfers happy, apart from the experts, that is, whose main mission is making barrels at brutally intense waves like El Quemao.

The North Atlantic can send through large northwest-to-north swells of up to 18 ft (5.5 m). The peak of this action is between November and February, which also coincides with reasonably favorable east–northeast trade winds.

Lanzarote has a pleasant semiarid climate. Temperatures average 57–70°F (14–21°C) in winter and 70–84°F (21–29°C) in summer. Rainfall is minimal. With water temperatures averaging 64–72°F (18–22°C), full wetsuits or springsuits are the usual attire. Hazards include sea urchins and shallow, breaking waves. For the surfer, September to April are the best months.

the Hawaii of the Atlantic?

Along with Ireland, the Canary Islands have often been dubbed the "Hawaii of the Atlantic." Lanzarote in particular has powerful waves breaking over sharp volcanic reef that certainly live up to this billing. Unfortunately, the island also has a reputation for gnarly locals, although respectful travelers, especially those who make an effort to use basic Spanish, are unlikely to encounter problems.

1 El Quemao

El Quemao is a pipelinelike left-hand reef break in front of the small harbor at La Santa on Lanzarote's west coast. There's a big peak takeoff, followed by a huge barrel, and an end section over shallow urchin-covered lava reef. Definitely not for beginners.

WAVE TYPE Left

WAVE HEIGHT 3–12 ft (0.9–3.7 m)

BREAK TYPE Reef

BEST SWELL NW–N

BEST WIND E

BEST TIDE Mid–high

BEST TIME October–March

HAZARDS Powerful waves, shallow and sharp reef, sea urchins, strong currents, territorial local and expat surfers

DIRECTIONS From Lanzarote airport on the east coast, follow signposts to the town of La Santa on the west coast; El Quemao is directly in front of the harbor.

2 Morro Negro

A long and powerful right point break on the northwest coast of Lanzarote, Morro Negro can hold major winter swells. Easily accessible and less localized than other nearby spots, this wave is popular with both locals and visitors.

WAVE TYPE Right

WAVE HEIGHT 3–12 ft (0.9–3.7 m)

BREAK TYPE Point

BEST SWELL NW–N

BEST WIND E

BEST TIDE All

BEST TIME October–March

HAZARDS Powerful waves, slippery rocks, sea urchins, strong currents

DIRECTIONS From Lanzarote airport on the east coast, follow signposts to the town of La Santa on the west coast. From there, the prominent point of Morro Negro is easy to find.

3 Playa de Famara

This large open beach break takes all swells and can be very good with offshore south winds. Playa de Famara is a popular spot for surf schools and their students as it is one of the few sand beaches on volcanic Lanzarote.

WAVE TYPE Left and right

WAVE HEIGHT 3–6 ft (0.9–1.8 m)

BREAK TYPE Beach

BEST SWELL NW–N

BEST WIND S–SW

BEST TIDE Mid–high

BEST TIME October–March

HAZARDS Strong currents, territorial locals

DIRECTIONS From Lanzarote airport on the east coast, follow signposts to the village of Playa de Famara on the northwest coast. Although there's accommodation in the village, most surfers stay in the La Santa area and make a day trip to the break.

4 Jameos del Agua

A left-hand point break on the northeast coast of Lanzarote, Jameos is a good option when there's a large swell and northwest wind. The wave is a long left with various sections, and there can be a strong current on a big swell.

WAVE TYPE Left

WAVE HEIGHT 3–6 ft (0.9–1.8 m)

BREAK TYPE Point

BEST SWELL NW–N

BEST WIND W–NW

BEST TIDE Mid–high

BEST TIME October–March

HAZARDS Sharp and shallow reef, sea urchins, strong currents, territorial locals

DIRECTIONS From Lanzarote airport on the east coast, follow signposts to the town of Jameos del Agua on the northeast coast. There's parking on the black lava near the point.

Morocco

Morocco's pleasant climate and exposure to the North Atlantic's swells make it an attractive surfing destination, especially given its close proximity to Europe. The coast from Rabat to Agadir is liberally dotted with beach breaks, reefs, and points, and the coastal highway gives easy access.

Several consistent, uncrowded waves, such as Dar Bouazza, exist on the northwest-facing coast around the cities of Casablanca and Rabat. The majority of surfers bypass them, however, heading directly south to the world-class rights just north of Agadir. These waves get big and challenging, yet break over smooth, forgiving reefs, meaning they're relatively user-friendly for the paddle-fit.

Openly exposed to the Atlantic Ocean, Morocco's coast receives an abundance of northwest-to-north swell up to 18 ft (5.5 m) during the best surfing months of November to March. The northwest-facing coast around Casablanca and Rabat receives more swell than the southwest-facing points such as Anchor Point, although northeast trades blow cross-shore, so early mornings and evening glass-offs are worth considering. The waves around Taghazout have natural wind protection from a cape, which can switch northeast trade winds to offshore breezes.

Casablanca, with its international airport, is a major travel hub. Rather than fly in, many surfers prefer to cross the Mediterranean by ferry with their vehicles from Spain, arriving at Tangier.

The arid climate has hot days and cool nights. From November to April, when the water temperature averages 63°F (17°C), full wetsuits are required. The water averages 70°F (21°C) for the remainder of the year, when it may or may not be warm enough to swap the full suit for a springsuit.

1 Dar Bouazza

This is the hottest left in Morocco, with long waves peeling through predictable cutback sections and fast walls. The point and nearby Jack Beach host national contests. Crowds are a problem, but a good ride here is worth the wait. Beware of tangling with the rusty ship's boiler, *la bobine*, on the inside.

WAVE TYPE Left

WAVE HEIGHT 3–10 ft (0.9–3.1 m)

BREAK TYPE Point

BEST SWELL NW

BEST WIND S

BEST TIDE Low

BEST TIME October–April

HAZARDS Sea urchins, rocks, crowds, wreck debris

DIRECTIONS Drive south from Casablanca on Azemmour Rd. Take Dar Bouazza Rd and park in front of the wave, just before the town.

2 Safi – Le Jardin

In big swells, Safi sparkles, offering speed and power; it's the jewel in the Moroccan surf crown. Its fast, tubing waves rival those of Jeffreys Bay in South Africa. It is, however, heavily localized, very challenging, and at times populated by a Quiksilver training camp.

WAVE TYPE Right

WAVE HEIGHT 3–10 ft (0.9–3.1 m)

BREAK TYPE Point

BEST SWELL N

BEST WIND E

BEST TIDE Low

BEST TIME November–February

HAZARDS Localism, currents, crowds, rocks

DIRECTIONS Drive north from Essaouira on Casablanca Rd. Take Safi Rd, and drive 1¼ miles (2 km) north of Safi city.

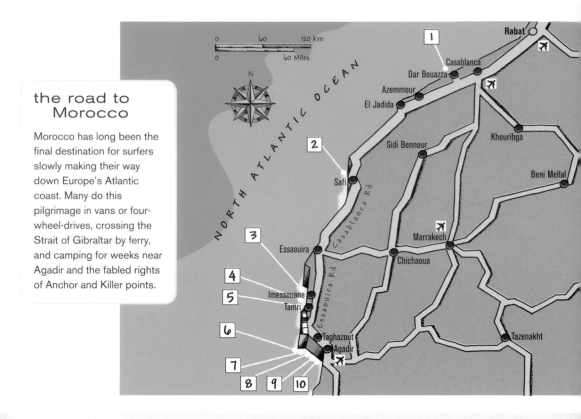

the road to Morocco

Morocco has long been the final destination for surfers slowly making their way down Europe's Atlantic coast. Many do this pilgrimage in vans or four-wheel-drives, crossing the Strait of Gibraltar by ferry, and camping for weeks near Agadir and the fabled rights of Anchor and Killer points.

---

3 Imessouane – La Cathédrale

La Cathédrale is an exposed sand-bottom point break framed by ancient Moroccan fishing cottages. On a medium swell with light winds, the shifting rights offer a perfect canvas for free expression, including long drops, bowling cutbacks, and strong momentum into the beach break. Once little surfed and uncrowded, this wave is now better known, but the scene remains friendly and relaxed.

WAVE TYPE Right

WAVE HEIGHT 3–8 ft (0.9–2.4 m)

BREAK TYPE Point, beach

BEST SWELL N

BEST WIND E

BEST TIDE Mid–high

BEST TIME October–March

HAZARDS Rocks, rough seas, crime

DIRECTIONS Drive north from Agadir on Essaouira Rd. Follow the road closest to the sea, and park above the wave before Imessouane village.

---

4 Pointe d'Imessouane – The Bay

This is a smooth longboard wave that rarely gets messy, or big, and peels over soft sand for 300 yards (300 m). An easy paddle in the channel either side of the break makes this a must for fun-seekers.

WAVE TYPE Right

WAVE HEIGHT 1–3 ft (0.3–0.9 m)

BREAK TYPE Point

BEST SWELL NW

BEST WIND NE

BEST TIDE Low

BEST TIME November–February

HAZARDS Crowds, access

DIRECTIONS Drive north from Agadir on Essaouira Rd, and take Imessouane Rd toward the harbor. About 500 yards (500 m) after the turnoff, pull in at the lookout spot to get a bird's-eye view of the swell and crowd conditions. Continue to the harbor, park, and walk east to where the wave is nestled deep in the bay.

5 Tamri Plage

This is a swell-magnet beach with hollow lefts at low tide and easy peaks at high. It's worth the drive when the south is flat. Don't be fooled by the deserted-looking landscape. Tens of children will appear from the rocks and hassle you. Agree to pay one local a few dirhams, or some food, and your car will be safe.

WAVE TYPE Left and right

WAVE HEIGHT 1–12 ft (0.3–3.7 m)

BREAK TYPE Beach

BEST SWELL NW

BEST WIND E

BEST TIDE All

BEST TIME October–April

HAZARDS Crime, rough seas, broken glass on cliff path

DIRECTIONS Drive north from Taghazout on Essaouira Rd. About 2 miles (3.2 km) before Tamri town, turn down the dirt track next to the river mouth.

6 Boilers

Boilers offers heavy and thrilling rights over slippery rocks, close to a narrow paddle-out keyhole. This is a great spectator spot, where local topography keeps the faces clean when the rest of the coast is messy. Don't wipe out close to the ship's boiler or sharp cliff face.

WAVE TYPE Right

WAVE HEIGHT 3–8 ft (0.9–2.4 m)

BREAK TYPE Point

BEST SWELL NW

BEST WIND NE

BEST TIDE Mid

BEST TIME November–February

HAZARDS Rough seas, sharp rocks, wreck debris, access

DIRECTIONS Drive north from Taghazout on Essaouira Rd. Turn off just before Cap Rhir lighthouse, and drive along the dirt track.

The long rides at Dar Bouazza give surfers time for some neat cutbacks.

7 Killer Point

Here you'll find beautiful bowling rights exposed to all swells. The long walk and even longer paddle mean it rarely gets busy. At size, fast 300-yard (300-m) rides are common and smiles widespread.

WAVE TYPE Right

WAVE HEIGHT 3–10 ft (0.3–3.1 m)

BREAK TYPE Point

BEST SWELL NW

BEST WIND E

BEST TIDE All

BEST TIME November–February

HAZARDS Access, rough seas, rocks

DIRECTIONS Killer Point is a short drive north of Taghazout on Essaouira Rd, or a 30-minute walk from Taghazout. If driving, turn off 2 miles (3.2 km) from the town, at the parking area 100 yards (100 m) past the old anchor factory. Walk and then paddle north toward the point.

8 La Source

This crisp, playful, and atmospheric reef is at its best on small swells. Women used to dry laundered rugs on the sandstone rock face before apartments were built. Taghazout has been on the hippie trail since the 1960s, so the people are used to visitors, but it still has a timeless feel.

WAVE TYPE Left and right

WAVE HEIGHT 2–4 ft (0.6–1.2 m)

BREAK TYPE Reef

BEST SWELL NW

BEST WIND NE

BEST TIDE Mid–high

BEST TIME November–February

HAZARDS Rocks, crowds, sea urchins, broken glass on cliff path

DIRECTIONS La Source is a short drive north of Taghazout on Essaouira Rd, or a 20-minute walk from Taghazout. If driving, turn off 2 miles (3.2 km) from the town, at the parking area 100 yards (100 m) past the old anchor factory.

9 Anchor Point

This legendary long, peeling right has that quintessential Moroccan wall – not too steep, not too hollow, just right. The consensus is that Anchors only comes alive with size. It's crowded and localized, longboarders aren't welcome, and occasional fights erupt in the lineup. Some claim that the sand bottom is not as good as it was in the sixties.

WAVE TYPE Right

WAVE HEIGHT 4–10 ft (1.2–3.1 m)

BREAK TYPE Point

BEST SWELL NW

BEST WIND NE

BEST TIDE Low

BEST TIME November–February

HAZARDS Localism, crowds, rocks, rough seas

DIRECTIONS Anchor Point is a short drive north of Taghazout on Essaouira Rd, or a ten-minute walk from Taghazout. If driving, go 1 mile (1.6 km) out of town, and park near the old anchor factory.

10 Devil's Rock

Devil's Rock offers a rolling right wedge and an open-faced left – both perfect for beginners. There's a rustic café on the beach, camel herds, and a welcoming long- and shortboard crew. Families relax and have picnics here on weekends, making it a great place to experience Moroccan culture.

WAVE TYPE Left and right

WAVE HEIGHT 2–4 ft (0.6–1.2 m)

BREAK TYPE Beach

BEST SWELL NW

BEST WIND NE

BEST TIDE Mid–high

BEST TIME November–February

HAZARDS Rocks

DIRECTIONS Drive south from Taghazout on Agadir Rd. Just past Tamrhakht, next to the bus stop, turn on to the dirt track and drive a short distance to the beach.

Cape Verde

Cape Verde is a group of ten islands that lies about 380 miles (612 km) off the coast of Africa. The focus of surfing interest is Sal, the third-smallest island, situated in the northeast corner of the archipelago. Besides a couple of inconsistent beach breaks, the island's waves, most of which are on the west coast, are typically short, heavy reefs breaking over lava. Monte Leão and Ponta do Sinó are both longish rights that buck this trend, yet both are disappointingly fickle. The biggest drawcard on Sal is world-class Ponta Preta, with its long, hollow, and powerful rights (take a helmet for protection against rocks).

The best months for surfing are November to February, when northwest swells of up to 12 ft (3.7 m) light up the west coast. Northeast trade winds blow offshore at many of the waves, and can also create windswell waves on the east coast. Several Cape Verde islands lie south of Sal, blocking almost all south swell, although occasional southwest swells from March to August can bring Santa Maria and Ponta do Sinó (near Ponta Preta) to life.

Sal has a dry, desertlike climate with temperatures averaging 70–82°F (21–28°C) in summer and 66–77°F (19–25°C) in winter. Between January and April, a springsuit is the norm, which many surfers will discard for boardshorts when the water temperatures increase to around 79°F (26°C).

Sal has an international airport just south of the town of Espargos. There are regular flights from Portugal and charter flights from the United Kingdom. Portuguese is the official language of the Republic of Cape Verde.

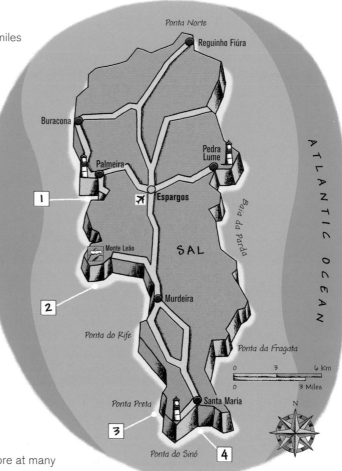

the next Costa del Sol?

Cape Verde could be the next big thing in tourism. Windsurfers discovered Sal's most famous wave, Ponta Preta, in the late 1980s, although the island remained a laid-back surfing destination. This could be about to change, however, especially now there are direct flights from the UK for sun-seeking Brits. The foreign investment boom has arrived in the islands, just as it did in the Canary Islands and Spain's Costa del Sol.

1 Palmeira

This good-quality, hollow left offers relatively short rides. It suffers from the same blown-out conditions that affect many of Sal's waves, and the area also receives more windswells than quality groundswells, with sloppy waves to match. But it's a good barrel if you have the time or are lucky enough to score the wave in prime conditions.

WAVE TYPE Left

WAVE HEIGHT 3–10 ft (0.9–3.1 m)

BREAK TYPE Reef

BEST SWELL NW

BEST WIND SE

BEST TIDE All

BEST TIME November–February

HAZARDS Rocks, sea urchins

DIRECTIONS From the west-coast town of Palmeira, the wave is a 500-yard (500-m) walk south along the coast.

2 Monte Leão

This nicely shaped, high-quality wave breaks over a shallow reef. It gets hollow, powerful, and potentially very clean thanks to the nearby Monte Leão (Sleeping Lion Mountain), which juts out into the sea and can shelter the wave from the wind. It's reasonably consistent, and there are also beach-break peaks close by.

WAVE TYPE Right

WAVE HEIGHT 3–12 ft (0.9–3.7 m)

BREAK TYPE Reef

BEST SWELL WSW

BEST WIND NNE

BEST TIDE High

BEST TIME November–February

HAZARDS Rocks, sea urchins, sharks

DIRECTIONS The wave is on the south shore of Monte Leão, halfway up Sal's west coast. From the airport, head south ⅔ mile (1 km) past the end of the airport runway on the island's main road. Veer west for the south side of Monte Leão for 1¼ miles (2 km).

3 Ponta Preta

This world-class wave works equally well in small or big swells. Deep tubes can be ridden here, as well as rides several hundred yards long. A much shorter yet intense left also breaks off the peak and terminates close to the inside rocks. Wear a helmet on lower tides, as there are submerged rocks.

WAVE TYPE Right

WAVE HEIGHT 3–12 ft (0.9–3.7 m)

BREAK TYPE Point

BEST SWELL NW

BEST WIND E

BEST TIDE Low–mid

BEST TIME October–December, February–April

HAZARDS Rocks, sea urchins, sharks

DIRECTIONS From Santa Maria in the very south, Ponta Preta is a 30-minute walk. Alternatively, drive to the western limit of Santa Maria and take the only road leading north. This road passes within 500 yards (500 m) of the wave.

4 Santa Maria

Santa Maria can be fun and sometimes hollow, although most swells are windswells lacking size and power. There are also reasonable lefts and rights on the beach break. It's not a particularly consistent wave due to the fact that the other islands in the Cape Verde archipelago block south swells.

WAVE TYPE Left and right

WAVE HEIGHT 3–9 ft (0.9–2.7 m)

BREAK TYPE Reef and beach

BEST SWELL SW

BEST WIND N

BEST TIDE Mid–high

BEST TIME March–September

HAZARDS Sea urchins, sharks

DIRECTIONS The town of Santa Maria is on the south coast of the island. The beach is next to the town's pier.

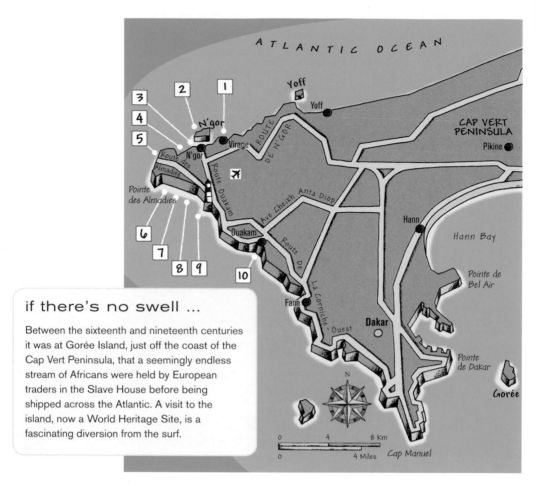

ATLANTIC OCEAN

Yoff
Yoff

CAP VERT
PENINSULA

N'gor

Pikine

Virage

N'gor

Route des Almadies

Route Ouakam

Ave Cheikh Anta Diop

Hann

Hann Bay

Pointe des Almadies

Ouakam

Route De La Corniche Ouest

Pointe de Bel Air

Fann

Dakar

Pointe de Dakar

Gorée

N

0   4   8 Km

0   4 Miles   Cap Manuel

if there's no swell ...

Between the sixteenth and nineteenth centuries it was at Gorée Island, just off the coast of the Cap Vert Peninsula, that a seemingly endless stream of Africans were held by European traders in the Slave House before being shipped across the Atlantic. A visit to the island, now a World Heritage Site, is a fascinating diversion from the surf.

Senegal

The most interesting part of the 310-mile (500-km) coastline of Senegal is the Cap Vert Peninsula, which is also the westernmost point of the African continent. It's here, in the area around Pointe des Almadies, just north of the capital city, Dakar, that most surf trips begin and end. Both the north- and southwest-facing coasts have several quality reef breaks within walking distance of one another, so it's a simple matter of surfing whatever coast has the best conditions at the time. Dakar's airport is a short distance from Pointe des Almadies.

Between October and March, northwest-to-north swells of up to 12 ft (3.7 m) hit the north coast and wrap around the peninsula, creating slightly smaller but cleaner surf on the south-west coast. The north coast is best surfed early

in the day, before the northeast trades blow cross-shore, when it's time to hit the southwest coast as it becomes offshore.

Once you've gone stir crazy on the peninsula it's worth exploring the river mouth and beach break options farther north toward Mauritania, although most of this coastline is straight and relatively uninteresting, and is also susceptible to northeast trade winds.

The climate is hot and dry year-round apart from July to October, the hot and humid rainy season. The temperature range is 64–86°F (18–30°C). The water gets chilly between January and April and a full wetsuit or springsuit is required. For the rest of the year, the water temperature ranges between 70 and 79°F (21–26°C) — ideal for boardshorts or a springsuit.

1 Le Virage

Le Virage is rarely crowded and easy to get to, but due to the less than epic nature of its waves, it will only appeal to beginners. Tribal Surf, a surf shop near the break, rents boards.

WAVE TYPE Left and right

WAVE HEIGHT ½–3 ft (0.2–0.9m)

BREAK TYPE Reef

BEST SWELL NW

BEST WIND SE

BEST TIDE Mid

BEST TIME November, March

DANGERS Sharp rocks, occasional sharks

DIRECTIONS From central Dakar, head north on Route de la Corniche-Ouest and Route Ouakam. Turn right into Route de N'Gor, which runs past N'Gor village to Virage. You'll find the break as the road meets the coast, in front of a restaurant.

2 N'Gor Rights and Lefts

N'Gor Island lies 600 yards (600 m) off the northwestern coast of the Cap Vert Peninsula. Here, a good but fickle right and a mediocre left break from opposite sides of the island. The wind is often onshore, but the walled-up right can get epic, occasionally dishing out barrels.

WAVE TYPE Left and right

WAVE HEIGHT 3–8 ft (0.9–2.4 m)

BREAK TYPE Reef, point

BEST SWELL NW

BEST WIND SE–S

BEST TIDE All

BEST TIME November–March

DANGERS Sharp rocks, sea urchins, strong currents, occasional crowds

DIRECTIONS From central Dakar, head north on Route de la Corniche-Ouest and Route Ouakam to N'Gor village, on the coast. Although you can paddle across to the island from here, most surfers prefer to go by local fishing boat, which is quick (three minutes) and cheap.

3 La Baie des Carpes

Also known as Carpes Rouges, this is not the best wave in the area, but it's usually uncrowded and can be fun if there are no waves anywhere else. It's located near a jetty, right in front of a garbage dump, so watch out for trash in the often-dirty water.

WAVE TYPE Left and right

WAVE HEIGHT 3–5 ft (0.9–1.5 m)

BREAK TYPE Reef

BEST SWELL N

BEST WIND SE

BEST TIDE All

BEST TIME April–October

DANGERS Pollution, the occasional shark

DIRECTIONS From central Dakar, head north on Route de la Corniche-Ouest and Route Ouakam. Turn left onto Route des Almadies and drive to the jetty near the garbage dump (just before the Hotel Méridien President).

4 La Gauche de Loic

La Gauche is the most north-facing of all the waves in the area and is thus exposed to a lot of swell, which makes it quite consistent. However, it's rarely surfed as it falls inside the compound of the Hotel Méridien President, so unless you're staying there, you're probably better off finding waves elsewhere.

WAVE TYPE Left

WAVE HEIGHT 3–8 ft (0.9–2.4 m)

BREAK TYPE Point, reef

BEST SWELL NW

BEST WIND NE, E

BEST TIDE Mid–high

BEST TIME November–March

DANGERS Sharp rocks, hotel security

DIRECTIONS From central Dakar, head north on Route de la Corniche-Ouest and Route Ouakam. Turn left onto Route des Almadies, which will take you to the Hotel Méridien President.

5 Club Med

Due to its position near Pointe des Almadies, where it's very exposed to onshore wind, Club Med (aka Le Club) is even more fickle than N'Gor but is arguably better, with sucky bowls offering up barrels and long sections. It doesn't work often, but it's worth a look if the other spots in the area are working but crowded.

WAVE TYPE Right

WAVE HEIGHT 3–8 ft (0.9–2.4 m)

BREAK TYPE Reef

BEST SWELL WSW–W

BEST WIND N–NNE

BEST TIDE Mid–high

BEST TIME November–March

DANGERS Sea urchins, weekend crowds

DIRECTIONS From central Dakar, head north on Route de la Corniche-Ouest and Route Ouakam. Turn left onto Route des Almadies and follow it to Club Med Les Almadies. You can access the break from the south side along the shore.

6 Secret 1

The rocky beach at Secret 1 is the most accessible on this stretch of coast, which is littered with small coves and surf spots featuring short, punchy waves. Surfers gather at the small bar-restaurant on the beach. This is one of the social hubs of the wave-riding scene in the area, as you can see the waves at Club Med from it and hike to breaks to the south.

WAVE TYPE Left

WAVE HEIGHT 3–6 ft (0.9–1.8 m)

BREAK TYPE Reef (with sandbars)

BEST SWELL SW

BEST WIND N, NE, E

BEST TIDE All

BEST TIME May–September

DANGERS Sharp reef, crowds

DIRECTIONS From central Dakar, head north on Route de la Corniche-Ouest and Route Ouakam. Turn left onto Route des Almadies and stop at the beach just past the Lieu de Prière. You can also walk from Club Med.

7 Secret 2

Adjacent to Secret 1, Secret 2 is a fun right-hander that works in similar conditions to its namesake and can occasionally get very good. There's an informal café-restaurant where you can socialize with local surfers and leave your stuff while you surf.

WAVE TYPE Right

WAVE HEIGHT 3–6 ft (0.9–1.8 m)

BREAK TYPE Reef (with sandbars)

BEST SWELL SW

BEST WIND N, NE

BEST TIDE All

BEST TIME May–September

DANGERS Sharp reef, crowds

DIRECTIONS From central Dakar, head north on Route de la Corniche-Ouest and Route Ouakam. Turn left onto Route des Almadies and stop at the beach just past the Lieu de Prière. You can also walk from Club Med.

8 Le Vivier

Le Vivier is a fun right-hander that breaks over a shallow shelf featuring the odd barely submerged rock. Due to its shallow nature, it's favored by bodyboarders and skilled local surfers who know the wave well. It can offer good barrels for those brave enough.

WAVE TYPE Right

WAVE HEIGHT 3–6 ft (0.9–1.8 m)

BREAK TYPE Reef

BEST SWELL SW

BEST WIND NE

BEST TIDE All

BEST TIME March–November

DANGERS Shallow water, sharp rocks, sea urchins, occasional crowds

DIRECTIONS From central Dakar, head north on Route de la Corniche-Ouest and Route Ouakam. Turn left onto Route des Almadies and stop at the beach just past the Lieu de Prière. Walk to Le Vivier.

9 Le Vivier Gauche

Adjacent to Le Vivier, Le Vivier Gauche is a shallower, more sucky, and slightly shorter version of its right-breaking counterpart. And like Le Vivier, it's largely the domain of bodyboarders and confident surfers.

WAVE TYPE Left

WAVE HEIGHT 3–6 ft (0.9–1.8 m)

BREAK TYPE Reef

BEST SWELL SW

BEST WIND NE

BEST TIDE High

BEST TIME March–November

DANGERS Very shallow reef, sea urchins

DIRECTIONS From central Dakar, head north on Route de la Corniche-Ouest and Route Ouakam. Turn left onto Route des Almadies and stop at the beach just past the Lieu de Prière. Hike south to Le Vivier Gauche.

10 Ouakam

The break, which offers a left and a right, is in the fishing village of Ouakam and is widely regarded as one of the best waves in Senegal, if not the whole of West Africa. The setting is beautiful: in a small bay in front of a mosque just south of Les Mamelles lighthouse.

WAVE TYPE Right and occasional left

WAVE HEIGHT 3–10 ft (0.9–3.1 m)

BREAK TYPE Reef

BEST SWELL SW, S

BEST WIND N, NE

BEST TIDE Low–mid

BEST TIME March–October

DANGERS Sharp rocks, crowds

DIRECTIONS From central Dakar, head north on Route de la Corniche-Ouest to Ouakam village. The break is directly in front of the mosque.

With its two solid barrel sections, world-class Ouakam attracts a lively crowd of talented surfers.

Ghana

Bordering the Gulf of Guinea, Ghana has a lush, green 335-mile (539-km) coastline (the Gold Coast), which is dotted with old slave forts and castles. There's a variety of waves with beach breaks, reefs, river mouths, and points to be found along the country's predominantly southeast-facing coast. With warm water and consistent, albeit mellow, waves, it's one of the more relaxed African countries to surf in.

Ghana receives southwest swell from the South Atlantic Ocean. The best months are April to September, when swells of up to 10 ft (3 m) are possible, with waves occasionally getting hollow and powerful. Most of the time the surf is head-high, however, as Ghana's main problem is a lack of solid swell, making it a good idea to take a fish, longboard, or any other high-volume board. The best time for surfing is early in the day, before sea breezes from the west blow out many waves, although some waves are sheltered from the wind.

Accra has an international airport. The climate is tropical and humid, with year-round temperatures averaging between 74 and 90°F

beginner's paradise in Africa

Ghana is home to a good range of waves that rarely get overly big or powerful. Combine this with friendly local people, a stable, democratic government, low prices, and an almost complete lack of surfers, and you have the perfect African surf destination for the beginner or intermediate surfer.

(23–32°C). Downpours offer brief periods of cool relief, the wettest months being May and June. Water temperatures average 79°F (26°C), so there's usually no need to bring anything other than boardshorts, except in August to September, when it's a few degrees cooler and a springsuit may be required.

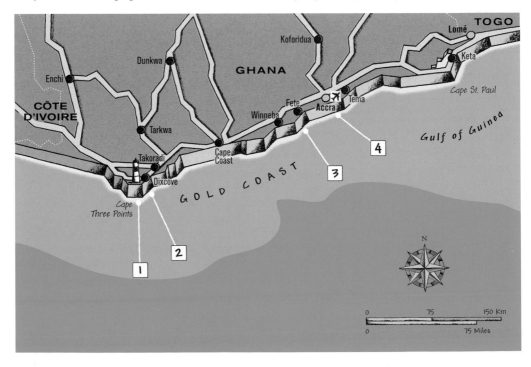

1 Cape Three Points

There are three exceptional and easy-to-ride points at the southern tip of Ghana. The first is the biggest, the second the cleanest and best, and the third is the slowest and leads into a suicidal shore break. An American has built a house in front of the waves, and enjoys months of empty sessions in a West African paradise.

WAVE TYPE Right

WAVE HEIGHT 2–8 ft (0.6–2.4 m)

BREAK TYPE Point

BEST SWELL S–SW

BEST WIND NE

BEST TIDE Mid

BEST TIME April–September

HAZARDS Currents, rocks, rough seas

DIRECTIONS Drive west from Takoradi on Axmin Rd, then turn onto Prince's Town Rd. At the coast, drive southeast along the dirt track until you reach the lighthouse.

2 Dixcove

Dixcove offers a well-shaped, easy-to-handle right-hander amid stunning tropical scenery, with no crowds or local surfers. Pollution from the river mouth can be a drawback, but that's outweighed by the great fun to be had at this point break.

WAVE TYPE Right

WAVE HEIGHT 2–8 ft (0.6–2.4 m)

BREAK TYPE Point

BEST SWELL S–SW

BEST WIND NE

BEST TIDE Mid–high

BEST TIME April–September

HAZARDS Pollution, murky water, rough seas, rocks

DIRECTIONS Drive west from Takoradi on Axmin Rd. At Agona Junction take Dixcove Rd, then park at Fort Metal Cross, the old slave fort.

3 Fete

Fete is a sweetly formed and mellow point with zippy pockets and sloping walls. Against the current, the paddle is tiring, but the interaction with the local fishing community is rewarding. Sometimes fishermen catch the shoulders in their boats. Trouble is, the beach is the village toilet, so on the rising tide, when the wave heats up, it gets smelly.

WAVE TYPE Right

WAVE HEIGHT 1–6 ft (0.3–1.8 m)

BREAK TYPE Point

BEST SWELL S

BEST WIND NW–N

BEST TIDE Mid

BEST TIME April–September

HAZARDS Pollution, rocks

DIRECTIONS From Accra, drive west on Winneba Rd for about 20 miles (32 km). Take Senya Beraku Rd and drive along the dirt track into Fete. Walk the rest of the way or access the beach through the White Sands Beach Resort.

4 Labadi Beach

This lively beach break with soft breaking peaks is at the tourist epicenter of Ghana. The water's warm and there's no surf culture, despite the beach featuring in the 1966 movie *The Endless Summer*. Pollution can be bad after rainfall. But on the positive side, you'll quickly have a network of friends to cater for your every need, and you'll enjoy the bars, music, and dancing.

WAVE TYPE Left and right

WAVE HEIGHT 1–6 ft (0.3–1.8 m)

BREAK TYPE Beach

BEST SWELL S

BEST WIND NW–N

BEST TIDE High

BEST TIME May–October

HAZARDS Pollution, rocks

DIRECTIONS From Accra, drive east on Tema Rd, then take Labadi Rd for a short distance. Pay a small fee to access the beach through large red gates.

Namibia

Bordered by the massive sand dunes of the Namib Desert, Namibia's 925-mile (1,489-km) coastline is harsh and wind-blown. Cape Cross, on the Skeleton Coast, has a couple of world-class lefts, which are offshore in the predominant south winds. Farther south are numerous reefs and points around the resort town of Swakopmund. Namibia's waves get seriously hollow and powerful and, with few local or traveling surfers, it's a matter of whether you're comfortable surfing with few people, when the waves are solid, the waters cold, and sharp-toothed marine life lurks below. Note that armed guards from diamond-mining companies block access to certain parts of the coast, limiting surf exploration.

Between March and October, Namibia's west coast receives consistent doses of southwest swell of up to 15 ft (4.6 m). The prevailing south-to-southeast wind blows

the Skeleton Coast

The Skeleton Coast, running north from around Cape Cross, has a ghostly feel, with constant coastal fog and dozens of rusting shipwrecks. There's also abundant bird life and huge seal colonies. Around here, the only creatures you're likely to share the waves with are seals and, quite possibly, sharks, which feed on the seals. On land, hyenas and jackals stalk the inhospitable desert.

offshore on many of the waves, and the real key is getting the right combination of tide and swell at any given spot.

The capital, Windhoek, has an international airport. Temperatures are low at night and high during the day. Rain is almost nonexistent in this desert climate. A full wetsuit and optional boots and hood are required throughout the year as water temperatures average 57°F (14°C) from May to October and 64°F (18°C) for the rest of the year.

1 Cape Cross

Cape Cross is reputed to be one of the world's longest waves, delivering rides of up to ½ mile (0.8 km) in length. The break is in a seal reserve. Depending on population levels, seals can be just an irritant or make the wave unsurfable.

WAVE TYPE Left

WAVE HEIGHT 3–8 ft (0.9–2.4 m)

BREAK TYPE Point

BEST SWELL SW–W

BEST WIND S, SW

BEST TIDE Mid–high

BEST TIME March–September

DANGERS Thousands of occasionally aggressive seals; sharks; very cold water

DIRECTIONS Cape Cross is 75 miles (120 km) north of Swakopmund along the coastal road via Henties Bay. This salt-dirt road is passable for most regular motor vehicles. Once you get to the Cape Cross Seal Reserve and pay your entrance fee, don't mistake the first point for the main wave, which is a little farther to the south.

2 Lockjoint

Sometimes jokingly referred to by the locals as Namibia's answer to Hawaii's Pipeline, this is a short, sucky, powerful wave favored by bodyboarders and surfers comfortable with quick takeoffs. It has two fast sections that deliver thick, doubling-up tubes. Lockjoint is located smack in the center of Swakopmund.

WAVE TYPE Left

WAVE HEIGHT 3–6 ft (0.9–1.8 m)

BREAK TYPE Reef

BEST SWELL SW–W

BEST WIND NE–E

BEST TIDE Low–mid

BEST TIME May–September

DANGERS Sharks, sharp rocks, shallow reefs, very cold water, strong currents, occasional crowds

DIRECTIONS In Swakopmund, drive to the end of Sam Nujoma Ave and turn left into Strand St. Lockjoint is on the north side of the jetty and is easily accessible from the parking lot on the beach. If it's breaking, you'll see it.

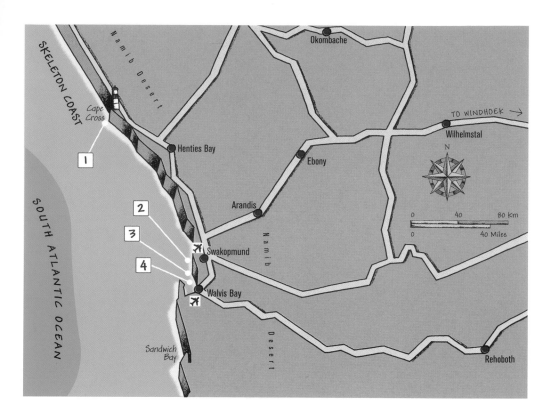

3 Guns

Although predominantly a left, below 4 ft (1.2 m) Guns offers a short, punchy right and a slightly longer left with a nice outside bowl, which wraps into a cutback section before unloading into a closeout on the beach. Above that size it becomes a left only, which offers a steep drop, very smackable wall, and the odd tube ride before ending in the shore break.

WAVE TYPE Left and right under 4 ft (1.2 m); left only above 4 ft (1.2 m)

WAVE HEIGHT 3–8 ft (0.9–2.4 m)

BREAK TYPE Reef

BEST SWELL SW

BEST WIND NE or none

BEST TIDE All

BEST TIME May–September

DANGERS Sharks, very cold water

DIRECTIONS Guns is a 20-minute drive south, in the direction of Walvis Bay, from Swakopmund on Nathaniel Maxuilili St. Look out for the small, black concrete building just north of the break.

4 Mussels

This spot (named after the shellfish, but sometimes mistakenly written as "Muscles") is widely regarded by local surfers as one of the best waves in the region. But, as it requires a rare combination of wind and swell directions, it hardly ever delivers. When it's on, it's mainly a long, walled-up right-hander serving up the occasional tube ride.

WAVE TYPE Right

WAVE HEIGHT 3–6 ft (0.9–1.8 m)

BREAK TYPE Reef

BEST SWELL Big W

BEST WIND NE

BEST TIDE All

BEST TIME June–August

DANGERS Sharks, sharp rocks, very cold water

DIRECTIONS Mussels is 40 minutes' drive south, in the direction of Walvis Bay, from Swakopmund on Nathaniel Maxuilili St. The break is on the right-hand side just before Walvis Bay, hidden by the dunes, adjacent to a private holiday resort.

Western South Africa

The Western Cape, from Lamberts Bay to the Cape of Good Hope, is a surf-blessed region, catering for the tastes of all surfers who can handle the large waves and the cold waters. There are several waves around Lamberts Bay, the pick being the five-star Elands Bay, which is a powerful, hollow left point. Farther south, the Cape Peninsula has every wave under the sun, from beach breaks, reefs, points, and genuine big-wave spots like Sunset, Crayfish Factory, and Dungeons, the latter being one of the world's biggest, most ominous waves. Surfing in this region is all about asking yourself, "How hard do I want to charge?"

Between March and October, there's an abundance of southwest swell, which breaks anywhere up to 21 ft (6.4 m). March and April can be the most stable time, with favorable south-to-southeast winds. The winter months of June to August have the biggest swell, but conditions are often stormy and it can be a frustrating wait for a settled period to provide quality surfing conditions.

Cape Town, with its international airport, is the main entry point. Summers are warm, averaging 61–79°F (16–26°C), and winters mild, 46–66°F (8–19°C). Water temperatures are extremely chilly, thanks to the cooling effect of the Benguela Current. The average year-round water temperature is 57–61°F (14–16°C), which requires a thick wetsuit and usually a hood and boots.

the pull of the bull

Surfing among bull kelp at spots like Outer Kom and 365s on the Cape Peninsula can be an eerie experience for the uninitiated. Paddling in or out, the trough between swell lines can leave you stuck on top of the kelp unable to paddle until the next crest raises the water level, releasing you from the grip of the rubbery kelp.

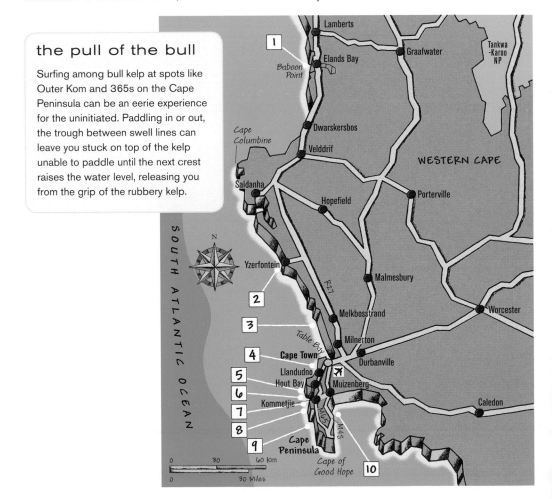

1 Elands Bay

For decades, the long, winding left-handers of Elands Bay have attracted surfers from around South Africa. It's best to head up to Elands when it's 6+ ft (1.8+ m) in Cape Town. If you get it working, you'll find yourself riding some of the most memorable lefts of your life.

WAVE TYPE Left

WAVE HEIGHT 3–8 ft (0.9–2.4 m)

BREAK TYPE Point

BEST SWELL SW

BEST WIND SE

BEST TIDE Mid

BEST TIME March–May, August–October

HAZARDS Rocks

DIRECTIONS Heading north from Cape Town, drive about 155 miles (250 km) along the R27. Go through Velddrif and past Dwarskersbos, then carry on straight until you go over a hill and cross some train tracks. You enter Elands Bay from the top of the point. Follow the road to the beach, and park at the base of the point.

2 Yzerfontein

Very exposed to the open ocean, the bay at the small town of Yzerfontein is a great option when everywhere else on the Cape Peninsula is too small. The punchy waves can offer some very hollow tubes, but it's best to look elsewhere when there's any decent swell running.

WAVE TYPE Left and right

WAVE HEIGHT 2–5 ft (0.6–1.5 m)

BREAK TYPE Beach

BEST SWELL SW–W

BEST WIND Light NE

BEST TIDE Low–mid

BEST TIME Whenever the swell is small

HAZARDS Sharks, strong rips with bigger swells

DIRECTIONS Drive about 37 miles (60 km) north from Cape Town on the R27 and take the signposted left turn to Yzerfontein. Once you get into the town, stick to the left; the main surfing beach is in front of some houses on the bay.

3 Melkbosstrand

The fun, barreling waves of Melkbosstrand offer a great option when the swell is too big for many of the other spots around Cape Town. The beach is protected from the wind, and the offshore kelp beds break up the larger swells, which then re-form into high-performance rides on the inside.

WAVE TYPE Right

WAVE HEIGHT 2–5 ft (0.6–1.5 m)

BREAK TYPE Beach

BEST SWELL SW

BEST WIND NE

BEST TIDE High

BEST TIME Year-round

HAZARDS Occasional crowds

DIRECTIONS Follow the R27 north from Cape Town, passing through Milnerton and Bloubergstrand, then take a left into Melkbosstrand (clearly signposted). The road takes you onto the beachfront where there's a choice of peaks.

4 Llandudno

A consistent and popular Cape Peninsula spot, Llandudno's picturesque, white sandy beach offers fast and powerful waves that can serve up some thick, throaty barrels when conditions are right. The only drawback is that the offshore southeaster, while making the water a beautiful blue, causes a rapid drop in sea temperature.

WAVE TYPE Left and right

WAVE HEIGHT 2–6 ft (0.6–1.8 m)

BREAK TYPE Beach

BEST SWELL SW

BEST WIND SE

BEST TIDE Low–mid

BEST TIME Year-round

HAZARDS Crowds

DIRECTIONS From Cape Town, take the M62 through Camps Bay until you are on Victoria Rd. It's a winding 6-mile (10-km) coastal drive until you reach the Llandudno turnoff. Follow the turnoff to the beach — the best waves are in the northern corner.

5 Dungeons

Gaining ever-growing publicity and attracting hellmen from around the world, Dungeons has affirmed its place as one of the premier big-wave spots on the planet.

WAVE TYPE Right

WAVE HEIGHT 8–30+ ft (2.4–9.1+ m)

BREAK TYPE Reef

BEST SWELL WSW

BEST WIND Glassy or N–NE

BEST TIDE Low

BEST TIME Year-round

HAZARDS Sharks, kelp, lips thicker than your car

DIRECTIONS Dungeons is situated at the base of Sentinel Mountain in Hout Bay, a short distance from central Cape Town. While it can be accessed by paddling out through deep, shark-infested waters after a long walk around the cliffs, nearly everyone who rides Dungeons takes a boat from Hout Bay harbor.

6 Dunes

When the wind and swell come together just right, Dunes delivers among the most perfect barrels anywhere in the Cape Town area. As at Llandudno, the water can be as cold as it is beautiful. Be prepared for a long walk along the beach, but it's more than worth it.

WAVE TYPE Left and right

WAVE HEIGHT 3–8 ft (0.9–2.4 m)

BREAK TYPE Beach

BEST SWELL SW

BEST WIND SE

BEST TIDE Low

BEST TIME Year-round

HAZARDS Sharks, some heavy waves

DIRECTIONS Coming from Hout Bay, along Chapmans Peak Dr, turn right into Avondrust Circle and then right into Beach Rd. Follow the road to the parking lot and walk about 1¼ miles (2 km) to the south.

7 Long Beach

This is the epicenter of surfing on the Cape Peninsula and the entry-level spot for surfing the powerful waves of the west coast. Three peaks – Pebbles, Main, and Crons – are ridable when everywhere else is closing out. The high-performance lefts and rights, plus the tubes at Crons, have seen Long Beach become the venue for most contests in Cape Town.

WAVE TYPE Left and right

WAVE HEIGHT 2–5 ft (0.6–1.5 m)

BREAK TYPE Beach

BEST SWELL SW–W

BEST WIND SW

BEST TIDE Mid–high

BEST TIME Year-round

HAZARDS Crowds after work and at weekends

DIRECTIONS From Muizenberg, drive south on the M4S into Fish Hoek and then follow the road signs to Kommetjie. In Kommetjie, turn right into Kirsten Ave — opposite the gas station — and follow the road to the parking lot.

8 Outer Kom

The powerful left-handers of Outer Kom have been a Cape Town proving ground for decades. Offering anything from high-performance, rippable walls to grinding, sectiony beasts, Outer Kom delivers long rides and even a few tubes to the more experienced surfer.

WAVE TYPE Left

WAVE HEIGHT 5–10+ ft (1.5–3.1+ m)

BREAK TYPE Point

BEST SWELL SW

BEST WIND Light NE

BEST TIDE Low–mid

BEST TIME April–June

HAZARDS Rocks, kelp

DIRECTIONS From Muizenberg, drive south on the M4S into Fish Hoek and then follow the signs to Kommetjie. Drive through the town, and turn right into Von Imhoff Rd, immediately left into Lighthouse Rd, and right again into Nerina Ave.

Heavy, cold, and unforgiving, Dungeons has been surfed at waves measuring up to 60 ft (18 m) on the face.

9 365s

A powerful and hollow reef break, 365s is so named because it's 5 degrees rounder than 360 degrees. A tricky hop over the rocks followed by a paddle through dense kelp beds will reward you with rippable right-hand walls and thick, long tubes that can be cover-of-the-magazine perfect in the right conditions.

WAVE TYPE Right (occasional lefts on a S swell)

WAVE HEIGHT 3–8 ft (0.9–2.4 m)

BREAK TYPE Reef

BEST SWELL WSW

BEST WIND Glassy or NE

BEST TIDE Mid

BEST TIME Year-round

HAZARDS Rocks, very thick kelp beds

DIRECTIONS From Kommetjie, take the M65, and turn right into the Soetwater Reserve. After the gates, drive 1¼ miles (2 km) or so until the road curves back on itself, pass the tidal pool, and park just on the far side of a small hill. .

10 Kalk Bay Reef

This is a gnarly, ledging left-hander that explodes over a shallow slab. When Kalk Bay Reef is firing, it offers some of the most intense barrels around. It can be fickle, so you're far from guaranteed to get it going off, plus you have to wait your turn while the hardcore locals take their pick of the best rides.

WAVE TYPE Left

WAVE HEIGHT 2–6 ft (0.6–1.8 m)

BREAK TYPE Reef

BEST SWELL ESE

BEST WIND SW

BEST TIDE Mid

BEST TIME May–August

HAZARDS Train tracks, shallow bottom, crowds, heavy locals

DIRECTIONS From Muizenberg, take the M4S and keep driving south on the coast road past St. James until you reach the parking lot at Kalk Bay (near the station). Walk across the train tracks to the water. It's easy to spot the break.

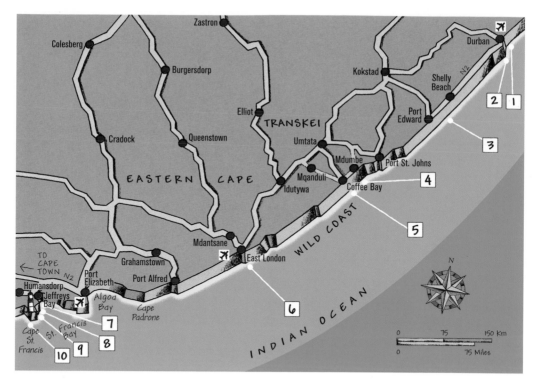

Eastern South Africa

The Eastern Cape has umpteen right point breaks, interspersed by reefs, beach breaks, and river mouths. Durban's coast has hollow beach breaks, with Cave Rock an exceptional reef barrel. Point break heaven begins on the crowd-free Wild Coast. The access can be difficult here, but the quality and variety of waves make it worthwhile. The high density of quality waves continues all the way to St. Francis Bay, where the world's best right point is located, at Jeffreys Bay. The main concern with surfing the east coast is the sharks, which include great whites, a problem Durban has overcome with shark nets.

March to October is the best time for surfing as North Atlantic lows track east beneath the coast. Southeast to southwest swells of up to 17½ ft (5.3 m) can arrive, lighting up even the most sheltered points. From December to March, occasional tropical cyclones can create east swells. The predominant wind is southwest to west, which is reasonably favorable for the southeast-to-east-facing waves.

In Durban, water temperatures range from 68 to 77°F (20–25°C), warm enough for a springsuit. From January to April board shorts will suffice. St. Francis Bay's water temperature is remarkably cold and a full wetsuit is required year-round, apart from January to March when hardier surfers don springsuits.

Durban and Port Elizabeth have airports, which have connections to the international hubs, Johannesburg and Cape Town.

shark threat

With great whites and bull sharks on the prowl, the threat of shark attack is usually somewhere in most surfers' minds in South Africa. Jeffreys Bay offers surfers some respite, however, as large pods of dolphins pass through the bay on an almost daily basis, riding the waves often in tandem with a lucky surfer. The presence of the dolphins soothes the nerves of surfers, especially those who believe that these marine mammals repel sharks.

1 New Pier

The high-performance surfing capital of South Africa, New Pier is the premier surf spot on the Golden Mile beaches of Durban, South Africa's Surf City. The long, hollow rights that peel over the sandbars formed by the pier on the south end of Dairy Beach are home to most of the country's top pro surfers, and the venue hosts numerous top-class surf contests.

WAVE TYPE Left and right

WAVE HEIGHT 2–8 ft (0.6–2.4 m)

BREAK TYPE Beach

BEST SWELL SE

BEST WIND SW

BEST TIDE Low

BEST TIME February–June

HAZARDS Crowds, fishermen on the pier

DIRECTIONS Durban is well signposted, with many roads leading to the beachfront. Head for the Central Beaches and park on Marine Pde near the Ocean Sports Centre (to the north of the Holiday Inn).

2 Cave Rock

Cave Rock's heaving barrels explode over a shallow slab and can deliver the tube of a lifetime. Not a place for beginners, this spot has dished out more than its fair share of injuries. For those who can get it wired, however, it's a must.

WAVE TYPE Right

WAVE HEIGHT 4–12 ft (1.2–3.7 m)

BREAK TYPE Reef

BEST SWELL SE

BEST WIND Glassy or NE

BEST TIDE Mid

BEST TIME May–September

HAZARDS Rocks

DIRECTIONS Come down the Southern Freeway from central Durban, turn left into Edwin Swales Dr and across Bluff Rd into Old Mission Rd. Turn left into Tara Rd and right into Club Dr. Go across into Marine Dr and carry on through to Foreshore Dr. Go past Ansteys Beach and park at the end of the road.

3 St. Michaels-on-Sea

A right-hand reef, point, and beach break that starts outside a tidal pool and breaks all the way though to the beach on the inside, St. Mikes can deliver perfect barrels and rippable, fun walls. Very consistent, it is also ridable in bigger swells with easy entry from the pool wall. St. Mikes is protected by shark nets and is the venue for most surfing events in the region.

WAVE TYPE Right

WAVE HEIGHT 2–10 ft (0.6–3.1 m)

BREAK TYPE Reef, point, beach

BEST SWELL SW

BEST WIND SW

BEST TIDE Mid

BEST TIME April–August

HAZARDS Crowds; rocks; annual sardine run (May–July) sees surfing banned at times

DIRECTIONS Follow the N2 south from Durban, and take the Shelly Beach turnoff (R102). Take a right onto Marine Dr and turn left at the sign for St. Michaels-on-Sea.

4 Mdumbe

Mdumbe offers a right-hand point leading into a playful beach break, and a gnarly reef just around the headland. The place has a great atmosphere. Check that the backpacker hostel has beds available before making the trek as it's the only accommodation in the area.

WAVE TYPE Right

WAVE HEIGHT 2–8 ft (0.6–2.4 m)

BREAK TYPE Point, reef, beach

BEST SWELL Solid SE

BEST WIND SW

BEST TIDE Low

BEST TIME May–September

HAZARDS Rocks, sharks, no medical facilities

DIRECTIONS From Durban, drive through Umtata and look for the Coffee Bay turnoff about 18½ miles (30 km) on. From East London, drive through Idutywa and after 37 miles (60 km) turn off toward Coffee Bay. Go on through Mqanduli and then drive for almost an hour before you reach the signposted Mdumbe turnoff.

5 Coffee Bay

Coffee Bay offers a fun right-hand point break and, near the river mouth, a peaky beach break that delivers good rides. As with anywhere else in the Transkei, be wary of sharks. Check accommodation availability before traveling.

WAVE TYPE Right

WAVE HEIGHT 2–6 ft (0.6–1.8 m)

BREAK TYPE Point, beach

BEST SWELL SE

BEST WIND W

BEST TIDE Low

BEST TIME May–September

HAZARDS Rocks, sharks, no medical facilities

DIRECTIONS From Durban, drive through Umtata and look for the Coffee Bay turnoff about 18½ miles (30 km) on. From East London, drive through Idutywa and after about 37 miles (60 km) turn off toward Coffee Bay. Keep going through Mqanduli and then drive for around an hour. Stick on the same road the whole way until you approach Coffee Bay, which is signposted.

6 Nahoon Reef

One of the most consistent waves in the country, Nahoon Reef is a great right-hander that works on a variety of swell directions. Sometimes a mean, barreling slab on the takeoff, at other times a mellow, workable wall, this spot has something for everyone.

WAVE TYPE Right

WAVE HEIGHT 2–8 ft (0.6–2.4 m)

BREAK TYPE Reef

BEST SWELL SW

BEST WIND NW

BEST TIDE Low

BEST TIME Year-round

HAZARDS Rocks, sharks, occasional crowds

DIRECTIONS From central East London, drive along the esplanade and turn right just in front of the Holiday Inn into John Bailey Rd. Take a right at the second four-way intersection (a badminton hall, which looks like a metal barn, is on your right) and continue toward James Pierce Park. Turn right at the turnoff to Nahoon Reef.

Damien Fahrenfort scales the face of a solid wave at New Pier, the surfing hub of the east coast.

7 The Point

The Point is a mellow wave, ideal for hot-dogging, particularly for longboarders. It can offer plenty of juice in the right conditions and provides long rides after a hollow takeoff on the outside. Tubes, the next break up toward Supertubes, gives faster, hollower, shorter rides.

WAVE TYPE Right

WAVE HEIGHT 2–6 ft (0.6–1.8 m)

BREAK TYPE Point

BEST SWELL SSW

BEST WIND SW

BEST TIDE Low

BEST TIME May–September

HAZARDS Rocks, crowds, sharks

DIRECTIONS Jeffreys Bay is a 45-minute drive west of Port Elizabeth on the N2. Driving north along Da Gama Rd in Jeffreys Bay, take the next right after Pepper St. The road eventually comes to a lookout above Tubes, where you can check the waves. Another 100 yards (100 m) brings you to the parking lot at The Point.

8 Supertubes

From the heaving peaks at the top of Boneyards through the speedy barrels of the parking-lot section, to the huge tubes of Impossibles, Supers is the planet's premier performance point break. It's surfable from 2 to 12 ft (0.6–3.7 m), but best at 6–8 ft (1.8–2.4 m).

WAVE TYPE Right

WAVE HEIGHT 2–12 ft (0.6–3.7 m)

BREAK TYPE Point

BEST SWELL SSW

BEST WIND SW

BEST TIDE Low

BEST TIME May–August

HAZARDS Sharks, rocks, crowds, some heavy locals, jelly legs

DIRECTIONS Jeffreys Bay is a 45-minute drive west of Port Elizabeth on the N2. Driving north along Da Gama Rd in Jeffreys Bay, turn into Pepper St and park as close to the lookout deck as possible. On busy days, you may have to park over 200 yards (200 m) away.

9 Bruce's Beauties

Made famous by Bruce Brown's *The Endless Summer* movie in the mid-sixties, these perfect peeling right-handers have suffered in recent years due to housing developments disrupting the sandbank along the point. Bruce's still gets epic on the right day, however, with user-friendly barrels and long, speedy rides.

WAVE TYPE Right

WAVE HEIGHT 2–8 ft (0.6–2.4 m)

BREAK TYPE Point

BEST SWELL Big E

BEST WIND SW

BEST TIDE Low

BEST TIME February–June

HAZARDS Rocks, tricky entry

DIRECTIONS From Humansdorp, just off the N2, drive southeast for 12½ miles (20 km) to St. Francis Bay. Take the third turn to the left into the town and turn left again when you reach the T intersection. Turn right at Harbour Rd, right again, and drive to the parking lot at the end.

10 Seal Point

This popular wave at Cape St. Francis can see perfect right-handers the length of the point. Beware of Full Stop rock, halfway down the point, which can offer either an insane tube or a painful drive to the doctor. The beach break also delivers insane barrels. Once a quiet getaway, Cape St. Francis has become more crowded in recent years.

WAVE TYPE Right

WAVE HEIGHT 2–6 ft (0.6–1.8 m)

BREAK TYPE Reef, point, beach

BEST SWELL SSW

BEST WIND SW

BEST TIDE Low

BEST TIME May–September

HAZARDS Rocks, sharks, seasonal crowds

DIRECTIONS From Humansdorp, just off the N2, drive southeast to St. Francis Bay, a distance of about 12½ miles (20 km). Simply stay on the same road all the way to its end, approaching the lighthouse, until you reach Seal Point Blvd.

Glossary

A-frame A tall, symmetrical wave with the peak at its center.

air As in "get air," "boost air." When surfer and board jump off the water, creating a gap, or air, between board and sea.

ASP Association of Surfing Professionals, the governing body of professional competitive surfing, which organizes international competitions.

backdoor To enter the wave from behind the peak and surf through a gap or the barrel to the front.

barrel The space formed inside a wave as the lip falls ahead of the face. Also called a tube.

bathymetry The measurement of ocean depths and, hence, the shape of the seafloor.

beach break A wave that breaks on sand.

bodyboard A small board made of foam rubber, normally ridden lying down.

break When the crest of a wave collapses forward in front of the face.

carve To make deep, smooth turns, achieved by thrusting one edge of the surfboard into the water.

cleanup set A wave or a set of waves that breaks farther offshore than normal, often as a result "cleaning" away the line of surfers waiting closer to shore.

closeout When a wave breaks along its entire length at once, instead of breaking gradually from one side to another. This prevents a surfer riding along the wave.

combo swell A combination of swells coming from different directions. This creates irregular wave patterns, which can be fun at beach breaks, but tend to spoil reef and point breaks.

crest The top part of the wave, often white, which falls forward and breaks. Also called the lip.

cutback A maneuver in which a surfer makes a sharp turn back toward the breaking edge of the wave, often used when the surfer has got too far ahead of the wave.

cyclone A large-scale weather system that rotates around an area of low pressure, often generating rain and strong winds. Cyclones turn counterclockwise in the Northern Hemisphere and clockwise in the Southern Hemisphere. In Australasia, the term is also used to mean a hurricane or typhoon.

down the line Along the full length of the wave. A down-the-line wave moves the surfer rapidly along its face.

drop-in The initial leap made by a surfer from the top of the wave onto its face. Also refers to the action of getting onto the wave in front of another surfer who is already on it – a major breach of standard surf etiquette!

duration The time a wind blows across an area of ocean.

face The front of a wave; the part that surfers ride along.

fetch The area of ocean over which a wave-generating wind blows.

fish A wide, thick, short surfboard with a swallowtail and two fins.

glass-off When a lack of wind results in a calm, waveless ocean with a surface like glass. Hence "glassy."

gnarly Used to describe difficult conditions, usually due to rough seas or rocky shoreline.

goofyfoot A left-footed surfer, who surfs with the right foot forward and the body facing the wave on left turns.

grommet A novice surfer.

groundswell A powerful swell (one with a period of at least 11 seconds between waves), usually generated by a large storm system, whose energy may reach down to the ocean floor (hence "ground"). See **windswell**.

gun A large surfboard used for surfing big waves.

hold-down When a powerful wave pins a surfer under the water.

hollow A wave with a well-defined barrel or tube.

hot-dog wave A wave that allows surfers to practice a wide variety of maneuvers.

hurricane A large tropical storm system that generates winds of more than 74 miles per hour (120 kph).

inside The position at the front of the lineup where the surfer will drop into the wave. If a surfer is on the inside, it means they have right of way, it's their wave.

ISA International Surfing Association, surfing's international governing body, which promotes and coordinates the development of the sport around the world.

kook A novice surfer or, in some contexts, an inept surfer who thinks he or she is an expert.

leash The cord that ties the surfboard to the surfer's leg. Also called a legrope.

lineup The area where surfers wait for waves to break; or the surfers waiting there.

lip The top, or crest, of a wave. Hitting or whacking the lip is a maneuver in which the surfer turns the board upward to strike the lip at the top of the wave.

localism Intimidation of visiting surfers by locals.

longboard A surfboard measuring more than 8 ft (2.4 m) in length, with a rounded tip. A longboard offers greater stability than a shortboard and is therefore favored by some beginners.

longshore drift The action by which waves, moving at an angle to the shore, push ocean sediments along the shoreline.

mushy Used to describe waves that are weak and hard to ride.

nose ride Riding with the feet placed on the front 12 inches (30 cm) of a surfboard.

offshore Used to describe a wind blowing from the land out to sea. Such winds normally create good surfing conditions because they slow down waves nearing land, making them stand taller and form better-defined barrels.

onshore Used to describe a wind blowing from the sea toward land. Such winds normally result in poor surfing conditions because they break up waves, creating a choppier surface.

overhead Used to describe a wave that is taller than the height of an average surfer. Often used in measurements such as double overhead, triple overhead.

peak A wave that has a prominent high point along its crest. Such a wave will usually break outward on both sides of the peak, allowing surfers to ride the wave on either side.

peel When a wave breaks steadily, from one end to the other, all the way along its length.

point break A wave that breaks onto a peninsula or promontory jutting out to sea.

rash vest A shirt worn by surfers to protect against jellyfish stings and sunburn.

reef break A wave that breaks over rock or coral.

rip A strong, potentially dangerous current running parallel to or away from the shore.

section A part of a wave that breaks separately from the rest.

set A series of waves. Sets of waves are separated by lulls.

setup The combination of features and circumstances that constitute a surf break at any given time, including the landforms, ocean depth, and swell and wind conditions.

shortboard A surfboard measuring 5–7 ft (1.5–2.1 m), used for high-performance surfing involving tight, quick turns.

shoulder The unbroken part of the wave just below the part that is breaking.

skeg A fin on a surfboard.

springsuit A wetsuit with short sleeves and legs, normally used in temperate conditions.

steamer A wetsuit with long sleeves and long legs.

surfari A journey undertaken with the prime objective of surfing waves.

swell A series of powerful waves, usually generated by a storm system far out to sea, whose energy often extends well below the surface.

swell direction The direction from which a swell is coming.

takeoff The maneuver whereby the surfer stands up on the board and drops into the wave.

tow-in The use of a motorized watercraft such as a jet-ski to tow a surfer and board out to the lineup, usually to reach big waves.

tube See **barrel**.

typhoon The name used for a hurricane in Eastern Asia.

tsunami A wave generated by a seismic activity such as an undersea earthquake or eruption.

wavelength The distance between successive wave crests.

WCT The World Championship Tour, the principal professional tour circuit, run by the ASP.

wetsuit A suit worn by surfers to protect them from the cold, normally made of a synthetic material called neoprene. The thicker the material, the warmer the suit. Most modern wetsuits are thicker on the torso than on the legs and arms. A 3/2 wetsuit means that it is 3 mm thick on the torso and 2 mm thick on the arms.

window An opportunity to drop into a wave, or the best time to drop into a wave.

windswell A swell generated by local winds blowing over the surface of the ocean (one with a period of less than 11 seconds between waves) that is more localized than groundswell and its energy doesn't extend as far beneath the surface of the ocean.

wipeout When a surfer falls or is knocked off the board.

WQS World Qualifying Series, a competition run by the ASP, success in which provides entry to the WCT.

Surfing the World Wide Web

The following websites, recommended by our authors, will provide further information on the surf spots featured in this book, as well as general travel information.

general

www.globalsurfers.com
http://magicseaweed.com/
www.savethewaves.org
www.surfersvillage.com
www.surf-forecast.com
www.surfinside.com
www.surfrider.org
www.wannasurf.com
www.wetsand.com

north america

CANADA

www.bruhwilersurf.com
www.coastalbc.com
www.livetosurf.com
www.longbeachsurfshop.com
www.pacificboarder.com
www.pacificsurfschool.com
www.sitkasurfboards.com
www.surfsister.com

UNITED STATES

www.bouyweather.com
www.surfermag.com
www.surfingthemag.com
www.surfline.com
www.transworldsurf.com
www.wetsand.com

MEXICO

www.surfinginmexico.com
www.surfing-waves.com/travel/ mexico
www.waterwaystravel.com

central america and the caribbean

EL SALVADOR

www.puntamango.com
www.wannasurf.com/spot/ Central_America/El_ Salvador
www.waterwaystravel.com/ elsalvador
www.wavehunters.com/ elsalvador/elsal.asp

NICARAGUA

http://centralamerica.com/ nicaragua/surfing

www.globalsurfers.com/ country_details. cfm?land=Nicaragua
www.nicaraguasurfreport.com
www.nicasurf.com
www.surfaricharters.com
www.surfnicaragua.com
www.wavehunters.com/ nicaragua/nicaragua.asp

COSTA RICA

www.crsurf.com
www.lymanphotos.sbpix.com
www.surfingcr.net
www.surfingtravel.com
www.surfridercostarica.org
www.surftheplanet.org

PANAMA

www.panamainfo.com/
http://panamasurfexpeditions. com/
www.panamasurftours.com/
www.panama-travel-bureau. com/panama_surf_report. html
www.surfeapanama.com
www.surferparadise.com/
www.visitpanama.com

PUERTO RICO

www.curao.com
www.geocities.com/Pipeline/ Dropzone/8964/pr.html
www.playero.com
www.surfpr.com

BARBADOS

www.bsasurf.net
www.surfbarbados.com
www.surfbarbados.net
www.surfing-barbados.com
www.zedssurftravel.com

south america

ECUADOR

www.globalsurfers.com/ country _details.cfm?land= Ecuador
www.surfing-waves.com/travel/ ecuador.htm
www.wavehunters.com/ ecuador/ecuador.asp.

PERU

www.peruconcept.com
www.peruecosurf.com
www.surfpenascal.com

CHILE

www.aricasurf.cl
www.notv.cl

www.surfchicas.cl
www.surfchile.cl
www.surfeando.cl

ARGENTINA

www.elsurfero.com
www.laesco.com.ar
www.welcomeargentina.com/ turismo-aventura/nauticas_ i.html
www.xigma.com.ar

BRAZIL

www.brazilsurftravel.com
www.justbrazil.org
http://ricosurf.globo.com
www.surfing-waves.com/travel/ brazil.htm

the pacific ocean islands

PAPUA NEW GUINEA

www.surfingpapua newguinea.org.pg

NEW CALEDONIA

www.jayaksurfari.com
http://nc-surf.ifrance.com
www.nekweta.com
www.newcaledoniatourism- south.com
www.ouanosurf.com

NEW ZEALAND

www.metservice.co.nz
www.snow.co.nz
www.surf.co.nz
www.swellmap.com
www.wind.co.nz

FIJI

www.batiluva.com
www.bulafijinow.com/surfing
www.fijiguide.com/Recreation/ surfing.html
www.fijisurf.com
www.fijisurfshop.com
http://primophotos.com/fiji.html
www.waidroka.com
www.waitui.com
www.wavehunters.com/fiji/ Outer_Islands_Fiji.asp

TONGA

www.surfingtonga.com
www.tonga.islands-holiday.com
www.tonga.spto.org
www.tongaholiday.com

SAMOA

www.samoa.resortspacific.com
www.samoanaresort.com

www.surfsamoa.com
www.visitsamoa.ws

FRENCH POLYNESIA

www.chopu.com
www.mooreaisland.com
www.tahiti.pacific-resorts.com
www.tahiti-tourisme.com

HAWAII

www.bigisland.org
www.gohawaii.com
http://hasasurf.org/
www.kauai-hawaii.com
www.nssahawaii.org
www.triplecrownofsurfing.com
www.visitmaui.com
www.visitmolokai.com
www.visit-oahu.com

australia

www.australianexplorer.com
www.coastalwatch.com
www.isurfing.com
www.realsurf.com
www.stormsurf.com
www.surfingaustralia.com
www.surfline.com
www.surfrider.org.au
www.swellnet.com.au

WESTERN AUSTRALIA

www.countrywide.com.au
www.lifesavingwa.com.au
http://scarboro.info/surf/index. htm
www.slswa.com.au
www.therealaustralia.com
www.westernaustralia.com/au

SOUTH AUSTRALIA

www.atn.com.au/surf.html
www.fleurieupeninsula.com.au
www.southaustralia.com
www.surfrescue.com.au
www.surfsouthoz.com

VICTORIA

www.epa.vic.gov.au/water/ coasts/surf_diatoms.asp
www.gippslandinfo.com.au
www.lifesavingvictoria.com.au
www.surflifesaver.com.au
www.surfworld.org.au
www.torquayslsc.com.au
www.visitvictoria.com

CENTRAL NEW SOUTH WALES

www.brontesurfclub.com.au
www.coogeesurfclub.com.au
www.cronullasurfclub.com

www.manlylsc.com
www.maroubraslsc.com.au
www.northbondisurfclub.com
www.surflifesaving.net
www.surflifesavingsydney.
com.au
www.sydney-australia.biz
www.sydneysurf.com.au
www.sydney.visitorsbureau.
com.au

NORTH COAST, NEW SOUTH WALES

www.bayweb.com.au
http://bhslsc.midcoast.
com.au/
www.byron-bay.com/byron
bay/beachguide.html
www.holidaycoast.net.au/
www.surflifesaving.com.au/
surflife_cms
www.tropicalnsw.com.au/

GOLD COAST, QUEENSLAND

www.burleighcam.com.au
www.goldcoastaustralia.com
www.hellogoldcoast.com.au
www.lifesaving.com.au
www.surfersparadiseslsc.
com.au/
www.surfersparadise.com/
the_beach/

SUNSHINE COAST, QUEENSLAND

www.onsurfari.com.au
www.sunshinecoast.org
www.sunshinecoasttourism.
com
www.wavesense.com.au

eastern asia

INDONESIA

www.baliwaves.com
www.grajagan.com
www.indosurf.com.au
http://mentawaiblue.com/
www.mentawairesorts.com
www.sumateratourism.com

PHILIPPINES

www.philippines-travel-guide.
com/philippines-surfing.
html
www.aurora.ph/tourist-surfing.
html
http://surigaoislands.com/
surfing.html

JAPAN

www.japansurf.com
www.jpsa.com/surfer
www.d2tb.com
www.namiaru.tv

www.wavehuntersjapan.com
www.go-naminori.com
www.holdyourline.com

the indian ocean

MADAGASCAR

http://buoyweather.com/
www.lavanono.com
http://mada.moreorless.au.com
www.mada-surfari.com
www.madonline.com
www.masombahiny.com/
Madagascar_Information.
html
www.surfermag.com/photos/
magazine/mdgascrgallry/
www.tourisme.gov.mg

RÉUNION

www.la-reunion-tourisme.com
www.saintpaul-lareunion.com/
index-uk.php

MAURITIUS

www.mauritius.net/index.php
www.tourism-mauritius.mu
www.tourisminmauritius.com
www.travelmauritius.info/
surfing.html

MALDIVES

www.atolltravel.com
www.meteorology.gov.mv
www.tropicsurf.net
http://surf.allianceholidays.
com/index.html
www.visitmaldives.com

SRI LANKA

www.arugam.info
www.srilankaecotourism.com
www.srilankan.aero
www.srilankatourism.org
www.srilankatravelguide.com

western europe

www.eurosurfing.org
www.getaforecast.com
www.mediterraneanweather.
com/forecasts.htm
www.meteosim.com/wave/
atl.hs.anim.gif
www.surferdream.com
www.surfeuropemag.com

IRELAND

www.ireland.ie
www.isasurf.ie

UNITED KINGDOM

www.a1surf.com
www.bbc.co.uk/weather/
ukweather/
www.britsurf.co.uk

www.chrisold.co.uk/webcam
www.cornwalltouristboard.
co.uk/
www.errantsurf.co.uk/
www.gwithianlines.com
www.magicseaweed.co.uk
www.metoffice.gov.uk/
weather/uk/surface_
pressure.html
www.sas.org.uk
www.supertubes.co.uk

FRANCE

www.beachwizard.com/
country.asp?country
=FRANCE
http://magicseaweed.com/
France-Surf-Forecast/2/
www.meteo-france.com
www.seignosse-surf-school.
com
www.surfingfrance.com
www.surfing-waves.com/travel/
france
www.surf-report.com

SPAIN

www.globalsurfers.com/
country_details.
cfm?land=Spain
http://magicseaweed.com/
Spain-Portugal-Surf-
Forecast/8/
www.purevacations.com/surf/
spain
www.surfing-waves.com/travel/
spain.htm
www.surfspain.co.uk
www.wannasurf.com/spot/
Europe/Spain
www.winterwaves.com

PORTUGAL

www.beachwizard.com/
country.asp?country
=PORTUGAL
http://magicseaweed.com/
Spain-Portugal-Surf-
Forecast/8/
www.wannasurf.com/spot/
Europe/Portugal

AZORES

http://magicseaweed.com/
The-Azores-Surf-
Forecast/67/
www.surfing-waves.com/travel/
azores.htm
www.wannasurf.com/spot/
Europe/Azores

ITALY

www.italiasurfexpo.it
www.photorepetto.com/
pag-italian_waves.htm
www.surfcorner.it

www.surfingitalia.org
www.wannasurf.com/spot/
Europe/Italy
www.wavecam.it

africa

MADEIRA

www.flytap.com
www.madeiratourism.org
www.madeira-web.com
www.savethewaves.org

CANARY ISLANDS

www.canarias.org/eng/
turismo/turismo.html
www.canaries-live.com
www.canary-travel.com
www.lanzarote.com/surf
www.surflanzarote.com

MOROCCO

www.errantsurf.com
www.globalsurfers.com/
morocco.cfm
www.moroccosurf.com
www.purevacations.com
/surf/morocco
www.surfing-waves.com/
travel/morocco.htm
www.surfmaroc.co.uk

CAPE VERDE

www.capeverdeinfo.
org.uk
www.capeverdetravel.
com
www.capoverdenews.com
www.datrip.com
www.ecaboverde.com
www.surfcaboverde.com

SENEGAL

www.africaguide.com/
country/senegal
www.ausenegal.com
www.senevolu.org

GHANA

www.ghana.co.uk/travel/
travelling/beaches.htm
www.surf-forecast.com/
breaks/Fete.shtml

NAMIBIA

www.namibia-travel.net
www.namibweb.com
www.swakop.com

SOUTH AFRICA

www.kahunasurf.co.za
www.wavescape.co.za
www.zigzag.co.za
www.surfingsouthafrica.
co.za

Acknowledgments

Global Book Publishing would like to thank Kylie Mulquin for creating the icons and the tide illustrations on page 19; Dannielle Doggett for her assistance in the production of the book; Mario Viera and Nelly Viera for their assistance with Spanish-language translation; and Joanne Holliman, Suzanne Keating, and Lynn Lewis for their help during the conceptualization process prior to production. Special thanks go to Shane Clark (Surfing Association of Papua New Guinea), Marilu Cornejo (*Surfeando* magazine, Chile), and Gustavo Huici (Surfrider Foundation Argentina) for their expert guidance.

The consultants would like to acknowledge the team at Coastalwatch for their advice and suggestions throughout the production of this book, along with the excellent information on ocean conditions and terminology they supplied.

Photo Credits

Captions for Preliminary Pages and Section Openers

Page 1 A surfer takes to the air off Emma Wood State Beach at Ventura, California, USA. **2–3** Assessing the conditions at Waimea Bay, Hawaii, USA **4–5** Riding one of the outstanding barrels at Grajagan (G-Land), Java, Indonesia **6–7** A view from beneath the waves, Queensland, Australia **8** Exploring the shore of Christmas Island, Central Pacific **10–11** Pacific swells can generate enormous waves like this one off Maui, Hawaii, USA. **22–23** A typically photogenic wave at Salt Creek, Southern California, USA **46–47** Riding the last waves of the day at Tamarindo, Costa Rica **64–65** World-class beach breaks lie just a short distance from downtown Rio de Janeiro, Brazil. **86–87** Hawaiian surfer Pancho Sullivan bottom-turning at one of the world's heaviest waves, Teahupoo in Tahiti **124–25** Surfers warming up for their heats during the Rip Curl Pro competition at Woolamai Beach, Phillip Island, Victoria, Australia **152–53** David Weare performs a lay-back turn in southern Sumatra, Indonesia **172–73** South African surfer Royden Bryson in the Maldives **192–93** Hawaiian surfer Andy Irons in competition at Mundaka, Spain **218–19** Sunset waves at Kalk Bay on South Africa's West Coast